SHIFTING PARADIGMS

AMERICAN PHILOLOGICAL ASSOCIATION
American Classical Studies

Series Editor

Matthew S. Santirocco

Number 27

Shifting Paradigms

by
Bernard Frischer

Bernard Frischer

SHIFTING PARADIGMS
New Approaches to Horace's *Ars Poetica*

Scholars Press
Atlanta, Georgia

SHIFTING PARADIGMS

Bernard Frischer

© 1991
The American Philological Association

Library of Congress Cataloging in Publication Data

Frischer, Bernard.
    Shifting paradigms : new approaches to Horace's Ars poetica / Bernard Frischer.
    p. cm. — (American classical studies ; no. 27)
    Includes bibliographical references and index.
    ISBN 1-55540-619-X. — ISBN 1-55540-620-3 (pbk.)
    1. Horace. Ars poetica. 2. Horace—Aesthetics. 3. Aesthetics, Ancient. 4. Poetics. I. Title. II. Series.
PA6393.E7F7 1991
871'.01—dc20   91-22285
                                                            CIP

Printed in the United States of America
on acid-free paper

Uxori
doctissimae·karissimaeque
ob·eius·merita
d·d·d

TABLE OF CONTENTS

List of Plates viii

List of Tables viii

Preface xi

Introduction 1

Chapter 1: The Title of the Poem—Ancient and Medieval Evidence
  vs. Renaissance Speculation 5

Chapter 2: The Date of the Poem 17

Chapter 3: Interpretive Implications of Chronology—The *Ars Poetica*
  in Its Cultural Context 51

Chapter 4: Genre of the *Ars Poetica*—Epistle, Didactic Poem, or
  Tertium Quid? 87

Appendix I: Key Documents for the Renaissance Theory that the
  Ars Poetica is an Epistle 101

Appendix II: Calculating the Odds of Finding Matched Pairs of
  Trend Lines in the Lyrics and Hexameters 109

Appendix III: Piso in Pola. The Date of *Inscr. Ital.* X.i.81 115

Abbreviations and Bibliography 127

General Index 137

Plates *(bound at end)*

Fig. 1—*Inscr. Ital.* X.i.65 (Pola, Lapidarium of Arheoloski muzej Istre 214)

Fig. 2—Detail from Frieze of the Temple of the Divine Julius Caesar, Rome (DAI Rome 63.1233)

Fig. 3—Detail of Wall Painting from Left Ala, House of Livia, Rome (DAI Rome 56.435)

Tables

I	Position of the *Ars Poetica* in the Mss. of Horace	7
II	Chi-Square Test of Data in Duckworth's Table I	24
III	Chi-Square Test of Duckworth's First Four Patterns	25
IV	Chi-Square Test of Duckworth's Last Four Patterns	25
V	Function Words *Ad, Per,* and *Sed* in Horace	33
VI	Table V Recalculated to Minimize Effect of "Rest"	35
VII	Comparisons of the Full and Various Collapsed Models of the Data in Table V	35
VIII	Frequency of *Nec* in Horace	38
IX	Table VIII Controlled for "Rest"	38
X	Comparisons of the Full and Various Collapsed Models of the Data in Table VIII	39
XI	Chi-Square Test of the Frequency of Unique and Non-Unique Strings in Horace	42
XII	Alternative Models for Grouping the Data of Table XI	43
XIII	Approximate Publication Dates of Horace's Poetry	44
XIV	Percentage of Unique Strings in Horace's Non-Hexameter Poetry	45

Table of Contents ix

XV	Percentage of Unique Strings in Horace's Hexameter Poetry	46
XVI	Best and Worst Regression Models for Dating the *Ars Poetica* by Means of Function Words	48
XVII	Monsters in Wall Painting, Stuccoes, and Sculpted Friezes from the City of Rome, ca. 35-20 B.C.	78
XVIII	Concluding Topics in Horace's *Epistles*	94
α	Types of Potential Patterns in Horace's Use of Function Words in the Lyrics	110
β	Types of Potential Patterns in Horace's Use of Function Words in the Hexameters	111
γ	Combinations of Two 5-Point Line Types in Each Set	112
δ	Conversion of 3-Point Line-Types to Their Exact 5-Point Equivalents in the Sets {L}, {C}, and {R}	113
ε	Classification of Function Word Patterns in Horace's Lyrics and Hexameters	113
η	Results of Binomial Test, N=16, π=.010974	114
A	Frequency of Certain Function Words in Horace	143
B	Graphs of Randomly Occurring Function Words (1): *Atque, Aut*	144
C	Graphs of Randomly Occurring Function Words (2): *Cum, Et*	145
D	Graphs of Randomly Occurring Function Words (3): *Iam, In*	146
E	Graphs of Randomly Occurring Function Words (4): *Non, Nunc*	147
F	Graphs of Randomly Occurring Function Words (5): *Si, Sic*	148
G	Graphs of Randomly Occurring Function Words (6): *Ut, Vel*	149
H	Graph Showing Frequency of *Ad* in Horace	150
I	Graph Showing Frequency of *Per* in Horace	150

J	Graph Showing Frequency of *Sed* in Horace	151
K	Graph Showing Frequency of *Ad*, *Per*, and *Sed* in Horace	151
L	Graph Showing Frequency of *Nec* in Horace	152
M	Graph Showing Frequency of *Ne* and *Nec* in Horace	152
N	Graph Showing Average Number of Characters Per Word in Horace	153
O	Graph Showing Ratio of Words to Stops in Horace	153
P	Graph Showing Unique and Non-Unique Strings in Horace's Poetry	154
Q	Graphs of Best and Worst Regression Models for *Sed* in Horace	155
R	Graphs of Best and Worst Regression Models for *Per* in Horace	156
S	Graphs of Best and Worst Regression Models for *Nec* in Horace	157
T	Graphs of Best and Worst Regression Models for *Ad* in Horace	158

PREFACE

"You're going to include *this* in your book on the *Ars Poetica?*" asked my friend, Ann Scott, looking incredulously at my tables and charts on the date of the poem. The idea of publishing the material that follows as a separate book was born that day. My motivations in dividing my work on the poem into at least two publications are several. First, the methodological and literary styles of the following work are quite different from those in the purely interpretative book that I also hope to publish on the *Ars Poetica*. The two works may thus appeal to two rather different readerships, neither very interested in the concerns of the other. Secondly, since the longer, interpretative book I plan to publish elsewhere contains a re-reading of the poem as a parody, it makes sense to precede that book with the present study, which provides some of the background assumptions and scholarly underpinnings for my new reading. Not that my new interpretation could not stand on its own, in the event that the following study falls on deaf ears or on minds more mathematically, or prosopographically, agile than mine.

The statistical analyses that follow are based on the digitized text of Horace edited by F. Klingner and kindly made available to me in Macintosh™ format by Tad Brennan of Princeton University with the consent of the publisher, the Packard Humanities Institute. I wish to thank Dr. David Packard for permission to use the text and Dr. John Gleason for helping me to obtain a copy. Mr. Brennan informs me that "the Horace files were created using the Ibycus Scholarly Computer; the P.H.I. Demonstration CD-ROM #1, a collection of Latin texts published by the Packard Humanities Institute; and Ibyxfer, a file-transfer program written by Wilkins Poe of Yale University. The Packard Humanities Institute CD-ROM describes itself as 'partially corrected,' and this must be taken at face value; errors are sure to exist." I have not had the resources to proofread the text nor to do more than correct a few errors that I happened to note in the course of these investigations. Since there are over 40,000 words of Horace extant, I would hope that any textual errors that may have crept into the P.H.I. text will have but little impact on the statistical studies that follow.

Once transferred to Macintosh format, analysis of the text was aided by the text-processing program, Doug Clapp's Word Tools™, published by Aegis Development, Inc. Most of the statistical analyses and graphics were produced with the help of the statistics package, Systat 3.2™, published by Systat, Inc. I also used the Data Desk—Student Version™.

Readers who are unfamiliar with statistics will inevitably be disappointed to find that this book presumes at least a basic understanding of the field and does not attempt to provide more by way of background than references to the first-year college textbook that I myself used in getting started (A. Agresti and B. Finlay, *Statistical Methods for the Social Sciences* [San Francisco and London, 1986^2]). Before tackling such a work, students of literature may be directed to A. J. Kenny's approachable book, *The Computation of Style* (Oxford 1982), which introduces many of the fundamental concepts of statistics through literary examples and problems.

I wish to thank the following for helpful discussions and comments about this and related aspects of my work on Horace: William S. Anderson (Classics Dept., Berkeley), Ernst Badian (History Dept., Harvard), David Blank (Classics Dept., UCLA), Irene Bragantini (University of Naples), Dee Clayman (Classics Dept., Brooklyn College, CUNY), Enrica Croda (Economics Dept., University of Venice), Andrew Dyck (Classics Dept., UCLA), Karin Einaudi (Fototeca Unione, Rome), Carlo Ferrari (School of Engineering, University of Padua), Nathan Greenberg (Classics Dept., Oberlin), Patricia M. Greenfield (Psychology Dept., UCLA), Erich Gruen (History Dept., Berkeley), William Harris (History Department, Columbia University), Richard Janko (Classics Dept., UCLA), Daniel Javitch (Comparative Literature Dept., New York University), Rudolf Marloth (Senior Scientist, Radar Systems Group, Hughes Aircraft Co., Los Angeles), Charles Murgia (Classics Dept., Berkeley), Michael Putnam (Classics Dept., Brown University and currently Mellon Professor of Classical Studies at the American Academy in Rome), Lorenzo Quilici (University of Rome), Annalise Quintavalle (Dept. of Statistics, University of Padua), Peter Rockwell (Rome), Ann Scott (Classics Dept., University of Delaware), Russell T. Scott (Dept. of Latin, Bryn Mawr College), Volker Michael Strocka (Archaeological Institute, Freiburg University), and Laura Weiss (Psychology Dept., UCLA). Responsibility for the opinions expressed and the statistics reported here is of course mine alone.

David Konstan (Classics Dept., Brown University) was kind enough to examine the manuscripts of Charisius in Naples for me. Robert Matijasic, of the Archaeological Museum of Istria, graciously supplied information about the Pola inscriptions mentioning L. Calpurnius Piso and also provided a photograph of *Inscr. Ital.* X.i.65. Dott. M. L. Veloccia Rinaldi and Arch. Costantino

Centroni of the Soprintendenza Archeologica per il Lazio provided helpful information about Horace's Villa at Licenza as well as access to archaeological material housed in the Licenza Museum. Mr. Clyde James, Director of the California State Library, Sutro Branch, answered an important bibliographical question about a copy of Lambinus' Horace edition in his collection. I am also very grateful to the German Archaeological Institute in Rome for permission to publish the photographs in figures 2 and 3 and to the Soprintendenza Archeologica per il Lazio for permission to make my own photographs of material housed in the museum of Licenza. Joan Gruen kindly lent me her camera (which I regret to say I inadvertently damaged) for photographing Horace's Sabine Villa; Mr. Antonio von Marx let me use his apartment (which I believe I returned no worse for the wear) when I visited London to work in the British Library (I did, however, manage to crash his Macintosh). Speaking of computers, I owe an enormous debt of gratitude to Apple Computer, Inc. for its generous gift of Macintosh computers to the Division of Humanities of UCLA. Anne Rivera of Apple took an early interest in my work, providing much needed help and advice.

I was fortunate to be able to work in the following libraries, whose staffs I wish to thank for their many kindnesses: the Biblioteca Apostolica Vaticana; the Biblioteca Civica of Bergamo; the Biblioteca dell'Accademia dei Concordi in Rovigo; the Biblioteca Marciana; the British Library; the University Research Library of UCLA; and in Padua, the Biblioteca Civica, the Biblioteca Universitaria, and the Biblioteca dell'Istituto di Filologia Latina. The librarians Marino Zorzi, Marco Buonocore, Leonard E. Boyle, O.P., and Lucilla Marino facilitated my work in many ways.

Special thanks are also due to Nicholas Horsfall (Rome)—who read drafts of the manuscript and made many encouraging comments and helpful bibliographical suggestions—and to Eleanor Winsor Leach (Classics Dept., University of Indiana)—who provided some very valuable suggestions, particularly about how to arrange the various sections of this work. Matthew Santirocco (Classics Dept., University of Pennsylvania) has not only discharged his duties as editor in exemplary fashion but, *Quintilii ritu*, has become a good friend as well. Finally, it is a pleasure once again to acknowledge the support generously given this research by the Academic Senate of UCLA and to thank Prof. Joseph Connors, Director of the American Academy in Rome, for giving me permission to stay in the Academy while researching this book in Rome.

On this numerically highly significant day in our lives, I dedicate this book to my wife, Jane Crawford, who will, I am sure, be even happier than I am to see it completed and sent on its way—at least, as long as *nescit vox missa reverti*.

—Padua, December 1, 1989
revised in Los Angeles, April, 1991

INTRODUCTION

About one instance of the relationship between historical background and poetic foreground in the works of Catullus, Sir Ronald Syme wrote:

> The proconsul and his 'comites', Veranius and Fabullus, have a chronological bearing on the life and writings of Catullus, that imbroglio of problems where dogma and ingenuity have their habitation, where argument moves in circles, and no new passage in or out.[1]

These words might seem to provide an inappropriate—or, at least, inauspicious—beginning to a new study of the centuries-old and interrelated problems of the title, date, addressees, and genre of the poem we call Horace's *Ars Poetica*. Dogma and ingenuity have certainly found their habitation in scholars' treatment of these problems, too. About this work, Horace's longest and most influential, we know much less than we sometimes assume. Moreover, much of what we think we know about these topics is subject to doubt and perhaps even revision. The purpose of this study is to support these claims, which, once demonstrated, set the stage for the new interpretation of the poem as a parody of Peripatetic poetics that I will adumbrate here and present with full details elsewhere.

By subtitling this book, *New Approaches to Horace's Ars Poetica,* I want, first of all, to allude to Syme's phrase, "new passage in." By using the plural, I also want to suggest that a historical reading of a poem as complex and elusive as the *Ars Poetica* requires that we make our way not along a single royal road, but through a variety of approaches, old and new, if we are to stop moving in the same interpretive circles. Progress in this as in any scholarly project comes from our ability to bring to bear new evidence, new methods, or

---

[1]*Roman Papers,* vol. 1, ed. E. Badian (Oxford 1979) 301-302 (= *Classica et Mediaevalia* 17 [1956] 130-131).

both to address old problems. These methods help us to eke out more information from the evidence contained within the poem itself and to find more unexploited historical evidence that can help us to calibrate our reactions to the poem with the knowledge and assumptions of Horace's informed, contemporary readership. For the first, I would single out statistical stylistics, which, applied here for the first time to the problem of dating Horace's poetry, can rely on data within the poems themselves to suggest a probabilistic dating of the *Ars Poetica*. Applying art-historical analysis to the interpretation of the opening lines of the poem exemplifies the second way in which a newly applied methodology can provide a richer context for historical understanding of the *Ars Poetica*. Of course, traditional philological techniques have a contribution to make, too, e.g., in helping us to determine the poem's genre and to make sense of the ancient and medieval evidence about its title and position in Horatian manuscripts.

Progress can also be made by shifting our perspectives as critics. For far too long the *Ars Poetica* has been read as something that would be rather anomalous among Horace's poems: a sincere and almost confessional "how-to-do-it" booklet. Read in this way, the poem can be—and in this century generally has been—too easily dismissed as disappointing or worse. "The nineteenth century, like the twentieth so far, did without the *Ars*," wrote the translator C. H. Sisson with much justification.[2] In their history of literary criticism, Wimsatt and Brooks wrote rather dismissively that "the *Ars Poetica*...is a nice mélange of objective and critical rules with snatches of studio wisdom."[3] It is a telling fact that even the most historically-oriented literary critics of Horace have rarely found insights in the *Ars Poetica* that aid them in understanding his other poems. To cite perhaps the most striking example, in his influential book on Horace, Fraenkel did not discuss the poem at any length, mentioning it mainly in footnotes.[4] Yet, if the *Ars Poetica* were really Horace's poetic credo, it ought to be of some utility in the practical criticism of his poetry. Persona-theory, applied so fruitfully to other Roman poetry, including Horace's own, can also serve us well in this endeavor to break free of critical ruts and circles. Once we dis-

---

[2]C. H. Sisson, *The Poetic Art. A Translation of Horace's Ars Poetica* (Cheadle Hulme, Cheadle 1975) 19.

[3]W. K. Wimsatt, Jr. and C. Brooks, *Literary Criticism. A Short History* (New York 1957) 94. They go on to write: "Keep your pencils sharpened, carry a pocket notebook, drink a pint of beer with lunch...take your time in publishing. It is no derogation from such statements to say that they are not strictly parts of criticism. In the *Ars Poetica* of Horace they are, despite the random structure of the poem, not actually in great danger of being confused with criticism."

[4]E. Fraenkel, *Horace* (Oxford 1957). As far as I can tell, the only references to the poem occur at pp. 77n2, 125n3, 148n2, 177n2, 299, 308n1, 347n4, 365n1, 382, 389n3, 389n5, 393n3, and 398n4.

sociate Horace, the poet, from the speaker of the *Ars Poetica*, the poet's fictional creation, we can stop having to explain or edit away the poem's deficiencies and dullness, and we can begin to appreciate in it the same techniques of wit and satire that are so characteristic of Horace's poetry.[5]

The itinerary we will pursue through these approaches is as follows. In *Chapter 1* I discuss the ancient and medieval evidence about the title of the poem and its location in the ancient manuscripts of Horace's poetry, showing that modern editors' habit of printing the poem after or even with *Epistles* II and of giving it the title *Epistula ad Pisones* goes against the grain of the evidence and reflects the (in most cases probably unconscious) influence of some rather flimsy Renaissance theorizing. The evidence strongly suggests that we should view the poem as an independent work in the Horatian corpus. In *Appendix I*, the pertinent Renaissance texts for the letter-theory are reproduced.

In *Chapter 2* I tackle the problem of the poem's date, using statistical stylistics and more traditional historical and literary arguments to advocate an early date (i.e., 24-20 B.C.) against the currently fashionable late dating to the end of Horace's life. *Appendix II* presents some technical details.

In *Chapter 3* several of the major prosopographical and interpretive consequences of chronology are discussed. Of these, the first and perhaps most important is that the early dating does not force us—as has been assumed for over a century—into the uncomfortable position of having to identify Cn. Calpurnius Piso (cos. 23) as the senior addressee of the *Ars Poetica*. Rather, there is good reason to assign that role to L. Calpurnius Piso Caesoninus (cos. 58), a candidate never before considered, doubtless because of modern scholarly speculation that he died well before the *Ars Poetica* was written. In *Appendix III* is related the historical evidence from Pola supporting my suggestion that this speculation is probably wrong. Caesoninus—who had been memorably pilloried by Catullus for bad taste in choosing his literary companions and who had been branded the "Phalaris of *grammatici*" by Cicero—stood for bad literary taste in this period. The fact that the speaker of the *Ars Poetica* mentions him and Hor-

---

[5] I am aware of only one earlier attempt to apply persona-theory to the *Ars Poetica*: A. G. Wood, *Literary Satire and Theory. A Study of Horace, Boileau, and Pope* (New York and London 1985) passim. As will be seen below in *Chapters 3* and *4*, I do not agree with Wood's statements that "the 'I' of the [*Ars Poetica*] is portrayed much like the poet..." (p. 4) and that "we should not expect to find great differences between the texts and the stated beliefs of Horace. In the case of Horace it is extremely difficult to find inconsistencies between the poet and his personae" (p. 14). Wood's analysis, while claiming to be based on persona-theory, makes very little progress beyond earlier interpretations of the *Ars Poetica* precisely because it fails to find any inconsistencies between the poem and the behavior and "stated beliefs" of the poet.

ace's bête noire, Sp. Maecius Tarpa, as respected authorities on literature naturally calls the speaker's own authority into question—a suggestive piece of evidence for the parody-theory. This chapter concludes with a reading of the poem's opening lines, where I argue that through his misuse of rhetoric and his display of ignorance about new developments in Roman painting, the speaker is characterized right from the start as a pretentious pedant who abuses poetic license and is out of touch with the taste of Horace and his circle.

In *Chapter 4* I reconsider the generic classification of the poem, arguing that it more closely conforms to the features of Horatian *sermo* than to those of *epistula*—an exercise of interest for at least three reasons. First of all, refutation of the letter-theory reinforces the view that the *Ars Poetica* should not be printed with *Epistles* II or interpreted in the light of those poems. Secondly, the case for classifying the poem as *sermo* on the basis of formal features adds strength to the conclusion of *Chapter 2* that the poem was composed in the period between *Sat.* II and *Epist.* I: for, although, as *Carm.* IV shows, Horace could revisit a genre after a long absence, he generally did not do so, and hence our dating is more plausible to the extent that it puts the poem into a period of Horace's life when he was writing poetry of a similar kind. Finally, the classification of the *Ars Poetica* as *sermo* lends obvious support to its interpretation as a mock-didactic parody, since, especially in *Sat.* II, we find some striking passages and even whole poems in which Horace sends up pedants and their foolish dogmas.

Before joining the imbroglio that rages around these matters, I should stress that one of my main goals here is less to offer new solutions to the old problems than to reveal how speculative our answers to all these questions have been and—in view of the evidence—must, perforce, be. Another goal is to re-open discussion of these major problems facing a critic of the poem, something desirable, I think, because our most recent studies of the *Ars Poetica*, for all their virtues, have been lacking in this regard. Since some of these problems have not been thoroughly reconsidered for a century or more, solutions originally offered as speculations have almost come to have the status of facts. In pursuit of this second goal, I will be proposing some new solutions that, if not necessarily always more cogent than the possibilities encountered in the scholarly literature, are at least no more speculative than those they would replace.

As in the case of Catullus' poetry, which cannot be diachronically understood without bringing to bear what can be ferreted out about such historical personages as Piso, Veranius and Fabullus, the importance of this enterprise lies in the new framework for interpreting the *Ars Poetica* to which it gives rise. As we will see, once we show that there are new possible ways of solving such basic—if seemingly antiquarian—problems as dating and classifying the poem and identifying its addressees, we are well on our way to constructing a fresh reading of what may well be not merely the longest, but also the wittiest, of Horatian poems.

CHAPTER 1

THE TITLE OF THE POEM: ANCIENT AND MEDIEVAL EVIDENCE VS. RENAISSANCE SPECULATION

What we know, or think we know, about the background of a literary work can have a decisive effect on our interpretation. Clues provided by the author—particularly the title[1]—and facts uncovered, or commonplaces created, by scholars and recorded in introductions, prefaces, or even, in modern times, on dust jackets create certain expectations in us even before we read the first words of a text. As S. J. Wilsmore has recently written, "the literary work often possesses its title essentially in that it could not be the same literary work without it. Moreover, it often possesses many of its essential aesthetic properties—those that must necessarily be perceived if it is to be 'appreciated'—as titles reveal them."[2] J. Fisher noted that "the unique purpose of titling is hermeneutical: titles are names which function as guides to interpretation."[3] These points are so obvious that they need not be elaborated here. They bear repeating because they have often been forgotten, or at least ignored, by critics of the poem that, as I will show presently, should be called the *Ars Poetica* but which is all too often given the misnomer *Epistula ad Pisones*—as it is, for example, in two otherwise excellent new studies recently published by Rudd and Kilpatrick.[4]

[1] Cf. H. Adams, "Titles, Titling, and Entitlement To," *JAAC* 46 (1987) 7-21, at p. 17: "Titles don't come at the ends or middles of texts, so the relation that we have been considering is always one involving expectation...."
[2] S. J. Wilsmore, "The Role of Titles in Identifying Literary Works," *JAAC* 45 (1987) 403-408, at p. 408.
[3] J. Fisher, "Entitling," *Critical Inquiry* 11 (1984) 286-298.
[4] I refer to N. Rudd, *Horace. Epistles II and Epistle to the Pisones ('Ars Poetica')* (Cambridge 1989) 19; and R. S. Kilpatrick, *The Poetry of Criticism. Horace Epistles II and Ars Poetica* (Edmonton, Alberta 1990) ix, 33, 52, 56, 72. In his new book for the general reader, D. Armstrong calls the poem *Epist.* II.3 (*Horace* [New Haven 1989] 154), as does N. Rudd in his superb Penguin translation (*Horace, Satires and Epistles; Persius, Satires* [Harmonsworth, Middlesex, England 1979] 190-203).

5

It is thus useful to begin this study by reviewing what is known about the poem's title. The titles that we find in modern editions—*Ars Poetica, Epistula ad Pisones,* or *Epist.* II.3—are not supported by any evidence dating from Horace's lifetime. How Horace and his contemporaries referred to the poem is a mystery and is likely to remain one. Information about the title starts to become available about one hundred years after Horace's death in references to it by other writers. More information is contained in the late-antique scholia and in the medieval manuscript tradition. Now, normally such a wealth of material would be sufficient to establish something like the title of an ancient work, assuming, of course, that the evidence points in a certain direction, as it does in the present case. Why, then, do so many scholars use the titles *Epistula ad Pisones* or *Epist.* II.3 when the only title with strong ancient and medieval support is *Ars Poetica*?

Let us start by looking at the work's location in the ancient and medieval manuscripts of Horace's poetry and in modern printed editions. My aim is simple: not so much to add to our knowledge of such matters as to remind readers of Horace that the custom of printing the *Ars Poetica* at the end of the corpus with (or, next to) the "sincere" poetic letters to Augustus and Florus in *Epistles* II is modern and is not supported by any credible ancient evidence.

Where the *Ars Poetica* appeared in late-antique texts of Horace's works can be inferred from the arrangement of the poems in the principal medieval manuscripts and from the order in which the ancient commentator Porphyrio discusses the works,[5] as Vollmer's table (TABLE I, next page) indicates.[6]

Vollmer compiled this table in order to try to group the mss. into families—that is, for purposes of textual history and criticism. This attempt failed, as Brink trenchantly showed,[7] but the information is still useful for another purpose. With its help, we can easily see that in the ancient texts, the *Ars Poetica* came either fourth, after the *Carm. Saec.* (CLASS I), or else second, after the *Odes* (CLASS II). In either case, the poem was kept quite distinct from *Epist.* I and II. The ancients considered it an independent work in Horace's corpus.

We do not understand why, nor do we know exactly when, the poems of Horace were arranged in these ways. Wickham thought that the *Ars Poetica* and *Odes* appeared as the first two works because of their utility in the schools, but

---

[5]His commentary presumably follows the order of the works in the ancient edition he was using.

[6]See Brink, II, 14; F. Vollmer, "Die Überlieferungsgeschichte des Horaz," *Philologus Suppl.* 10 (1907) 290. The abbreviations for the *sigla* are from Brink (see II, 53); here and there Vollmer's differ.

[7]Brink, II, 15.

this arrangement only pertains to Vollmer's CLASS II.[8] Vollmer thought that the principle of arrangement of the second class was alphabetical order.[9]

CLASS I			
C(E)	B	A	D
1. Carm.	Carm.	Carm.	Carm.
2. Epod.	Epod.	Epod.	—
3. Carm. Saec.	Carm. Saec.	Carm. Saec.	—
4. *Ars Poetica*	*Ars Poetica*	—	—
5. Serm.	—	Epist.	Epist.
6. Ep./Serm.	Serm.	—	Serm.
CLASS II			
R λ1 δπφψ	V(?)		Porphyrio
1. Carm.	Carm.		Carm.
2. *Ars Poetica*	*Ars Poetica*		*Ars Poetica*
3. Epod.	Epod.		Carm. Saec.
4. Carm. Saec.	Carm. Saec.		Carm. lib. V [=Epod.]
5. Epist.	Serm. (?)		Serm.
6. Serm.	Epist. (?)		Epist.

TABLE I: POSITION OF THE *ARS POETICA* IN THE MSS. OF HORACE

What is, in any event, clear is that before Henricus Stephanus (Henri Estienne), whose influential edition of Horace was first published in 1549, almost no editor placed the *Ars Poetica* after *Epist.* II at the very end of the Horatian corpus.[10] It is also clear that Stephanus' location was not immediately accepted by everyone: for example, the new version of the great variorum edition of Parrasio, Badius van Assche, Poliziano, Sabellico, et al., published in Venice

---

[8]E.C. Wickham, *Quinti Horatii Flacci, Opera Omnia*, vol. 2 (Oxford 1891) 327, 332.

[9]Vollmer, op. cit. (*supra* n. 6) 278n30. Brink rightly expresses scepticism at II, 14.

[10]H. Stephanus, *Q. Horatii Flacci, Opera Omnia* (Paris 1549) = Mills 147. A new edition is listed at Mills 199, 200, 209. Second editions of this are found at Mills 239 and 240; the third edition is at Mills 256. On Stephanus (1528-1598), see A. A. Renouard, *Annales de l'imprimerie des Estienne* (Paris 1837); J. Jehasse, *La renaissance de la critique* (Saint-Etienne 1976) 71-88.

An earlier edition to print the *Ars Poetica* as the last work in the Horatian corpus was that of Joannes Aloisius Tuscanus published in ca. 1474 (= Mills 32, with a date of ca. 1475; ca. 1474 is the date given in the British Library catalogue for I.B. 18046, which I have examined in London). There may well have been other pre-Stephanus editions to print the *Ars Poetica* last; I cannot claim to have inspected every printed edition of Horace predating 1549.

in 1553, kept the *Ars* in its old position after the *Carmen Saeculare* and before *Sermones* I, the position in **C(E)**.[11] This is the same place in which the anonymously edited *opera omnia* published *ex officina M. Vascosani* put the *Ars Poetica* in 1551.[12] In Georgius Fabricius' Horace edition, which appeared in Basel in 1555, the poem also appeared after the *Carmen Saeculare* and before *Sermones* I, and was to remain there as late as the Leipzig reprint of 1593.[13] That Stephanus' rearrangement of the corpus became canonical—and remains so to this day—is probably due to Lambinus' great edition with commentary of 1561, where the *Ars Poetica* is printed last, after *Epistles* II.[14]

As the material collected in *Appendix I* shows, no one seems to have called the *Ars Poetica* the *Epistola ad Pisones* before Jason De Nores, the professor of Moral Philosophy at Padua from 1577 to his death in 1590, who in 1553 wrote a commentary on the poem based on the ideas of his friend and teacher,

---

[11]*Q. Horatii Flacci Poetae Venusini Omnia Poemata* (Venice 1553) = Mills 154 (and cf. Mills 97, 112, 119, etc.). On Aulo Giano Parrasio and his work on Horace's *Ars Poetica*, see F. D'Episcopo, *Aulo Giano Parrasio, fondatore dell'Accademia Cosentina* (Cosenza 1982). In M.-A. Muret's edition published in Venice in 1555 (*Horatius. M. Antonii Mureti in Eundem Annotationes*), the *Ars Poetica* is printed as a separate work after *Epistles* II but before *Serm.* I. Muret entitled the work, "Q. Horatii Flacci De Arte Poetica Liber. Ad Pisones" (p. 189).

[12]*Q. Horatii Flacci Poemata* (Paris 1545-1551) = Mills 137. This edition appeared in five parts; the part containing the *Ars Poetica* was issued in 1551.

[13]See Mills 160 for the 1555 printing; I examined the 1593 reprint in the Bib. Marciana. On Fabricius (1516-1571), see *Biographie universelle*, 13 (Paris 1855) 294.

[14]Lambinus' work appeared in two volumes, of which the first contains the lyric poems and the second the hexameters: *Q. Horatius Flaccus, Ex fide, atque auctoritate decem librorum manuscriptorum, opera Dionys. Lambini Monstroliensis emendatus: Ab eodemque commentariis copiosissimis illustratus, nunc primum in lucem editus* (Lyon 1561) (= Mills 168); and *Q. Horatii Flacci sermonum libri quattuor, seu satyrarum, libri duo, epistolarum, libro duo, a Dionysio Lambino Monstroliensi ex fide novem librorum manuscriptorum emendati ab eodemque commentariis copiosissimis illustrati* (Lyon 1561) (= Mills 171). Note that Mills 171 = Mills 124, the copy in the California State Library, Sutro Branch, which Mills, following the Sutro catalogue entry, erroneously dates to 1541. As I suspected, and as Mr. Clyde Janes, Director of the Library, kindly confirmed in a personal communication, the title page of the Sutro copy dates the book to MDLXI, which was apparently misread as MDXLI. Despite the possible implication of the title of the second volume containing the hexameters, Lambinus did not include the *Ars* in the second book of *Epistles* but printed it as an independent work after *Epist.* II. For an appreciation of Lambinus' edition, see C. O. Brink, "Horatian Poetry. Thoughts on the Development of Textual Criticism and Interpretation," *Wolfenbütteler Forschungen* 12 (1981) 7-17, at p. 10.

Padua professor Trifone Gabriele (*Appendix I* [3]).[15] In the preface to the work, De Nores gave a fairly detailed justification of this title, stating that the poem had the form of a letter, not of a technical treatise. Dismissing the testimony of Quintilian on the title, De Nores argues against possible critics of his new title by noting that letters can offer precepts and treat serious matters; he points out that in several of Horace's own indisputable letters, he does just this. De Nores also sees in the poem's lack of elaborate structure a further argument in favor of the letter-theory, since "the letter likes a certain familiarity of tone, and a highly precise structure tends more towards severity than familiarity."

It is likely that sensitivity of Gabriele and De Nores to the characteristics of the epistolary genre reflects the influence of earlier sixteenth-century works on the epistle, such as that by the northern Italian humanist, Marino Becichemo, who wrote a lengthy and perceptive treatise on this topic, without specific reference to the *Ars Poetica* (*Appendix I* [1]). Another possible influence was Erasmus.[16] At any rate, it is certain that De Nores knew the work of Francesco Robortello, whose career as public humanist took him to teaching positions in Venice, Bologna, and Padova.[17] In his *Paraphrasis* of the poem, printed in 1548 (*Appendix I* [2]) Robortello cautiously called the poem "Libellum...Qui Vulgo De Arte Poetica Inscribitur," and his introductory explanation for the poem's lack of structure foreshadowed De Nores' epistle-theory.

---

[15]On De Nores (?—1590), see the brief account of his life in *De Gymnasio Patavino Antonii Riccoboni Commentariorum Libri Sex* (Padua 1598) fol. 79r; *Biographie universelle*, 31 (Paris n.d.) 34; F. E. Budd, "A Minor Italian Critic of the Sixteenth Century: Jason Denores," *Modern Language Review* 22 (1927) 421-434. For his work on poetics, see B. Weinberg, *A History of Literary Criticism in the Italian Renaissance*, 2 vols. (Chicago 1961), especially pp. 316-319, 621-626.

[16]Becichemo's work on epistolography was still memorable enough to be singled out for special notice in A. Riccoboni's *De Gymnasio Patavino commentariorum libri sex* (Padua 1598) fol. 28v and in *Gymnasium Patavinum Iacobi Philippi Tomasini Episcopi Aemoniensis Libris V comprehensum* (Udine 1654) 340: "scripsit de ratione scribendarum epistolarum." On Becichemo (ca. 1468-1526), see C. H. Clough in *Biografia degli Italiani* 7 (1965) cols. 511-515; T. B. Deutscher in *Contemporaries of Erasmus*, vol. 1 (Toronto 1985) 114-115. On the epistolary genre in the Renaissance, see M. Fumaroli, "Genèse de l'épistolographie classique," *Revue d'histoire littéraire de la France* 78 (1978) 886-905; C. Fantazzi (ed.), *Juan Luis Vives, De conscribendis epistolis. Critical Edition with Introduction, Translation and Annotation, Selected Works of J. L. Vives,* vol. 3 (Leiden 1989) 5-14. Neither Fantazzi nor Fumaroli takes note of Becichemo.

[17]For a brief *vita* of and bibliography on Robortello (1516-1567), see W. McCuaig, *Carlo Sigonio. The Changing World of the Late Renaissance* (Princeton 1989) 9; *Cambridge History of Renaissance Philosophy* (Cambridge 1988) 835.

De Nores' work was to have great influence through the centuries. The idea of classifying the *Ars Poetica* as a letter first spread through northern Italy. In 1555, Marc-Antoine Muret—who had been living in the Veneto since the previous year, having fled charges of sodomy and heresy in his native France— also implicitly embraced De Nores' theory. In his *In Horatium Scholia* (Venice 1555) he called the poem "Epistola in Artem Poeticam" (*Appendix I* [4]).[18] Another French scholar in Italy in the 1550s was Muret's friend Denis Lambin, whose headnote to the *Ars Poetica* in his great Horace edition of 1561 (*Appendix I* [5]; and cf. above n. 14) repeats De Nores' defense of the letter-thesis against a possible attack that a letter should offer precepts and also suggests that the poem's length is no impediment to interpreting it as a letter. From Henri Estienne's *Schediasmatum* (*Appendix I* [10]), we learn that Lambin spent some time in Padua "many years ago" where he discussed Horace's poetry with Estienne. From Lambin's love letters to Lucia of Padua, we can date their Padua sojourn to 1549-1552.[19] It was doubtless in these years that Lambin and Estienne had their discussions, after exposure to Robortello's and De Nores' new ideas.

With Lambin, De Nores' ideas spread to northern Europe, and not a moment too soon. In 1561, Julius Caesar Scaliger, who praised Horace's lyric poetry, attacked the *Ars Poetica* for displaying a lack of craftsmanship (cf. *Appendix I* [6a-c]).[20] Scaliger's criticisms caught on among such non-scholarly writers as Claude Du Verdier and Henry Peacham, but fell on deaf ears among philologists, who grew ever more bold in their application of the epistle-

---

[18]Muret also called the poem an *epistola* in his *Variarum Lectionum Liber Duodecimus* in *M. Antonii Mureti Opera Omnia*, tom. 2, ed. D. Ruhnkenius (Leiden 1789) 302. On Muret (1526-1585) see *Biographie universelle*, 29 (Paris n.d.) 606-608; C. Dejob, *Marc-Antoine Muret, un professeur français en Italie dans la seconde moitié du XVIe siècle* (Paris 1881); *Cambridge History of Renaissance Philosophy* (Cambridge 1988) 827.

[19]See H. Potez and F. Préchac (eds.), *Lettres galantes de Denys Lambin, 1552-1554, Publications de la Faculté de l'Université de Lille* 6 (1941) x (for the chronology of Lambin's first Italian trip with Cardinal de Tournon), and 1-3 for a letter dated 5 December 1552 to Lucia, the last lines of which read: "Quoties ad me scribere voles, huic recte dare poteris. Habitat cum Legato Regio. Est huic nomen Henrico Stephano." On Lambin (1516-1572), see *Biographie universelle*, 23 (Paris n.d.) 58-59. Lambin's observation that some letters could be quite long was a Renaissance commonplace; cf. J. L. Vives, op. cit. (*supra* n. 16) 125-126 (§101).

[20]On Scaliger (1484-1558), see the bibliography cited in *La statue et l'empreinte. La poétique de Scaliger*, ed. by C. Balavoine and P. Laurens (Paris 1986) 193-195. On Scaliger's attack on the *Ars*, see M. Magnien, "Le statut d'Horace dans les Poetices Libri VII," ibid., 19-33.

thesis.[21] Thus, Johann Sturm—perhaps most famous as the teacher of Petrus Ramus[22]—suggested that the poem belonged in *Epistles* II. Rejecting as inconclusive the argument that the poem is a letter simply because it was addressed to the Pisones, Sturm rests his case on the facts that *Epistles* I has about 1,000 lines and that *Epistles* II would be approximately as long if the *Ars Poetica* is combined with the letters to Augustus and Florus (cf. *Appendix I* [9]). Sturm also points out that the *Ars Poetica* treats the same subject as *Epist.* II.1 and II.2. Despite his belief about the genre of the poem, Sturm retained the traditional title, *De Arte Poetica Liber*. Sturm's work was published in 1576 by his student Joannes Lobartus Borussus. It was not long before Iacobus Cruquius, in his Antwerp edition of 1578, took the next logical step and actually called the *Ars Poetica* "Epistola Tertia Libri Secundi, Ad Pisones De Arte Poetica."[23] Cruquius' new position and title were accepted by other scholars almost immediately. Petrus Gualterius Chabotius, for example, called the poem "Epistola Tertia Libri Secundi Ad Pisones De Arte Poetica" in his *Expositio analytica et brevis in universum Q. Horatii Flacci poema* (Paris 1582).[24]

Since the late sixteenth century, the speculations of Stephanus, De Nores, Sturm, and Cruquius have become deeply ingrained in our editions, literary histories, and therefore in our assumptions about the poem. Today it comes as a surprise to most non-specialists to discover that, in fact, the ancient and medieval evidence offers virtually no support to the placement of the poem with

---

[21]Cf. C. Du Verdier, *In Auctores Paene Omnes, Antiquos Potissimum Censio* (Lyons 1586) 57: "Horatius in Lyricis quidem apud Latinos primas tenet, in hexametris duriusculus esse videtur. Versus enim ut plurimum inexculte per monosyllaba desinere facit, quo nihil absurdius, ut illum, 'nascetur ridiculus mus' et innumerabilia id genus. De Poetica arte multa praecipit quae ipse non observat." H. Peacham, *The Compleat Gentleman* (Oxford 1906; originally published in 1622[1], 1634[2], 1666[3]) 89: "his Poetica [is] his worst peece, for while he teacheth the Art, hee goeth unartificially to worke even in the very beginning."

[22]On Sturm (1507-1589), see W. Ong, *Ramus, Method, and the Decay of Dialogue* (Cambridge, Mass. 1958) passim, especially pp. 231-236; N. W. Gilbert, *Renaissance Concepts of Method* (New York 1960) 72-73, 122-124.

[23]Cruquius wrote, in his edition of 1578 (= Mills 210), "iniuria ad Pisones epistola a suis coepistolis (ut ita dicam) est avulsa...." (apud Orelli-Baiter-Mewes, *Q. Horatius Flaccus,* vol. 2 [Berlin 1892] 568; I have not been able to find this passage in the copies of Cruquius I have seen). On the edition, see C. Zangemeister, "Über die älteste Horaz-Ausgabe des Cruquius," *RhM* 23 (1864) 321-339. On Cruquius (dates unknown; first appointed professor of Greek and Latin at Bruges in 1544), see *Biographie universelle,* 9 (Paris n.d.) 537-538.

[24]= Mills 219. On Chabotius (1516-1597), see A. Chalmers, *The General Biographical Dictionary,* 9 (London 1813) 59-60.

Epistles II nor even to its classification as a letter.[25] As we have seen, these humanist speculations were presented with great boldness but little argumentation. In particular, De Nores and Lambin did not so much positively establish that the poem is an epistle as defend the unargued epistle-thesis against hypothetical attacks about subject matter and length. Sturm's argument about book-length, while ingenious, is hardly compelling: 500 lines is not abnormal in this period, as Virgil's *Georgics* shows.[26] One can also argue that the *Epodes* (625 lines), *Ars Poetica*, *Epistles* II, and *Odes* IV (580 lines) give sufficient evidence for the existence of modest-sized, "Homeric" books in the Horatian corpus.

In this century, editions, commentaries, and translations either print the poem as *Epistles* II.3 or else put it in Stephanus' position after *Epistles* II.2, which, in both cases, gives the unwary reader the impression that the *Ars* is somehow to be associated with the second book of letters.[27] To the contrary, the evidence strongly suggests that—whatever the basis of the ancient arrangement of Horace's works—the *Ars Poetica* was a separate *liber*, not part of the *Epistles*. We may here express the hope that future editors will restore the *Ars* to its pre-sixteenth century position in the corpus, somewhere after the *Odes* and before the *Satires*. The point is not so much to put it back where Horace wanted it—for, in fact, we have no information that confirms Horace's participation in the planning of the ancient edition of his collected poetry—as to put the poem in a place that is at least not misleading.

As for the title, we have seen that in reclassifying the poem, neither De Nores nor Sturm cited any ancient evidence. Within a few decades of De Nores' treatise, Henri Estienne, in his *Diatribae* (1575), noted that, in two places, the late-antique grammarian Charisius quotes words from the *Ars* as coming from Horace's *epistulae* (cf. *Appendix I* [7]).[28] These are the passages:

---

[25] Cf. below, *Chapter 4*, where I show that the poem does not display the generic features of Horatian (or, for that matter, other ancient) letters.

[26] See, in general, J. Van Sickle, "The Book Roll and Some Conventions of the Poetic Book," *Arethusa* 13 (1980) 5-42, especially pp. 6-12 on book-length.

[27] By the words "somehow to be associated with" I mean that the poem is either part of *Epistles* II or else is at least written in the same style, genre, or spirit as the poems immediately preceding. While editors who print the *Ars* at the end of their editions as a separate work could claim to be implying nothing of the sort, we might ask why they have not simply kept the *Ars* in one of its less pregnant positions in the medieval mss. Cf. the perceptive comment of Brink (I, 239) on the tendency to date the *Ars* late: "without much reasoning [scholars] assigned to the *Ars* the last place in the chronology...often, one suspects, because H. Stephanus had assigned to it the last place in the sequence of the poems."

[28] See H. Stephanus' new edition of the *Poemata* of Horace, to which he appended (separately paginated) *Diatribae De Hac Sua Editione* (Paris 1575 = Mills 200; cf. Mills 199). On Charisius, see *Restauration und Erneuerung. Die lateinische Litera-*

[1] Charisius, p. 263.9-12 Barwick-Kühnert (= p. 202.26-29 Keil):
Impariter Horatius epistolarum, 'versibus impariter iunctis' [=*Ars Poetica* 75]; ubi Q. Terentius Scaurus in commentariis in artem poeticam libro X 'adverbium,' inquit, 'figuravit.'

Horatius *corr.* n[1] [= codex Neapolitanus IV A 9 saec. xv/xvi]
persius N [= codex Neapolitanus IV A 8, olim Bobiensis, saec. vii/viii]

[2] Charisius, p. 265.1-5 Barwick-Kühnert (= p. 204.5-10 Keil):
Longum clamet Horatius epistularum [*Ars Poet.* 459], 'licet succurrite longum clamet'; ut Maro quoque [*Ecl.* 3.79] 'et longum...Iolla.'

Aldus Manutius (II), in his commentary on the poem of 1576, summarily rejected Charisius' testimony, noting that it contradicts all other ancient evidence (see *Appendix I* [8]).[29] In favor of Manutius' position, we may note that Charisius, while generally reliable, is not perfect when it comes to citing titles. At 268.5 (Barwick), he refers to Lucretius 1.525 as *Lucretius...de rerum natura libro III*. At 100.18, he calls Caesar's *ad Pisonem* the *de Pisone*. The incipits and explicits of the manuscripts of the poem and the scholia are all but unanimous in calling the poem the *(Liber) De Arte Poetica*.[30] Charisius himself twice refers to Terentius Scaurus' second-century A.D. *Commentarii in Artem Poeticam*, thereby showing awareness of a very different title. One such reference comes in [1].[31] Even if unlikely, his reports that the poem belonged in the letters need to be examined in some detail here because they have been taken more seriously than they should by recent commentators.

We may begin by granting that it is, of course, possible that Charisius was correct in assigning the poem to Horace's *epistulae*. If so, we have no way of knowing, on the basis of Charisius, to *which* book of *Epistles* the *Ars* would have been attached (advocates of the epistle-thesis, following Sturm, too quickly assume *Epist*. II), and we can say that such a text, if it ever really existed, must have been late-antique. Vollmer's observation about Charisius remains valid, at least as far as the *original* publication of the *Ars* and the early ancient texts of Horace are concerned: "mit keiner in Hss. sich findenden Ordnung deckt sich, daß

---

tur von 284 bis 374 n. Chr., *Handbuch der lateinischen Literatur der Antike*, vol. 5, ed. R. Herzog and P. L. Schmidt (Munich 1989) 125-131; Schanz-Hosius, *Geschichte der römischen Literatur*, *HdA* IV.1 (Munich 1914) 165-169.

[29] For Aldus Manutius (II), Paulli filius, Aldi nepos, see his *In Q. Horatii Flacci Venusini Librum De Arte Poetica...Commentarius* (Venice 1576).

[30] The evidence is conveniently presented in the edition of O. Keller and A. Holder, vol. 2 (Jena 1925) 284, 320.

[31] Cf. Charisius 263.11-12, 272.27-28 Barwick.

Charisius gram. I 202,26 und 204,5 die ars poetica als *in epistulis* citiert, während doch schon Quintilian das gesonderte Buch kennt."[32] As Bowersock has aptly observed in another context, "the mere antiquity of a testimony is no guarantee, especially when it is testimony of some four hundred years after the text."[33]

However, even the hypothesis of a late-antique text of Horace calling the *Ars* a letter is subject to serious doubts. Charisius, his source(s), a glossator, or the scribe of Naples codex IV A 8 may have simply erred. Insufficient attention has been paid to how Charisius cites his literary parallels. There are, in general, two classes of citations: those with writers cited by name and frequently by title; and those often cited by name but never by title. In the first class belong quotations of, e.g., Cicero, Cinna, Sallust, and Virgil. In the second class are to be found Ovid,[34] Persius, Propertius, and Tibullus.[35] Where does Horace belong? In his grammar, Charisius cites passages of Horace a total of nineteen times. Aside from the problematic passages [1] and [2] above, he never gives the title. In four cases he does not even mention Horace's name.[36] The seventeen secure cases all but ensure that Charisius cited Horace without title and sometimes without name. On this basis, the title cited in [1] and [2] is suspect insofar as it cannot in all probability be supported by the authority of Charisius.[37]

[32]Vollmer, op cit. (*supra* n.6) 290n67.

[33]G. W. Bowersock, "A Date in the *Eighth Eclogue*," HSCP 75 (1971) 73.

[34]The passages in Charisius (= C., with pagination of Barwick's edition) are the following (*= no mention of Ovid's name): *De Medic. Fac.* 39 = C. 114.13; *Art. Am.* 1.249 = C. 91.29; *Art. Am.* 2.300 = C. 132.19; *Art. Am.* 2.375 = C. 131.28; *Art. Am.* 2.653 = C. 92.1; *Metam.* 1.13 = C. 82.6; *Metam.* 3.79 = C. 368.7*; *Metam.* 3.522 = C. 172.12; *Metam.* 4.494 = C. 102.10.

[35]*Persius* (= Ps.): 1.25 = C. 109.10 (as printed by Keil, not Barwick, i.e., without Putschen's supplement *in sat. I*); Ps. 4.43 = C. 332.3; Ps. 6.4 = C. 88.4; Ps. 6.10 = C. 124.18. *Propertius* (= P.): P. 2.33.37 = C. 137.25; P. 2.13.35 = C. 113.5; P. 3.11.15 = C. 131.19; P. 3.14.1 = C. 85.9. *Tibullus* (= T.): T. 1.5.3 = C. 184.1; T. 1.8.20 = C. 114.11; T. 1.8.26 = C. 109.16, 166.26; T. 2.4.31 = C. 160.8.

[36]The passages in Charisius (= C., with pagination of Barwick's edition) are the following (* = no mention of Horace's name): *Carm.* 1.1.33ff.= C. 350.30*; *Carm.* 1.4.1 = C. 104.2; *Carm.* 1.6.6 = C. 357.20; *Carm.* 1.12.41 = C. 133.11; *Carm.* 1.29.7ff. = C. 133.14; *Carm.* 1.36.8 = C. 351.1*; *Carm.* 2.18.7ff. = C. 127.15; *Carm.* 3.1.17ff. = C. 355.6*; *Carm.* 3.5.10 = C. 77.22; *Carm.* 3.14.9ff. = C. 83.5; *Epod.* 12.25 = C. 201.2; *Serm.* 1.1.94ff. = C. 295.7; *Serm.* 1.2.89 = C. 128.14; *Serm.* 1.9.13 = C. 123.2; *Serm.* 2.2.122 = C. 123.4; *Epist.* 1.7.22 = C. 352.11; *Epist.* 1.16.20 = C. 354.3.*

[37]It is reassuring that the same two classes with the same breakdown of authors are to be found in the fifth-century grammar of the Anonymus Bobiensis, which belongs to the "Charisius-group" of late-antique grammarians. See the edition of M. De Nonno, *La grammatica dell'Anonymus Bobiensis* (GL I 533-565 Keil), especially pp. xvi-xvii (on the "Charisius-group"); xix-xx (date); 89 (*index*

That Horace belongs to the second class is also suggested by the information in the *apparatus criticus* under [**1**]. Here we see that the original reading *Persius epistolarum* in N has been corrected in n[1] to *Horatius epistularum*. This is not the only corruption of an author's name in N. Some other examples are: Varrus instead of Varro (p. 69.2 Barwick); et Ennius instead of Titinius (p. 69.3); Plaustus instead of Plautus (p. 69.16); Aelius Cinna instead of Helvius Cinna (p. 101.23); Aedilius Cilo instead of Aelius Stilo (p. 106.8); Vergilius instead of Verrius (p. 107.14); Patulus instead of Pacuvius (p. 115.29); Lucilius instead of Lucretius (p. 116.8); Lucius instead of Lucilius (p. 125.1); Vergilius instead of Velius Longus (p. 145. 18); and Ninnius instead of Naevius (p. 184.16). These corruptions are all examples of errors arising from the confusion of similar letters, from the omission of letters, and the like. The corruption of Horatius into Persius is different. Two explanations are possible. Instead of a scribal confusion or omission of similar letters, we may have to do with a marginal note or a superscript written in a crabbed hand that was misread when added to the text of Charisius sometime between the first version in the fourth century and the transcription of N, three or four centuries later. The same hand was doubtless responsible for the similar notation (*Horatius epistularum*) that we see in the nearby passage [**2**].[38] That *Horatius epistolarum* in [**1**] is an intrusive note is furthermore suggested by the fact that Terentius Scaurus' commentary on the *Ars Poetica* is cited later in the sentence. Is it likely that the same person would have written in the same sentence "Horatius epistolarum" and "ubi Q. Terentius Scaurus in commentariis in artem poeticam?" As a parallel for adscripts of titles in the textual tradition of Charisius, we may cite the example of *in scauro* (at p. 97.19 Barwick) in the margin of N itself. Many citations in Charisius are without author or title, so the impulse for readers to add such notes is obvious.[39] A second possibility is more complicated but perhaps more likely: Charisius may originally have written *Verrius Flaccus epistolarum*, citing two passages where Verrius—who did write *epistulae* on grammatical problems—quoted

---

scriptorum); cf. also the review article by A. C. Dionisiotti in *JRS* 74 (1984) 202-205. In the Anon. Bob., Virgilian titles are cited rarely (only once out of 36 citations), suggesting that Virgil may have originally belonged to the second group and that most titles were added between the time of Anon. Bob. and N.

[38]The writer of the adscript may have correctly written *Horatius* in [1] and [2]. Another possibility, of course, is that [2] also had *Persius*, but this was corrected before or after N, or by the scribe of N himself. A reexamination of N, unfortunately, reveals nothing. Notoriously in a poor state of preservation, N may no longer be consulted in Naples. Prof. David Konstan informed me in a personal communication that the photographs of the manuscript in the Naples library are mostly black and illegible and that the legible parts do not include our passage.

[39]For examples, see s.vv. *incerti poetae* and *incerti scriptores* in Barwick's *index scriptorum* (p. 484).

Horatian examples without mention of Horace or the title of his work. Sometime between Charisius and N, *Verrius Flaccus* was changed to the two more famous Flacci: *Persius* in [1] and *Horatius* in [2].[40]

Thus, Charisius' testimony should not be allowed to cast doubt on the otherwise unanimous witness of ancient authors for three reasons. First, even if we suppose that *epistularum* in [1] and [2] was written by Charisius, this attests only a late textual tradition and cannot, in isolation, drive the unequivocal ancient evidence from the field. Secondly, even if written by Charisius, *epistularum* may be wrong, since we have parallels for incorrect titles in the *Ars Grammatica*. Finally—and most likely—the attribution to Horace's letters of the words cited in [1] and [2] may well be an intrusive note that postdates Charisius and predates N since Charisius never elsewhere cites Horace with title.

How, then, did the ancients refer to the *Ars Poetica*? The evidence is overwhelming that, no later than one hundred years after Horace's death, it was considered a separate book called either the *Ars Poetica*[41] or the *(Liber) De arte poetica*.[42] These titles are so similar that we need not expend any effort trying to choose between them. The fact that the poem consisted of only one book is attested by the latter title, by the *Vita Horatii* in Ps.-Acro,[43] and by a reference in Quintilian to the *prima parte libri de arte poetica*.[44] What, then, are we to call the poem? In several recent publications, Nicholas Horsfall has reminded us how unreliable our modern—and sometimes even our ancient—titles of the Latin classics really are.[45] The *Ars Poetica* presents an excellent case in point: despite modern speculation, we have no reason to think that Horace or most ancients called the poem an *epistula*. It is welcome news to report that in our latest Teubner editions of Horace by Borszak and Shackleton Bailey the proper titles are now used. However, as noted, these editors have still printed the poem in a misleading position at the very end of the corpus, just after *Epistles* II.

---

[40]Note that Charisius referred to Verrius as *Verrius Flaccus* at p. 73.9 Barwick. For a similar confusion of Flacci (Persius for Horace), cf. Servius on *Georg.* 3.363.

[41]Quintilian, *Epist. ad Tryph.* 2; Sidonius 9.223; [Probus] *De ultimis syllabis* 223.9 Keil; Priscian *Inst.*, vol. II, 271.19 Keil.

[42]Quintilian, *Inst.* 8.3.60; Terentius Scaurus *apud* Charisius, pp. 263.11-12, 272.27 (Barwick); Priscian *Inst.*, vol. I, 267.23, vol. II, 254.16, 331.15 (Keil); the second *Vita Horatii* in O. Keller's edition of the *Pseudoacronis Scholia in Horatium vetustiora,* vol. 1 (Leipzig 1902) 3 (line 6).

[43]"Scripsit autem carminum libros IIII, carmen saeculare, epodon, de arte poetica lib. I, epistularum lib. II, sermonum lib. II" (ed. Keller, ibid.).

[44]*Inst.* 8.3.60.

[45]See N.M. Horsfall, "Horace, Sermones 3?" *LCM* 4.6 (1979) 117-119; "Some Problems of Titulature in Roman Literary History," *BICS* 28 (1981) 103-114.

CHAPTER 2

THE DATE OF THE POEM

The argument for keeping the *Ars* separate from *Epistles* II can also be supported by chronology, for, as we will see, the *Ars Poetica* probably predates the two works in *Epistles* II. In any event, the date of the *Ars Poetica*, and, indeed, of any literary work, provides an indispensable framework for interpretation, and so the dating of the *Ars Poetica* would be worth reexamining for this reason alone.

Of all Horace's poems, the *Ars Poetica* is the hardest to date. Scholars have proposed dates ranging from the early 20s B.C. to the very end of Horace's life. In 1965, Duckworth published a useful overview of the various attempts at a date.[1] This may be updated, corrected and augmented as follows:

28-27, between *Satires* II and *Odes* I-III[2]
23-20, between *Odes* I-III and *Epistles* I[3]

---

[1] G. E. Duckworth, "Horace's Hexameters and the Date of the *Ars Poetica*," *TAPA* 66 (1965) 73-95, at pp. 84-85.

[2] J. Elmore, "A New Dating of Horace's *De Arte Poetica*," *CP* 30 (1935) 1-9. Elmore's dating is based on a rather arbitrary "correction" of Jerome's date for the death of Quintilius Varus (see Elmore, p. 5).

[3] J. H. Van Reenen, *Disputatio philologico-critica de Horatii Epistola ad Pisones* (Amsterdam 1806); A. Michaelis, "Die Horazischen Pisonen," *Commentationes Philologae in honorem T. Mommseni* (Berlin 1877) 420-432; H. Nettleship, "The *de Arte Poetica* of Horace," *JP* 12 (1883) 43-61; A. Y. Campbell, *Horace. A New Interpretation* (London 1924) 114-15; Schanz-Hosius, *Geschichte der römischen Literatur, HdA,* VIII.ii (Munich 1935[4]) 133; A. Rostagni, *Arte poetica di Orazio* (Turin 1930) xvi-xix; O. Immisch, *Horazens Epistel über die Dichtkunst, Philologus Suppl.* 24.3 (1932) 1-8; F. Villeneuve, *Horace, Epîtres* (Paris 1934) 193-96; F. M. Pontani, *Orazio. Arte poetica* (Rome 1953) xi-xiii; E. Pasoli, *Le epistole letterarie di Orazio* (Rome, n.d.) 31; P. Grimal, *Essai sur l'Art poétique d'Horace* (Paris 1968) 15-35.

20-19, between *Epistles* I and *Epistles* II.2[4]
18, between *Epistles* II.2 and the *Carmen Saeculare*[5]
17-16, after the *Carmen Saeculare* and before *Odes* IV[6]
15, before *Epist.* II.1[7]
13-8, after *Odes* IV, making the poem Horace's last[8]

In the absence of the kind of fairly reliable information that permits us to date Horace's other poetic books with some precision, how have scholars arrived at such widely divergent datings of the *Ars Poetica?* Three distinct approaches to chronology can be identified in the scholarship: (1) placing the *Ars* within some developmental pattern of Horace's ideas about poetry; (2) estab-

---

[4]A. S. Wilkins, *The Epistles of Horace* (London 1902) 330-32; E. Stemplinger, *RE* VIII s.v. Horatius (Stuttgart 1913) 2367 (in col. 2375 he dates the poem to 16); O. Immisch, op. cit. (*supra* n. 3) 1-8; J. C. Rolfe, *Horace. Satires and Epistles* (Boston 1935), Appendix, p. 13.

[5]J. Vahlen, "Über Zeit und Abfolge der Literaturbriefe des Horaz," *Monatsberichten der Berliner Akademie* 1878, 688-704 at pp. 702-703 (= *Gesammelte philologische Schriften* II [Leipzig and Berlin 1923] 46-61 at pp. 59-60); H. Schütz, *Q. Horatius Flaccus, Episteln* (Berlin 1883) viii; E. P. Morris, *Horace. The Epistles* (New York 1911) 188; C. Becker, *Das Spätwerk des Horaz* (Göttingen 1963) 111.

[6]A. Kiessling and R. Heinze, *Q. Horatius Flaccus. Briefe* (Berlin 1898[2]); cf. J. H. Kirkland, *Horace. Satires and Epistles* (Chicago 1893) 338-39.

[7]Richard Bentley, on the penultimate page of the unpaginated preface to his edition of Horace (Amsterdam 1713[2]), puts the *Ars Poetica* and *Epistles* II after the *Carmen Saec.* and *C.* IV, saying that they are *annis incertis*; A. Rostagni, op. cit. (*supra* n. 3) xix, xxii, xxxiv; W. Wili, *Horaz und die Augusteische Kultur* (Basel 1948) 309; A. La Penna, *Orazio e l'ideologia del principato* (Turin 1963) 158ff.; J. Perret, *Horace* (Paris 1959[2]) 190ff.; F. Cupaiuolo, *Tra poesia e poetica* (Naples 1966) 30n15; G. D'Anna, "La cronologia dell'epistola di Orazio ad Augusto," *Vichiana* 12 (1983) 121-135, at p. 125 (dating the poem specifically to 13); J.-M. Roddaz, *Marcus Agrippa, BEFAR* 253 (1984) 228n154. Note that Bentley's view on the date fluctuated, as Brink (I, 243n2) points out.

[8]G. Dillenburger, *Q. Horatii Flacci Opera Omnia* (Bonn 1848[2]) 517; L. Mueller, *Quintus Horatius Flaccus* (Leipzig 1880) 79-80; A. Waltz, *Des variations de la langue et de la métrique d'Horace dans ses différents ouvrage* (Paris 1881) 28; E. C. Wickham, *Quinti Horatii Flacci, Opera Omnia*, vol. 2 (Oxford 1891) 331-35; C. L. Smith, *The Odes and Epodes of Horace* (Boston 1894) xxxivf.; C. Cichorius, *Römische Studien* (Leipzig 1922) 340-341; T. Frank, *Catullus and Horace* (New York 1928) 260; J. W. H. Atkins, *Literary Criticism in Antiquity*, vol. 2 (Cambridge 1934) 66-69; O. A. W. Dilke, "When Was the *Ars Poetica* Written?" *BICS* 5 (1958) 49-57; J. Perret, op. cit. (*supra* n. 7) 190; Duckworth, op. cit. (*supra* n. 1) 91; Rudd, 19-21; R. Syme, "The Sons of Piso the Pontifex," *AJP* 101 (1980) 333-341, at p. 340 (= *Roman Papers*, vol. 3, ed. A. R. Birley [Oxford 1984] 1226-1232, at p. 1231).

lishing a *terminus ante-* and *post quem* based on historical persons mentioned in the poem; and (3) stylometrics, including diction and meter.

The first approach I will employ elsewhere to show that the ideas of the *Ars* differ so strongly from those found in Horace's other poetry that we cannot properly speak of an evolution of thought but must, instead, consider the possibility that in the *Ars Poetica* Horace contradicts himself. In earlier scholarship, the discontinuity between the *Ars Poetica* and Horace's other expressions of poetic belief was emphasized by L. Ferrero.[9] Ferrero interpreted the evidence in a biographical and rather psychological way, as the sign of an unresolved struggle in Horace's spirit. The parodic reading of the poem offers another and more simple explanation: the *Ars* contradicts much of what Horace says about poetry because it represents a send-up of a pedantic, academic view of poetry put into the mouth of a fictional speaker who we have no reason to suppose is Horace himself (or the Horatian poetic persona). At any rate, since the *Ars Poetica* does not fit into any discernible and datable pattern of Horace's intellectual development, I do not include here a history-of-ideas approach to chronology.

If we generalize this approach and look for any kind of relationship between the *Ars* and Horace's other poems, then we may observe that in the *Ars* there are two echoes of other works of Horace. In line 269 there is an allusion to *Epist.* I.19.11; in line 457 there is an echo of *Odes* I.1.35-36.[10] If either passage were the only one from Horace's corpus alluded to in the *Ars Poetica* we would not be able to make much use of it for the dating. With two such passages, so close in date (*Odes* I-III were published in 23; *Epistles* I in 20), we may guess that Horace echoed these passages because they were still fresh in his mind when he was composing the *Ars*. Later (see pp. 59-61), I will discuss some other important connections between *Epist.* I.19 and the *Ars Poetica,* perhaps implying an affinity in date. We do not know the date of *Epist.* I.19, but, as mentioned, the collection in which it appears was published in *c.* 20 B.C.[11]

The second approach is more solid. These contemporaries are mentioned in the *Ars:* [1-3] Calpurnius Piso and his two children (lines 6, 24, 235, 291-

---

[9]L. Ferrero, *La 'Poetica' e le poetiche di Orazio, Università di Torino Pubblicazioni della Facoltà di Lettere e Filosofia* vol. 5, fasc. 1 (1953) 9-13.

[10]Here are the texts: *AP* 269 nocturna versate manu, versate diurna ~ *Epist.* I.19.11 nocturno certare mero, putere diurno; *AP* 457 hic, dum sublimis versus ructatur et errat ~ *C.* I.1.36 sublimi feriam sidera vertice. In this connection, the repeated line *Sat.* 1.2.13 and *Ars Poetica* 421 (dives agris, dives positis in fenore nummis) is not relevant for dating (except as a *post quem,* assuming with, e.g., Shackleton Bailey that the earlier occurrence in the *Satires* is not an interpolation, as most modern editors suppose).

[11]So, e.g., Brink, III, 277 (ad *Epist.* II.2.20), and many others earlier.

292, 366, 388);[12] [4] Virgil (55); [5] L. Varius Rufus (55); [6] the booksellers Sosii (345); [7] M. Valerius Messalla Corvinus (371); [8] Aulus Cascellius (371); [9] Sp. Maecius Tarpa; and [10] Quintilius Varus (438).[13]

Of these ten, only numbers [4], [5], [7], and [10] are sufficiently well-known to help with chronology. Quintilius Varus [10] died in 24/23 B.C., and Horace uses the imperfect tense in speaking of him, so that it is clear that he is deceased when the *Ars Poetica* was published. This gives us a *terminus post quem* of 24/23 B.C. Virgil [4] and Varius [5] are mentioned in the poem as representatives of contemporary poetry, and so the implication is that they are still alive when the poem was published. This would give us a *terminus ante quem* of 19/15 B.C. (since Virgil died in 19 and Varius in *c.* 15),[14] if not for the fact that line 55 of the poem does not necessarily require that such famous poets as Virgil and Varius are still alive.[15] This is, however, the obvious interpretation of the line, and the fact that Aulus Cascellius [8], who was born in *c.* 100 B.C., would have been in his eighties after 20 B.C. could also be taken as supporting 19/15 B.C. as a *terminus ante quem*.[16] Nevertheless, the cautious conclusion to be drawn from a study of the historical persons mentioned in the *Ars Poetica* is that it provides a firm *post quem* but is only suggestive about a date *ante quem*.

A Reexamination of Duckworth's Metrical Arguments for Dating

To make further progress, we need to try to find stylistic criteria for dating Horace's poetry, and, as we will see, stylistic and metrical evidence also supports the conclusion that the *Ars Poetica* is an independent work in the corpus, less related to the second book of *Epistles* than to *Epistles* I or *Satires* II. Probably the most impressive attempt to date the *Ars Poetica* by stylometric means was undertaken by G. Duckworth. Although Duckworth read his evidence as linking the *Ars Poetica* to *Epist.* II.1, we will see, by reexamining his data, that if anything they suggest a date for the *Ars Poetica* in the period of *Epistles* I (i.e., 23-20 B.C.).[17]

---

[12]On whom, see below, pp. 52-59.
[13]On Tarpa and Quintilius, see below, pp. 61-62, 66-68.
[14]On the death of Varius, see P. L. Schmidt in *Der Kleine Pauly* 5 s.v. Varius III (Munich 1975) cols. 1130-1131.
[15]See, e.g., Brink, I, 240n3.
[16]But see Brink, I, 240n3, where, as in the case of Virgil, he points out that the text does not necessarily require that Aulus Cascellius was alive when the *Ars Poetica* appeared.
[17]G. E. Duckworth, op. cit. (*supra* n. 1) 73-95. Metrical features linking the *Ars Poetica* to *Epist.* I were earlier pointed out by H. Nettleship, op. cit. (*supra* n. 3) 46-47.

The reexamination will proceed in two stages: first we will present an inner critique of Duckworth's work by employing his own dubious statistical methodology to show that his numbers do not say what he thinks they do.[18] Second, we will develop an external critique in which Duckworth's naive methodology will be replaced with normal statistical tests used by statisticians. In this part of our study, we will perform new analyses of some, but not all, of Duckworth's data, limiting ourselves to those data sets that Duckworth thought most supported his late dating of the *Ars Poetica*.

Duckworth's methodology is quite simple: he tabulates metrical features and summarizes them as percentages according to poem or poetic book (*Satires* I, *Satires* II, *Epistles* I, *Epistles* II.1, *Epistles* II.2, and *Ars Poetica*). He assumes that when two or more poems or books show the same or nearly the same percentage, they must be close in date. When percentages are not close, he looks for trends in Horace's use of a certain metrical feature, assuming linear development from a lower to a higher percentage, or from a higher to a lower.

Duckworth's **first test** (p. 86) is the frequency of the four most common patterns of dactylic and spondaic feet. Of these, the *Ars Poetica* resembles *Epist.* II.1 for only the first pattern (*Epist.* II.1 = 11.85; *Ars Poetica* = 10.32; *Epist.* I = 12.82). For the rest, the *Ars Poetica* is closer to *Epist.* I than to *Epist.* II.1 (**Second Pattern**: *Ars Poetica* = 9.68; *Epist.* I = 10.74; *Epist.* II.1 = 11.11; **Third Pattern**: *Ars Poetica* = 8.62; *Epist.* I = 9.24; *Epist.* II.1 = 9.26; **Fourth Pattern**: *Ars Poetica* = 8.21; *Epist.* I = 8.05; *Epist.* II.1 = 9.26). So, the results of the first test place the poem closer to *Epist.* I than to *Epist.* II.1.

Duckworth's **second test** (p. 87) shows the same results. The percentage of the first four patterns in the three works is: *Ars Poetica* = 36.84; *Epist.* I = 40.85; *Epist.* II.1 = 41.48. For the second four, the percentages are: *Ars Poetica* = 29.05; *Epist.* I = 25.45; *Epist.* II.1 = 27.79. For the first eight, the percentages are: *Ars Poetica* = 65.89; *Epist.* I = 66.30; *Epist.* II.1 = 69.26. So, here, again, the *Ars Poetica* is closer to *Epist.* II.1 than to *Epist.* I in only one case.

In Duckworth's **third test** (p. 87), the results do show, as his thesis requires, the resemblance of the *Ars Poetica* to *Epist.* II.1. In the **fourth test** (pp. 87-88), the results are about equal. The percentage of units with eight or more different patterns in the *Ars Poetica* is 100%, as it is in *Epist.* II.1; however, the percentage for *Epist.* I is similarly high (97.67%)—a striking figure in view of the much lower results for *Epist.* II.2 (84.62%), *Sat.* I (83.64%), and *Sat.* II (86.67%).

---

[18] I omit Duckworth's tables and definitions of the various patterns he works with on the assumption that they serve no useful purpose here and can easily be found in the original publication. To have done otherwise would have meant taking up much valuable space recapitulating research that, as we will see, is inconclusive at best.

Duckworth's **fifth test** (p. 88) does not align the *Ars Poetica* with any of the other hexameter poems, and so need not be considered here. In the **sixth test** (of fourth-foot homodyne), the *Ars Poetica* (50.84%) again turns out to be closer to *Epist.* I (51.69%) than to *Epist.* II.1 (52.22). In the **seventh test** (p. 89)—rates of metrical repeats—the *Ars Poetica* (one every 12.2 lines) is closer to *Epist.* I (one every 12.2 lines) than to *Epist.* II.1 (one every 16.9 lines).

In three parts of the **eighth test** (pp. 89-90), the *Ars Poetica* is closer to *Epist.* I than to *Epist.* II.1; in one part it is closer to *Epist.* II.1 than to *Epist.* I; and in the fifth part, it is closer to *Sat.* II. Summing up, then, the eighth test favors the correlation of the *Ars Poetica* with *Epist.* I more than any of the other hexameter poems and indicates a date earlier than *Epist.* II.1. The **ninth test** (p. 90)—use of opposite metrical patterns—confirms Duckworth's thesis. The results of the **tenth test** (p. 90) partly confirm (part 2: ddsd—ssds) and partly disconfirm (sddd—dsss) the thesis. The **eleventh test** (p. 91)—reverse patterns—put the *Ars Poetica* (one every 25 lines) again closer to *Sat.* II (one every 25.8 lines) and *Epist.* I (one every 27.9 lines) than to *Epist.* II.1 (one every 54 lines).

To conclude this purely internal critique of Duckworth, of his eleven tests, six (1, 2, 6, 7, 8, 11) associate the *Ars Poetica* more closely with *Epist.* I than with *Epist.* II.1. In two tests (11 and the fifth part of 8), the *Ars Poetica* is most closely linked with *Sat.* II of *c.* 30 B.C. Only two tests (3, 9) confirm Duckworth's thesis. Three tests (4, 5, 10) are neutral.

Duckworth's methodology and his results can be attacked on several fronts. First, Duckworth's assumption of a correlation between date of composition and the metrical features he chose to study is assumed but nowhere defended. It is, however, possible, that the features Duckworth used for dating are not, in fact, chronometers. Second, Duckworth never explained the choice of features he selected for analysis. Some are intuitively obvious—for example, patterns of spondees and dactyls in the first four feet of the line. Others are less intuitively acceptable. For example, Duckworth pays attention to opposite patterns in adjacent lines consisting of spondees and dactyls in the first four feet of the line (dsss, sddd, etc.), as if poets strove for or avoided such patterns. Even if we grant that poets may sometimes have paid attention to such things, Duckworth still ought to have gauged the extent to which pure randomness affects his results. Thus, for example, for the *Ars Poetica* he reports 31 such opposites. Yet, random variation alone would lead us to predict 29.69 cases: since there are 16 metrical patterns, any of which can occur after any others (including itself), there are 16 * 16 = 256 possible pairs of patterns. Of these, 16, or 6.25%, are opposites. In the 476 lines of the *Ars Poetica*, there are 475 possible pairs of lines (lines 1 and 2, 2 and 3, 3 and 4, etc.). Multiplying 475 by .0625 gives us the number of opposites that we should have expected from chance alone, viz., 29.69. Our impression that the observed number (31) is not very far off from the expected number can be confirmed by a standard statistical test, the so-called z-test.[19] Let our null-hypothesis (H_0) be that the proportion of opposites in the *Ars Poetica* is the same as we should have expected by chance alone and let us (here, as elsewhere in this study) reject H_0 at alpha = .05. Our alternative hypothesis (H_a) is that the proportion of opposites in the *Ars Poetica* is larger than we should have expected by chance alone (the assumption behind Duckworth's work). The z-value is .244, giving us an alpha-value of .405. So, we do not reject H_0 in favor of H_a, and we conclude that the observed number of opposite patterns in the poem has no particular statistical significance.

Duckworth's main contention is that as time went on, Horace became more concerned about achieving metrical variety in his poetry. He writes: "To summarize, of the eleven categories listed above, some have more significance than others. Those dealing with larger totals, e.g., the frequency percentages of the first four and the first eight patterns, are the most decisive; they show a steady trend toward less concentration and greater variety...."[20] This hypothesis is, according to Duckworth, his most important, and it may be subjected to rigorous statistical testing in the form of a chi-square test of the data presented in Duckworth's first table (cf. TABLE II, next page).[21]

The chi-square test indicates that the hypothesis that the two variables of poem and metrical pattern are dependent fails at the alpha = .05 level, since the significance ("prob.") is .270. Thus, Duckworth has failed to find a significant correlation between the poems and the distribution of metrical patterns.

---

[19]See, in general, e.g., A. Agresti and B. Finlay, *Statistical Methods for the Social Sciences* (San Francisco and London, 1986²) 74-77, 146-147.

[20]Cf. Duckworth, op. cit. (*supra* n. 1) 91.

[21]Statisticians distinguish between three kinds of variables: nominal variables, which differ in some quality but not in quantity (e.g., different books of poems in Horace's corpus; different metrical patterns in the dactylic hexameter line); ordinal variables, which differ from each other according to quantities that are vaguely ranked (e.g., top score on an examination, second best score, worst score); and, finally, interval variables, which differ from each other according to a precisely defined quantitative scale (e.g., average number of words or verses in a poem). The chi-square and association tests are applied to nominal variables and determine the probability that the distribution of the actual values of the variables differs very much from their expected distribution. If the actual values do not so differ, then we say that the variables are independent; if they do differ, then we say that they are dependent. The association tests determine the degree of dependence obtaining between two variables. In the present case, no association tests have been reported (though they have been run) because we only test the strength of a dependence once the chi-square test indicates that the variables are not independent (which, as will be seen from TABLE II, is not the case). See, in general, e.g., A. Agresti and B. Finlay, op. cit. (*supra* n. 19) 14-16; 201-212.

Another way of stating this conclusion is that the overall distribution of metrical patterns does not give us a reliable chronometer for the date of a poem.

Duckworth's words cited above would lead us to expect the highest association between poem and metrical pattern in the four most frequent patterns.

MET. PAT.	SI	SII	EPI	EPII.2	EPII.1	AP	TOTAL
obs. dsss	132	152	129	30	25	49	517
obs. ddss	96	104	81	19	30	41	371
obs. dsds	104	104	93	24	25	46	396
obs. sdss	117	116	108	24	32	39	436
obs. ssss	92	80	62	13	16	31	294
obs. ddds	51	64	53	9	14	33	224
obs. ssds	64	69	64	13	13	34	257
obs. sdds	61	50	57	9	17	28	222
obs. dssd	67	67	69	14	24	37	278
obs. ddsd	37	55	54	8	17	21	192
obs. sdsd	42	48	61	16	17	34	218
obs. dsdd	39	42	43	12	14	25	175
obs. sssd	59	46	51	9	9	16	190
obs. ssdd	26	37	36	7	6	14	126
obs. dddd	30	17	23	1	3	10	84
obs. sddd	13	32	22	8	8	17	100
TOTAL	1,030	1,083	1,006	216	270	475	4,080
TEST STATISTIC			VALUE		DF		PROB
PEARSON CHI-SQUARE			82.063		75		.270

TABLE II: CHI-SQUARE TEST OF DATA IN DUCKWORTH'S TABLE I

Yet, the total of chi-square values for the first four patterns is only 13.78, far less than one-fourth the total value of chi-square; and when the first four patterns are considered in isolation from the rest of the table, the chi-square value is 17.67 with a significance of .609 (cf. TABLE III, next page). Thus, once again, the test of dependence fails, and we see that the four most frequent metrical patterns are not reliable chronometers for Horace's hexameters.

Much more of the chi-square value of Duckworth's first table is concentrated in the last group of metrical patterns. Yet, as TABLE IV (next page) shows, even here, where the chi-square value rises to 29.855 and the significance level reaches .072, the coefficients of association are quite low, indicating that the dependence between poem and metrical pattern is weak.

PATTERN	AP	EPII.1	EPII.2	EPI	SI	SII	TOTAL
1	49	25	30	129	132	152	517
2	41	30	19	81	96	104	371
3	46	25	24	93	104	104	396
4	39	32	24	108	117	116	436
Rest	300	158	119	595	581	607	2360
TOTAL	475	270	216	1006	1030	1083	4080

TEST STATISTIC	VALUE	DF	PROB
PEARSON CHI-SQUARE	17.669	20	.609

TABLE III: CHI-SQUARE TEST OF DUCKWORTH'S FIRST FOUR PATTERNS

PATTERN	AP	EPII.1	EPII.2	EPI	SI	SII	TOTAL
13	16	9	9	51	59	46	190
14	14	6	7	36	26	37	126
15	10	3	1	23	30	17	84
16	17	8	8	22	13	32	100
Rest	418	244	191	874	902	951	3580
TOTAL	475	270	216	1006	1030	1083	4080

TEST STATISTIC	VALUE	DF	PROB
PEARSON CHI-SQUARE	29.855	20	.072
COEFFICIENT	VALUE	ASYMPT STD ERROR	
CRAMER V	.0428		
CONTINGENCY	.0852		
LAMBDA	.0087	.00410	
UNCERTAINTY	.0024	.00081	

TABLE IV: CHI-SQUARE TEST OF DUCKWORTH'S LAST FOUR PATTERNS

In TABLE IV the chi-square value is more indicative of the non-independence of the variables than was the case with the first four metrical patterns, but the significance level (.072) still fails to meet the test of alpha = .05. Examination of the various tests of association (the Cramer V, Uncertainty Coefficient, etc., all of which vary from 0 to 1.0) confirm that the variables of poem and metrical pattern are weakly associated.

Our conclusion is thus that Duckworth has failed to find any useful indicator of date in his metrical studies. The search for a valid chronometer of Horace's hexameter poems must turn elsewhere for clues—our next task.

Dating the *Ars Poetica* through Style: A Statistical Approach

The foregoing has shown the utility of statistics for disproving a quantitative argument about the date of the poem. Statistical tests can, of course, also have a more positive, albeit never probative, value.[22] In what follows, I will present some new studies of word frequency which suggest that the *Ars Poetica* should be dated in the period of the composition of *Epistles* I and before the publication of *Epistles* II.2, i.e., *c.* 24-20 B.C.

This is not the place for even a brief history of stylometrics.[23] Suffice it to say, by way of introduction, that statistical studies of vocabulary have had some success in identifying reliable quantitative chronometers for attribution and relative chronology of works by different authors. They have less often been used for relative chronology within a single author's corpus.[24] Recent work by Lindsay and Mackay suggests that for the latter, the word class that offers the best hope for reliable results is that of the *function word* and the best analytical tool is the chi-square test.[25] In their classic study, Mosteller and Wallace define function words as: "the filler words of a language, such as a, an, by, to and that. Generally they include prepositions, conjunctions, pronouns, and certain adverbs, adjectives, and auxiliary verbs."[26]

---

[22] Cf. A. Agresti and B. Finlay, op. cit. (*supra* n. 19) 293: "we can never *prove* that one phenomenon is a cause of another, since causation is imputed by the observer but never actually observed. We can disprove causal hypotheses, however, by showing that empirical evidence contradicts them."

[23] For brief histories and bibliography, see, e.g., R. L. Oakman, *Computer Methods for Literary Research* (Athens, Ga. 1980, 1984) 139-171; K. L. Lindsay and T. W. Mackay, "An Authorship Study of the Pauline Epistles," an unpublished paper given at the *International Conference on Computers in the Humanities* (Brigham Young University, June 26, 1985) 1-13.

[24] F. Mosteller and D. L. Wallace, *Inference and Disputed Authorship: 'The Federalist'* (Reading, Mass. 1964) 20-21, note briefly that the function words *in* and possibly *from* may serve as chronometers for the works of President James Madison. They pay little attention to words in an author whose frequency changes in a patterned way over time (our third class of function words) since their concern is to distinguish one author (Madison) from another (Hamilton).

[25] Cf. Lindsay and Mackay, op. cit. (*supra* n. 23) 15-25, especially p. 25: "word frequency is the most sensitive wordprint." For the purposes of their interauthorial study of distinguishing Pauline from non-Pauline authorship of Biblical texts transmitted under Paul's name, "sensitivity" was not desirable and so Lindsay and Mackay do not use word frequency. For our intra-authorial study of Horace, it is precisely this high degree of sensitivity that makes function word frequency the proper tool.

[26] F. Mosteller and D. L. Wallace, op. cit. (*supra* n. 24) 17.

Function words are words useful for research on the authorship or chronology of texts because they are not dependent on content, context, or genre. Since, in Latin, about half are monosyllabic, Latin function words are also fairly independent of meter. Examples of such words are *et, in, ut, ad, sub,* etc. In addition to being fairly non-contextual, function words also have the advantage of being more frequent than other words, thus lending themselves more readily to statistical analysis. Since they are used so often and have so little connotative value, speakers of a language employ them with very little awareness of doing so. They are thus potentially good reflectors of a speaker's linguistic sense and development since it is generally through our more automatic behavior that we most plainly give ourselves away. In this sense, the stylometric use of function words is analogous in literary history to the Morellian method in art history.

Authors may use individual function words in any of three ways: (1) with little, if any, change over time; (2) with random fluctuation over time; and (3) with patterned variation over time. The first usage is most valuable for inter-authorial analysis, such as we find in the Mosteller-Wallace study of the authorship of certain *Federalist* papers.[27] On the other hand, it is of no help in determining the relative chronology of the works of one author's corpus. The second kind of usage is by far the most frequently encountered, as was pointed out in an important article by Damerau and as is confirmed by the case of Horace.[28] Function words displaying random fluctuation are of little, if any, use in stylometric analysis since they allow us neither to distinguish one author's works from another's nor to find trends in the individual works of an author's corpus.

For our purposes, then, words of the third type—relatively few as they may be—are the most important. These are words that meet four criteria: (1) as function words, they must, of course, be fairly independent of context, genre, and meter; (2) they must be common enough so that their frequency does not fall below five cases in any single unit of analysis more than 25% of the time;[29] (3) the frequency of their usage must vary according to a trend or pattern (whether linear or non-linear) from Horace's early to his late works; finally, (4) the number of words meeting the first three criteria must surpass, in a statistically significant way, the number expected from chance alone.

The third requirement brings up an important methodological consideration. For over a century, at least, the relative chronology of all the poems and poetic books in Horace's corpus, save the *Ars Poetica*, has been fairly well established on non-stylometric grounds. Even an approximate absolute chrono-

---

[27]F. Mosteller and D. L. Wallace, op. cit. (*supra* n. 24).

[28]F. J. Damerau, "The Use of Function Word Frequencies as Indicators of Style," *Computers and the Humanities* 9 (1975) 271-280.

[29]For this reason, the very short *Carm. Saec.* is left out of account.

logy has long been known.[30] In most cases in which stylometrics is used for attribution or dating, we are not so fortunate, and statistical arguments alone are used by default. Given what we think we know from non-stylometrical sources about the chronology of Horace's poetry, we would be ill-advised to limit our methodology to stylometrics alone, since that would be to forego a finer for a blunter instrument. Indeed, respecting "time order" is a principle of statistical methodology in any case.[31] Thus, I propose to start from the assumption that the conventionally accepted relative chronology is essentially correct and complete, with the exception of the *Ars Poetica*. I do not think this assumption is likely to be controversial. Since, as we have seen, non-stylometric information cannot narrow down the date of that poem to anything less than the long period between the deaths of Quintilius Varus and Horace (24-8 B.C.), we shall resort to the instrument of statistics only to see whether stylometrics (and, in particular, vocabulary analysis) can help decide the issue of whether I am correct in dating the poem to the early part of that period, or Duckworth and others are in putting it at the end. My approach to chronology is thus interdisciplinary: we will, so to speak, triangulate on the date with historical and statistical methods.

The analysis will proceed in two steps. First, the variable of poem will be considered nominal.[32] The object of this part of the study will be to model the data in the most economical way such that the value of the test statistic is optimized. The test statistic used is the chi-square test, which essentially gauges

[30]Cf., e.g., C. Franke, *Fasti Horatiani* (Berlin 1839), 80-81, where we already find the following chronology based primarily on historical references, prosopography, etc.: *Serm.* I, 41-34; *Serm.* II, 35-30; *Epod.* 41-30; *Carm.* I-III, 30-24; *Epist.* I, 24-20; *Carm. Saec.*, 17; *Carm.* IV, 17-13; *Epist.* II ("primo jam edito et post carmen saeculare scriptus est, sed incertum quo anno," p. 81). On the date of the *Ars Poetica*, Franke simply writes: "aetate nil constat" (p. 81). Modified by J. Vahlen's dating of *Epistles* II (op. cit. [*supra* n. 5] 46-61), Franke's chronology is still more or less accepted today; cf., e.g., K. Vretska, *Der Kleine Pauly* 2 s.v. Horatius (8) (Munich 1975) cols. 1219-1225, for the following dating of the composition and publication (indicated with an asterisk [*]) of Horace's works: *Epodes*–40-30*; *Sat.* I–35/34* ("or, 33?"–col. 1221); *Sat.* II–30/29*; *Carm.* I-III–c. 35 ("Horace began writing the Odes in the time of the Satires"; col. 1222)–23*; *Epist.* I–23-20*; *Epist.* II.2–"before 20"* (col. 1223); *Carm. Saec.*–17*; Epist. II.1–after 14*; Ars Poetica– 23-18* or 13-8*. Thus, Carl Becker, op. cit. (*supra* n. 5) 12-13, is correct to note that chronological studies of Horace are in a very fortunate position because "über ein ganzes Jahrzehnt hin—von 23 bis 14/13—lassen sich fast jedem Jahr horazische Dichtungen zuordnen." For work on Horatian chronology before Franke, see the survey in J. Tate, *Horatius Restitutus, Or the Books of Horace Arranged in Chronological Order according to the Scheme of Dr. Bentley* (London 1832[1], 1837[2]) 1-20.

[31]Cf., e.g., A. Agresti and B. Finlay, op. cit. (*supra* n. 19) 293.

[32]For a definition of this concept, see n. 21 above.

the degree to which actual values of the variables differ from values we would expect to find if the variables are independent. The greater the difference, the greater the chi-square value and the greater the likelihood that the variables in question are not independent. Modelling the data, in the present case, means combining values for the poems that relate to their expected values in the same way: the result is a grouping of poems according to actual values that are above, below, or about the same as what we would have expected. The assumption here is that the poems grouped together belong to the same period of composition.[33] At this first step of analysis, then, the dating of Horace's poetry—and, in particular, of the *Ars Poetica*—is quite approximate. At best, we can distinguish between early, middle, early-middle, middle-late, and late groups. The study of each function word will include a frequency graph, in which the poem will be arranged in order of relative chronology, with the *Ars Poetica* included in the appropriate group, but with no firm claim about its relative position in its group. In practice, this means that, although the tests indicate that the *Ars Poetica* belongs in Horace's middle period, we can only guess whether it is earlier or later than the other hexameter poem in the group, viz., *Epist.* I.

In a second step of the analysis, we will treat the poem variable as an interval variable. To do this, we will assign to all the poems except the *Ars Poetica* their generally accepted dates. We will then determine the most probable date for the *Ars Poetica* by inferential and exploratory statistical techniques. It should be stated here that each step of the analysis has an obvious weakness: the first step is too vague, the second too precise. These weaknesses are compensating, and our point is not so much to establish a precise date for the *Ars Poetica* as to demonstrate the greater probability that the poem is to be dated to Horace's middle period of poems than to his late period.

One final word about methodology. In studying the third class of function words, I have spoken till now only of a vague "trend" or "patterned development" in their usage, from, e.g., higher to lower frequency, or vice versa. I have also said that function words are, in general, attractive as chronometers because they are relatively non-contextual. At this point, one clarification should

---

[33]For a brief discussion of modelling by means of collapsing categories, see S. G. Levy, *Inferential Statistics in the Behavioral Sciences* (New York 1968) 210-213; and cf. P. M. Bentler, *Theory and Implementation of EQS: A Structural Equations Program* (Los Angeles 1985) 28: "when two models...are special cases of each other, chi-square difference tests can be used to evaluate the structural importance of the parametric constraints that differentiate two models. In the...most typical application, two models would differ in that one model would contain extra parameters beyond those provided by the other model: all other parameters would be the same. In such a case, the chi-square difference test evaluates whether the added parameters, considered simultaneously, are necessary to the model."

be made: few words (in Latin, at any rate) are completely "functional" and hence totally devoid of content and connotation. Accordingly, the rate at which a function word is used in Horace is modulated by the demands of genre, sometimes for reasons that may be unclear.[34] So, in establishing trends, we must keep the lyric poems separate from the hexameters, as far as frequency value is concerned; but we also must see the same pattern of development in both the lyric and hexameter group. In statistical terms, we must control for meter. As a result of doing so, another kind of triangulation becomes possible: the prime assumption behind chronology by stylometrics is that some aspects of an author's linguistic sense change in a measurable and consistent way over time. The fact that we can very neatly divide the Horatian corpus by meter and genre into two groups of poems and that members of each group represent Horace's early, middle, and late periods is thus extremely fortunate: it means that the probable explanation for any similarity in trends of function word use in both the lyric and hexameter groups is likely to be Horace's evolution as a speaker of the Latin language and not, e.g., metrical or generic exigencies.

Relative Chronology—Function Words as Chronometers of Horace's Poetry

To implement this methodology, we thus need to tabulate the frequencies in Horace of the major function words in Latin (see TABLE A). The following words seemed from inspection of the computer-generated frequency lists to have the greatest promise of surmounting the barrier of at least five cases in each unit of analysis (or, cell). Those in capitals and boldface turned out to satisfy the criteria of chronometers: sufficient frequency and the same pattern of development in the lyrics and hexameters. Most words turned out to be rejected because of low frequency—i.e., in at least 25% of the cells the frequency fell below 5 cases. These words are followed by "l.f." in parentheses. Other words passed the frequency test but failed the "trend" test of patterned development; Damerau's work had prepared us to expect to find just such words, whose random fluctuations make them unsuitable as chronometers. In the following list, they are followed by "n.p." (= "no pattern") in parentheses.[35]

---

[34]E.g., Horace's consistent preference for *sub* in the lyric [frequency: *c*. .0016] as opposed to hexameter [frequency: *c*. .001] poems. Let our null hypothesis be that the frequency in the two groups is the same; our alternative hypothesis is that the frequency of *sub* in the lyrics is greater than in the hexameters. The z-value of H_o is 3.94, giving a P-value of P < .000233. So we reject H_o in favor of H_a.

[35]The following function words were not studied since inspection of the word sorting and counting program's output indicated that they would fail to satisfy

a (l.f.)	cur (l.f.)	mox (l.f.)	post (l.f.)	sine (l.f.)
ab (l.f.)	de (l.f.)	nam (l.f.)	quia (l.f.)	sive (l.f.)
ac (l.f.)	donec (l.f.)	ne (l.f.)	quidem (l.f.)	sub (l.f.)
AD	dum (l.f.)	**NEC**	quodsi (l.f.)	tam (l.f.)
an (l.f.)	enim (l.f.)	neque (l.f.)	quoque (l.f.)	tamen (l.f.)
at (l.f.)	et (n.p.)	neu (l.f.)	saepe (l.f.)	tandem (l.f.)
atque (n.p.)	etiam (l.f.)	nisi (l.f.)	**SED**	ubi (l.f.)
aut (n.p.)	iam (n.p.)	non (n.p.)	seu (l.f.)	unde (l.f.)
autem (l.f.)	in (n.p.)	nunc (n.p.)	si (n.p.)	ut (n.p.)
cum (n.p.)	inter (l.f.)	**PER**	sic (n.p.)	vel (n.p.)
				velut (l.f.)

Twelve of the sixteen words passing the frequency test could not be used as chronometers because their distribution among the poems was more or less random, which in this context means that the trends observed in the hexameters (no matter how the *Ars Poetica* is dated) is different from that seen in the lyrics. Since these words will not be of interest, it would be tiresome to discuss them all (see TABLES B-G). *Cum* may serve as a typical example. As the frequency graph of *cum* shows (TABLE C, top), the word changes its frequency with a nonlinear (probably convex parabolic) pattern in the hexameter poems, while in the lyrics, it is used much more often in the epodes of the mid-30s than in the odes of the middle or late periods. In fact, the pattern of the lyrics is linear, with a negative slope. Thus, *cum* fails our test because the linear pattern of the lyrics is not mirrored in the hexameters, with their nonlinear trend. Without a metrical control for *cum*, we are helpless in trying to situate the *Ars Poetica:* arguments can be imagined justifying its location just about anywhere on the graph. For example, it might be considered the low point of the hexameter parabola, in which case we would date the *Ars Poetica* between *Epistles* I and *Epistles* II.2. Contrariwise, if we posit a change in Horace's *Sprachgefühl* from high to low use of the word *cum*, then we might decide to dismiss as anomalous the high frequency of the word in *Epistles* II.1 and place the *Ars Poetica* last among the hexameters so that the result is a linear pattern with negative slope in both the hexameters and lyrics. The point is that such arguments are merely speculative, because we cannot control for meter.

Before proceeding to discuss the four words that satisfy our first three criteria to be considered as chronometers, let us see if our fourth criterion is satisfied, viz., that the number of words satisfying the first three criteria exceed, in a statistically significant way, the number expected from chance alone (*supra,* p. 27). The details of the argument may be found in the *Appendix II*. In brief,

---

the frequency requirement: *ante, at, circum, contra, denique, ex, extra, haud, ita, num, numquid, ob, olim, pacto, porro, praeter, quare, quin, siquid.*

our three-point lines (i.e., lyrics) have nine possible distinct trend lines. Our hexameters form eighty-one five-point lines; of these, eight may be considered equivalent to the relevant three-point lines. Thus, we have 9 x 81 different combinations of three-point and five-point lines, for a total of 729. Of these, 8 are possible matched pairs, so that the odds of finding a matched pair are 8/729, or 0.010974. In our study, we have sixteen cases of function words with sufficient frequency: hence, we would expect 16 x 0.010974 matched pairs, or 0.176. Instead of the expected number of zero or, at most one matched pair, we have two exactly matched pairs and two similar pairs. We run a binomial test to determine the probability of our result. The test shows that there is less than a 1.2% probability that this could happen by chance. We may conclude that our fourth criterion is satisfied because there is only a very small possibility that our four words display similar trend lines in the hexameters and lyrics due to random variation alone.

The words that satisfy our criteria and hence are useful for chronology divide into two types: a group of three words *(ad, per, sed)* whose frequency has a high-low-high pattern (i.e., Type I) in the early *(Epodes* and *Satires)*, middle *(Carm.* I-III, *Epistles* I) and late *(Epistles* II, *Carm.* IV) periods; and a second type *(nec)* whose pattern (Type II) is the mirror-reversal of the first. In all four cases, as we will see, the *Ars Poetica* falls between *Epistles* I and *Epistles* II.2

TABLE V shows a tabulation and chi-square test of the data from the first group of function words. The chi-square test statistic (99.2, with twenty-four degrees of freedom) tells us that the variables are not independent: in fact, its probability level of 0.000 far surpasses our requirement that alpha < .05. The degree of dependence, or association, of the variables can be gauged by the Cramer V, Contingency, Lambda, and Uncertainty coefficients, which are measures appropriate to nominal variables. To interpret these, we need to know that all these coefficients vary between 0, indicating little or no association, and 1.0, indicating the highest degree of association. In the present case, the values for the coefficients appear, at a first glance, to be quite low.

Before concluding that the function words *sed* and *ad* are only weakly associated with Horace's poems, and hence are poor chronometers, we need to determine why the coefficients are so much closer to 0.0 than to 1.0. The reason is not far to seek: the category "rest"—with 43,066/43,415 (or, 99.2%) of the cases and with an observed distribution very close to what was expected—is so predominant that there is very little scope for the remaining data to be distributed in a way that appears strong according to the association tests.

WORD	S1	S2	EP1	EP2.1	EP2.2		TOTAL
AD	21	28	21	9	7		
PER	5	13	16	10	1		
SED	12	21	15	11	5		
REST	6957	7160	6634	1733	1406		
TOTAL	6995	7222	6686	1763	1419		
WORD	AP	EPD	C1-3	C4			
AD	13	12	12	8			131
PER	5	11	32	22			115
SED	6	7	16	10			103
REST	3058	2965	10634	2519			43066
TOTAL	3082	2995	10694	2559			43415
TEST STATISTIC					VALUE	DF	PROB.
PEARSON CHI-SQUARE					99.201	24	0.000
LIKELIHOOD RATIO CHI-SQUARE					89.662	24	0.000
COEFFICIENT			VALUE		ASMPT. STD		ERROR
CRAMER V			.0276				
CONTINGENCY			.0477				
LAMBDA			.0006				.00027
UNCERTAINTY			.0005				.00011

TABLE V: THE FUNCTION WORDS *AD*, *PER*, AND *SED* IN HORACE

That the association tests are quite sensitive to such a condition is clear from their formulae. For example, the Contingency Coefficient (C) is defined as follows:

$$C = \sqrt{\frac{\chi^2}{(\chi^2 + n)}}$$

Thus, the greater the number of cases (n) whose observed values do not depart very much from their expected values (that is, whose chi-square values are low), the smaller the value of C. To give a fair interpretation to our results, we must accordingly determine how high the coefficients can rise toward their theoretical limit of 1.0, given the limitations of the present case. This we do by an experiment in which we control for the category "rest" by keeping it constant while putting the greatest possible number of cases of *ad, per,* and *sed* into the cells of *Ep.* II.2 (hexameters) and the *Carm.* IV, where they will generate the maximum values for the coefficients since these works are both late and have the fewest words. The fact that both poems are late is important: it means that the trend in the hexameters and lyrics is the same—another requirement of our test. The other cells are given the minimum number of cases needed to satisfy our requirement that no more than 25% of all cells have fewer than 5 cases.[36] The results are given in TABLE VI (on the next page).

In this experiment, the chi-square value rises to 2171.8 and that of the coefficients go up about sixfold. Thus, we may say that, controlling for "rest" and taking into account our frequency and trend requirement, the degree of association that we find in Horace's use of *sed* and *ad* is approximately 15-20% of what is actually possible for a function word fulfilling our minimum conditions for consideration as a chronometer. Seen in this light, *ad, per,* and *sed* may be considered modestly useful chronometers.

Our next question is what the distribution of *ad, per,* and *sed* suggests about the date of the *Ars Poetica*. Since we are now treating poems as nominal variables, we have no way of determining a precise date. What we can do is attempt to model the data to see if we can combine the *Ars Poetica* with any other poem in such a way that there is no loss of significance. Our working assumption is that the most parsimonious model is the best and that poems grouped together belong to the same period of composition. In trying different combinations, we will, of course, respect time order and genre. In practice this means an experiment in which the *Ars Poetica* is combined with *Epistles* I, *Epistles* II.2, and *Epistles* II.1, first singly and then in the various combinations (e.g., *Ep.* I + *AP* + *Ep.* II.2; *AP* + *Ep.* II.2 + *Ep.* II.1; etc.).

TABLE VII (next page) reports the results of experiments run using the data in TABLE V. In TABLE V, we have a "full model" of the data: that is, the frequency of each word is studied in each poem or poetic book. The resulting test statistic is reproduced at the top of TABLE VII (under model I = "FULL"). In the following lines of the table, the data from the *Ars Poetica* are combined with those from the other hexameter poems (with the exception of the very early *Sat.* I) in an attempt to simplify and clarify the analysis: the strategy is to find the combinations of poems that give us the maximum and minimum values of the test statistic. The maximum values tell us the most likely period of composition of the *Ars Poetica*; the minimum values tell us the least likely date. Since we are, in effect, comparing the same test statistic at different levels (or, "degrees of freedom" ["DF"]), we must standardize our results by comparing our various collapsed models to the full model. To do this, we simply subtract the χ^2 values

---

[36]In practice, this means that the remaining cells are given values of 5 for these words. This we do because we would not be considering a function word as a possible chronometer in the first place if its distribution throughout Horace's poetry violated the requirement that it occur at least five times in 75% of the poems. Since *Carm.* IV and *Epist.* II.2 are late works (or middle-late, in the case of *Epist.* II.2), the resulting trend lines are similar in the lyrics and hexameters—a second important criterion for consideration of a function word.

WORD	S1	S2	EP1	EP2.1	EP2.2	TOTAL
AD	5	5	5	5	66	
PER	5	5	5	5	25	
SED	5	5	5	5	45	
REST	6980	7207	6671	1748	1283	
TOTAL	6995	7222	6686	1763	1419	

WORD	AP	EPD	C1-3	C4		
AD	5	5	5	30		131
PER	5	5	5	55		115
SED	5	5	5	23		103
REST	3067	2980	10679	2451		43066
TOTAL	3082	2995	10694	2559		43415

TEST STATISTIC		VALUE	DF	PROB.
PEARSON CHI-SQUARE		2171.8	24	0.000
LIKELIHOOD RATIO CHI-SQUARE		0876.3	24	0.000

COEFFICIENT	VALUE	ASMPT. STD. ERROR
CRAMER V	.1291	
CONTINGENCY	.2183	
LAMBDA	.0049	.00042
UNCERTAINTY	.0050	.00042

TABLE VI: TABLE V RECALCULATED TO MINIMIZE THE EFFECT OF "REST"

MODEL	χ^2	DF	PROB	DIFFERENCE IN χ^2 FROM FULL MODEL (I)	DF	SIGNIFICANT AT $\alpha = .05$?
I	99.20	24	.000	—	—	—
II	98.25	21	.000	0.951	3	NO
III	97.84	21	.000	1.362	3	NO
IV	97.71	21	.000	1.493	3	NO
V	83.16	21	.000	16.042	3	YES
VI	96.42	18	.000	2.778	6	NO
VII	95.01	18	.000	4.193	6	NO
VIII	80.73	18	.000	18.472	6	YES

MODELS: I = FULL; II = AP+S2; III = AP+E1; IV = AP+EP2.2;
V = AP+EP2.1; VI = AP+S2+E1; VII = AP+E1+E2.2; VIII = AP+E2

TABLE VII: COMPARISONS OF THE FULL AND VARIOUS COLLAPSED MODELS OF THE DATA IN TABLE V

of the full and collapsed model, as well as the difference in their degrees of freedom. We can then consult a standard table of χ^2 distributions to see if the difference results in a significant gain or loss in probability. This is reported on the table in the last column: if, at the $\alpha = .05$ level, there is no loss in probability, then we enter "NO" in the column. If the collapsed model is inferior to the full model—i.e., if there is a loss in significance—we enter "YES" in the column.

As can be seen, however we model the data, the *Ars Poetica* is best grouped with *Sat.* II, *Epist.* I, and *Epist.* II.2. The best models are: AP+SII and AP+SII+EI. Models combining the *Ars Poetica* with *Epistles* II.2 are also good. The worst models are those in which the *Ars Poetica* is grouped with *Epistles* II.1. Since the *Epistle to Augustus* is generally considered a late hexameter poem, the implication of our study is that the *Ars Poetica* is most likely a middle-period, not a late-period, hexameter poem. On TABLES H-P, the *Ars* is placed in the position indicated by these tests.

On the graph in TABLE H (a chart showing the frequency of *ad* in Horace's poems), we can see similar nonlinear trends in the lyrics and hexameters. The pattern of usage in both groups is a convex parabola. In accordance with the principle of parsimony in model-building, we disregard the value of *Satires* I. In the hexameters, we find high frequency in the early poems, lower frequency in the poems of the 20s, and higher frequency in the late works. In the case of the non-hexameters, use of *ad* is highest in the early period, with the late *Carm.* IV showing a steep rise as compared to *Carm.* I-III, but not steep enough to overtake the rate of the *Epodes*. The *Ars Poetica* takes its place between *Epist.* I, the nadir of the curve, and *Epist.* II.2.

The somewhat different shapes and values of the curves here and elsewhere in this group are not unexpected or disturbing. They are presumably the result of differences of genre and meter; of the greater number of hexameter as opposed to non-hexameter poems; and of the fact that the time intervals between the different poems (hexameter and non-hexameter alike) are not uniform. Complicating the last factor is the probable overlap in time of the different poems and poem categories. For example, it is likely that Horace was writing some of *Carm.* I-III in the 30s,[37] when he was mainly composing his *Satires*. It is impossible for us to determine which odes date from which period, with a few possible exceptions, like the *Cleopatra Ode* (I.37) or the poem consoling Virgil for the death of his friend Quintilius (I.24). In general, this limitation does not matter since we are concerned with relative chronology and dating the *Ars Poetica* between *Epist.* I and *Epist.* II.2. For this task, it is sufficient that we assume

---

[37]See, e.g., R. G. M. Nisbet and M. Hubbard, *A Commentary on Horace: Odes Book I* (Oxford 1970) xxviii-xxx; Vretska, op. cit. (*supra* n. 30) col. 1222; E. A. Schmidt, "The Date of Horace, Odes 2.13," *BICS* Supplement 51 (1988) 118-125.

that the linguistic data of the various works reflect Horace's habits of speech in the year or so of revision before final publication.

On TABLE I we have a graph showing Horace's use of *per*. As can be seen, *per* resembles *ad* in its general development, except this time the word is used more frequently in the lyrics than in the hexameters and in both groups of poems the highest use occurs in the late works. The frequency of the *Ars Poetica* is closest to *Epistles* I, though it is harder to visualize whether the data for the *Ars Poetica* fit better before or after those of *Epistles* I. By the principle of parsimonious modelling, the slight increase in value of *Epistles* I is not interpreted as evidence counter to a parabolic trend.

On TABLE J, showing Horace's use of *sed*, we again see a definite non-linear pattern. The frequency of *sed* falls somewhat in the 20s from the level found in the 30s (disregarding, as in the case of *ad*, the data of *Satires* I), and we find this both in the hexameter and in the non-hexameter works. The *Ars Poetica* fits nicely after *Epistles* I in the middle-period poems, whose observed frequencies are lower than expected. In the late poems, the rate with which Horace used *sed* rose again. Thus, the graphs of both hexameters and non-hexameters are convex parabolas described by quadratic equations.[38] The similar trends observed for *ad, per,* and *sed* can be seen from the composite graph on TABLE K.

As mentioned, a fourth function word, *nec*, has the opposite trend—a concave parabola. We begin with a table of the data subjected to chi-square and association tests. The results show high statistical significance and non-independence of the variables (TABLE VIII, next page).

Once again, to interpret the degree of association, we need to determine the maximum possible level of association that can be obtained with our frequency requirement and in view of the preponderance of data in the "rest" category (43,146 / 43,415 = 99.38%). Running an experiment similar to that used for *ad, per,* and *sed*, we obtain the results seen on TABLE IX (next page). Compared to the maximum values we can expect to find in one of our chronometers, the degree of association actually observed for *nec* is about the same as we found for *ad, per,* and *sed*.

---

[38]In modelling the hexameters, we may legitimately ignore the departure of *Satires* I from the parabolic model without postulating a cubic model; on the principle of parismony in model-building, see A. Agresti and B. Finlay, op. cit. (*supra* n. 19) 363-64; P. Turney, "The Curve Fitting Problem: A Solution," *The British Journal for the Philosophy of Science* 41 (1990) 509-530.

WORD	S1	S2	EP1	EP2.1	EP2.2	TOTAL
NEC	23	23	35	5	1	
REST	6972	7199	6651	1758	1418	
TOTAL	6995	7222	6686	1763	1419	
WORD	AP	EPD	C1-3	C4		
NEC	13	22	26	118		269
REST	3060	2969	10576	2543		43146
TOTAL	3082	2995	10694	2559		43415

TEST STATISTIC	VALUE	DF	PROB.
PEARSON CHI-SQUARE	75.529	8	0.000
LIKELIHOOD RATIO CHI-SQUARE	76.994	8	0.000

COEFFICIENT	VALUE	ASMPT. STD. ERROR
CRAMER V	.0417	
CONTINGENCY	.0417	
LAMBDA	.0000	.00000
UNCERTAINTY	.0004	.00010

TABLE VIII: FREQUENCY OF *NEC* IN HORACE

WORD	S1	S2	EP1	EP2.1	EP2.2	TOTAL
NEC	5	5	5	5	112	
REST	6990	7217	6681	1758	1307	
TOTAL	6995	7222	6686	1763	1419	
WORD	AP	EPD	C1-3	C4		
NEC	5	5	5	112		259
REST	3077	2990	10689	2447		43156
TOTAL	3082	2995	10694	2559		43415

TEST STATISTIC	VALUE	DF	PROB.
PEARSON CHI-SQUARE	2064.2	8	0.000
LIKELIHOOD RATIO CHI-SQUARE	915.3	8	0.000

COEFFICIENT	VALUE	ASMPT. STD. ERROR
CRAMER V	.2180	
CONTINGENCY	.2130	
LAMBDA	.0033	.00033
UNCERTAINTY	.0053	.00042

TABLE IX: TABLE VIII CONTROLLED FOR "REST"

The Date of the Poem   39

Next, we run some modelling tests, combining the *Ars Poetica* with the other middle and late hexameter poems, to see whether we can improve on the results obtained from the full model. The best reduced model once again turns out to be the one combining the *Ars Poetica* and *Epistles* I, though this time, there is no close runner-up.

As TABLE X shows, in the reduced model combining the *Ars Poetica* with *Epistles* I, we lose just 1.24 of chi-square value at one degree of freedom, which is not statistically significant. Thus, this reduced model is preferable to the full model. The other reduced models, combining the *Ars* with other poems, are much less compelling: the *AP* + *Epist.* II.2 model, with a chi-square value of 68.99, actually represents a result significantly worse than the full model and hence can be rejected, as can that combining the *Ars* with *Sat.* II. The model combining *Ars Poetica* + *Epist.* II.1 is an acceptable reduction, but barely so and with less probability than the model collapsing *AP* + *Epist.* I. The *Ars Poetica* + *Sat.* II + *Epist.* I model, with a chi-square value of 72.16, is almost significantly worse than the full model: 75.53 - 69.55 = 5.98, with one degree of freedom. To reject a reduced model of this type, we would have had to have a remainder of 5.991 or more. As it is, we can simply say that it is much less probable than the reduction *Ars Poetica* + *Epist.* I.

MODEL	χ^2	DF	PROB	DIFFERENCE IN χ^2 FROM FULL MODEL (I)	DF	SIGNIFICANT AT $\alpha = .05$?
I	75.53	8	.000	—	—	—
II	70.05	7	.000	5.48	1	YES
III	74.29	7	.000	1.24	1	NO
IV	68.99	7	.000	6.54	1	YES
V	72.16	7	.000	3.37	3	NO§
VI	69.55	6	.000	5.98	2	NO*
VII	66.99	6	.000	8.54	2	YES
VIII	67.93	6	.000	7.60	2	YES

MODELS: I = FULL; II = AP+S2; III = AP+E1; IV = AP+EP2.2; V = AP+EP2.1; VI = AP+S2+E1; VII = AP+E1+E2.2; VIII = AP+E2

§The difference would be significant if it were 3.841 instead of 3.37.
*The difference would be significant if it were 5.991 instead of 5.980.

TABLE X: COMPARISONS OF THE FULL AND VARIOUS COLLAPSED MODELS OF THE DATA IN TABLE VIII

Having seen the strong evidence associating the *Ars Poetica* with *Epistles* I, we can now place the *Ars Poetica* on a frequency graph of the data for *nec* (see TABLE L). Although we once again put the *Ars Poetica* after *Epistles* I, we make no claim at this point of our argument about its relative position with respect to *Epistles*. I. As the graph shows, the *Ars Poetica* takes its place alongside *Epistles* I at the peak of the parabola, which falls off quickly in the late works. For the sake of parsimony, we do not postulate a cubic equation because of the anomalously low frequency of *Epist.* II.2.

It is interesting to note here that the trend in Horace's use of *ne* is much the same as that of *nec*, except that the overall frequency is in general quite a bit lower than it is for *nec*, and the effects of genre are just the reverse. Whereas for *nec*, the non-hexameters showed a higher rate of usage, for *ne* the frequency in the non-hexameters is quite low—so low, indeed, that *ne* has been excluded from our study on account of low frequency. So it must remain. Since *ne* and *nec* are so similar in sound and sense, it is at least worth reporting here the fact that the trends in Horace's use of them are similar, too. Although of no probative value for our argument, the resemblance of the trend of *ne* to that of *nec* may add support to the principal theoretical assumption of this study—namely, that some function words may serve as chronometers because their use changes in a patterned way over time according to quite unconscious linguistic processes.

As before for the first "concave" group, it is useful to combine the graphs of the "convex" group so that we may visualize just how closely the frequency trends of *nec* and *ne* resemble each other (cf. TABLE M). In so doing, we will use two scales to compensate for the fact that *ne* is so much rarer than *nec*. This is justified, needless to say, because we are interested only in the convexity of the pattern, and not in the absolute frequencies of the words in the Horatian corpus. Of course, the fact that *ne* peaks over *Epistles* I and *nec* over the *Ars Poetica* is equally irrelevant: there is no reason why the two words should follow the exact same development. As a further visual aid, we will use the bar graph for *nec* and superimpose a line graph for *ne*.

To conclude this part of our stylometric attempt to date the *Ars Poetica:* two classes of functions words emerge from a study of function words in Latin as satisfying the frequency and pattern requirements of chronometers. They are *ad/per/sed,* on the one hand, and *nec,* on the other. The first group has the pattern of a concave parabola; the second class, that of a convex parabola. In both classes, the *Ars Poetica* takes its rightful place next to *Epistles* I. In neither of the two classes do we find any compelling evidence that the *Ars Poetica* should be combined with Horace's late poetry.

Possible Macrochronometers: Characters, Strings, Strong Stops

Many other stylometric tests for relative chronology are conceivable, and, while it is not my intention to try to exhaust all the possibilities here, it is at least prudent to see if the results reached so far can be confirmed or disconfirmed by other means.

Up to now we have looked at one category of vocabulary—function words. To compensate for this rather restricted approach, let us consider some typical tests of Horace's entire vocabulary. By examining features common to all of Horace's use of language—which we may call *macrochronometers*—we will have looked at Horace's word usage from, so to speak, both ends of the telescope. Once again we will be trying to find some feature that can serve as a chronometer because its usage in the corpus shows patterned development.

Statisticians of style often look at such things as the average number of characters per word, words per sentence, and unique strings as a percentage of all strings. These will serve as our macrochronometers, and we may begin by measuring the average number of characters per word in the works of the corpus. From the graph on TABLE N, it can easily be seen that there is no developmental pattern here. Rather, Horatian usage remains quite stable from poem to poem and genre to genre. The mean values for the poems are 5.636, with a standard deviation of .052. If the Horatian mean turns out to be significantly different from that of other Latin writers, then it could serve as a criterion of attribution. It is clear, however, that it cannot be of much help for establishing a relative chronology of Horace's own works.

The situation is much the same for the ratio of words per strong stop, though for a different reason. Here the problem is not stability but random fluctuation—especially opposite trends in the hexameters and non-hexameters, as can be seen on TABLE O.

The hexameters show a steady rise from *Satires* II through *Epistles* II.2 and II.1 (leaving out of account, of course, the *Ars Poetica,* so as not to be guilty of a *petitio principii*). The hexameters are thus linear. The non-hexameters, on the other hand, have fewer words per stop in *Carm.* I-III of the mid-20s than they did in the *Epodes*, giving them a parabolic shape. It is perhaps just as well that this ratio turns out not to be useful: the pointing is completely dependent on the single text of Horace that has been digitized to date (Klingner's Teubner), and pointing is notoriously arbitrary. For this reason, I first converted all colons and semi-colons to periods before the computer scanned the text to tabulate "sentences." Nevertheless, although "strong stop" is a vaguer category than is "sentence," the result will hardly be found to agree with any other edition so modified. If for this practical reason words/stop is not a very reliable measure, then it is equally suspect on statistical grounds.[39]

Our last hope for a macrochronometer that can confirm or disconfirm the results of our study of function words is the ratio of unique strings to non-unique strings in Horace.[40] Normally, one would prefer to study words—i.e., lexemes—per se, not strings, or inflected forms of words. However, given the current lack of a parser for Latin, it is impractical to study a corpus as large as Horace's in this way. On the other hand, in the present case very little inaccuracy is likely to result from using for analysis strings, as opposed to words, since Latin does not have many homonyms like *uti*. TABLE P reports the rate at which unique and non-unique strings appear in Horace's works.

As can be seen from TABLE XI, our intuition that we have, indeed, identified a statistically significant pattern is confirmed by chi-square and associ-

STRING	S1	S2	EP1	EP2.1	EP2.2	TOTAL
UNIQUE	3691	3988	3804	1277	1036	
NON-UNIQ	3304	3234	2882	486	383	
TOTAL	6995	7222	6686	1763	1419	
STRING	AP	EPD	C1-3	C4		
UNIQUE	2048	2038	7529	1872		27283
NON-UNIQ	1034	957	3165	687		16132
TOTAL	3082	2995	10694	2559		43415
TEST STATISTIC			VALUE	DF		PROB.
PEARSON CHI-SQUARE			1147.6	8		0.000
COEFFICIENT	VALUE		ASMPT. STD. ERROR			
CRAMER V	.1626					
CONTINGENCY	.1605					
LAMBDA	.0042		.00245			
UNCERTAINTY	.0066		.00039			

TABLE XI: CHI-SQUARE TEST OF THE FREQUENCY OF UNIQUE AND NON-UNIQUE STRINGS IN HORACE

[39]See A. Q. Morton, *Literary Detection* (New York 1978); K. L. Lindsay and T. W. Mackay, op. cit. (*supra* n. 23) 8-9. For a similar functional definition of "strong stop," see I. Marriott, "The Authorship of the *Historia Augusta*," *JRS* 69 (1979) 65-77, at p. 66 with 66n4.

[40]This kind of "type/token" analysis was used by Grayston and Herdan in an authorship study of works in the New Testament attributed to Paul; see K. Grayston and G. Herdan, "The Authorship of the Pastorals in Light of Statistical Linguistics," *New Testament Studies* 6 (1959-60) 1-15; the study is usefully criticized by Lindsay and Mackay, op. cit. (*supra* n. 23) 6-7. Grayston and Herdan studied words, not strings (arrays of characters, i.e., forms of words).

ation tests of the data. The high chi-square value tells us that there is very little chance indeed that the figures for the strings are the result of chance and a very high probability that the variables of poem and string-type are not independent. Their degree of dependence is expressed by the various coefficients, which indicate a modest degree of association reflective of the fact that the slopes of the lines in TABLE P are so gentle.

Attempts to model the data by combining the *Ars Poetica* with other poems do not succeed in establishing a more economical model without loss of significance. In fact, collapsing the data in any of the ways used earlier results in significant losses of chi-square value, as TABLE XII shows. The fact that the full model is preferable to any reduction means that we have no basis at this point in the analysis for associating the *Ars Poetica* with one of the datable hexameter poems.

On TABLE P, the location of the *Ars Poetica* between *Epistles* I and *Epist*. II.2 is thus purely speculative, supported only by the smooth linear pattern that results. In a moment we will convert the nominal poem variables to interval variables. Our first order of business will then be to see whether other tests, appropriate only to interval variables, can confirm or disconfirm this speculation.

MODEL	LOSS OF χ^2 VALUE	DF	PROB.
AP + *Ep*. I	82.48	1	.000
AP + *Ep*. II.2	17.9	1	.000
AP + *Ep*. II.1	17.19	1	.000
AP + *Ep*. II	26.21	2	.000

TABLE XII: ALTERNATIVE MODELS FOR GROUPING THE DATA OF TABLE XI

Absolute Chronology: Conversion to Interval Variables

A number of statistical analyses were unavailable to us because the variables we have been considering so far were nominal, not interval. It is prudent to consider Horace's poems as simple categories; on the other hand, in view of their generally accepted absolute chronology, they can also be taken as points on an interval scale of time. If we do this with due awareness of how approximate our results must be, we can make a provisional attempt to determine whether the *Ars Poetica* should be dated before or after *Epistles* I and we can obtain added confirmation for our rejection of the late dating of the poem.

Because we did not make such a conversion, we could not mathematically describe the linear and quadratic equations that may describe Horace's evolving use of *ad, sed, ne,* and *nec* as well as his ratio of unique to non-unique strings. Only after arriving at such equations, by building linear and non-linear regression models,[41] can we attempt to make our date of the *Ars Poetica* more precise.

In what follows, the conversion to interval variables will be based on the publication dates given by Vretska (see n. 30 above), with the exception that the *Epodes*—which were written over such a long period of time—are dated to the approximate mid-point of their period of composition (*c.* 35 B.C.) and *Epistles* II.2 is dated to 19/18.[42] To circumvent the problem that dates B.C. are regressive, dates will be expressed variously in terms of Horace's age or in years *ab urbe condita* (AUC), as follows:

HEX	AUC	=AGE	NON-HEX	AUC	=AGE
S I	718	30	EPD	718	30
S II	723	35			
			C1-3	730	42
EP I	733	45			
EP II.2	735	47			
EP II.1	740	52	C4	740	52

TABLE XIII: APPROXIMATE PUBLICATION DATES OF HORACE'S POETRY

First, equations will be derived for the data from poems, excluding the *Ars Poetica*. Then, the *Ars Poetica* will be dated by means of the equations. As before, the hexameters and non-hexameters will be treated separately. We may note here that our results will only relate to the *terminus ante quem* of the *Ars Poetica* as we have it. No attempt will be made to determine whether the poem we have is, e.g., a revised version or a second edition of an earlier poem.

Let us first examine the unique strings in the non-hexameter poetry. As we recall, these showed a strong linear pattern of development, with increasing rates of unique strings as time went on. We want to see whether there is support for our speculation that the *Ars* belongs roughly in the period between the composition of *Epist.* I and *Epist.* II.2

---

[41]Cf. A. Agresti and B. Finlay, op. cit. (*supra* n. 19) 243-288, 316-356.

[42]Vretska says the date is "before 20," but most scholars put it in 19/18; see Brink, I, 184n1.

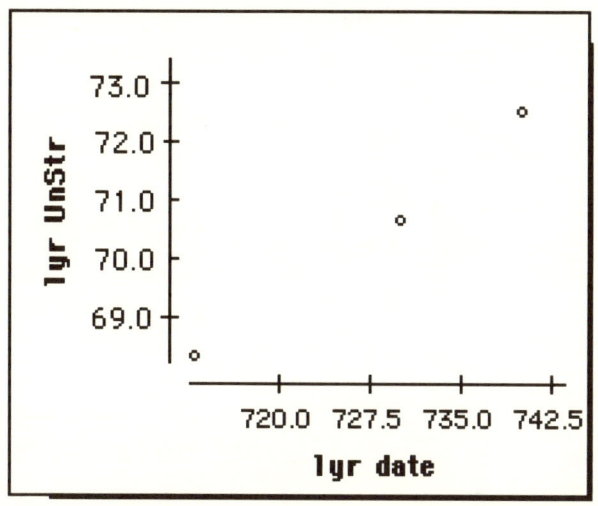

> Dependent variable is: lyr UnStr (lyric Unique Strings)
> $R^2 = 99.1\%$ R^2 (adjusted) = 98.3%
> s = 0.2781 with 3 - 2 = 1 degree of freedom
>
> | Source | Sum of Squares | DF | Mean Square |
> |------------|----------------|----|-------------|
> | Regression | 8.76931 | 1 | 8.7693 |
> | Residual | 0.077361 | 1 | 0.077361 |
>
> | Variable | Coefficient | S.E. of Coeff | T-ratio |
> |----------|-------------|---------------|---------|
> | Constant | -41.1566 | 10.49 | -3.93 |
> | lyr date | 0.153399 | 0.0144 | 10.6 |
>
> Formula: Y = -41.1566 + .153399X

TABLE XIV: PERCENTAGE OF UNIQUE STRINGS IN
HORACE'S NON-HEXAMETER POETRY

The figure R^2 is the coefficient of determination, which varies from 0 (indicating that the variables are independent) to 1.0 (indicating that they are strongly associated). In this case, the coefficient is practically 1.0, so that we may be quite confident that the rate of unique strings in a Horatian poem is determined by its date.

The frequency of unique strings in the hexameter poems also increases over time, as the table on the next page shows.

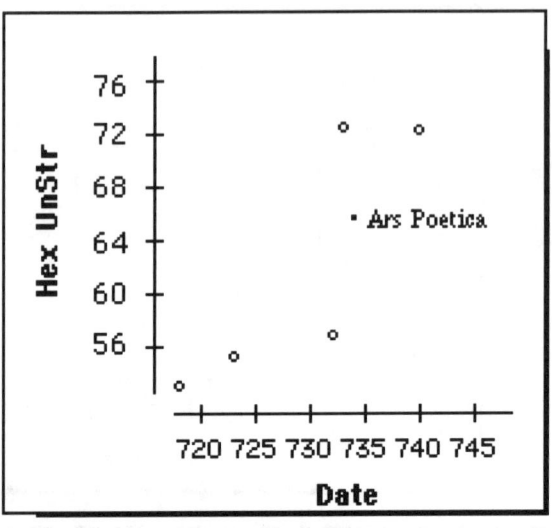

Dependent variable is: HexUnStr (hexameter Unique Strings)			
$R^2 = 69.6\%$ R^2 (adjusted) $= 59.4\%$			
$s = 6.119$ with $5 - 2 = 3$ degrees of freedom			

Source	Sum of Squares	DF	Mean Square
Regression	256.923	1	257.0
Residual	112.345	3	37.4482

Variable	Coefficient	s.e. of Coeff	t-ratio
Constant	-609.812	256.5	-2.38
Date	0.921136	0.3517	2.62

Formula: $Y = -609.812 + .921136X$
Date of *Ars Poetica*: $Y = 66.1$; $X = 733.78$ (21/20 B.C.)

TABLE XV: PERCENTAGE OF UNIQUE STRINGS IN HORACE'S HEXAMETER POETRY

In this case, the results are more scattered, but the coefficient of determination is still quite high at .696. This means that about 70% of the variability of unique strings from poem to poem is explained by the dates of the poems, as opposed to other (non-specified) factors. The formula resulting from our analysis gives us the Y-intercept and slope of the linear equation that best describes this data: $Y = -609.812 + .921136X$. With the Y-value for the *Ars Poetica* (66.1) in hand, we can solve the equation for X (i.e., for date) for the *Ars Poetica*. The answer is 733.728 a.u.c., or 21/20 B.C. On the scattergram, I have entered the poem into the locus indicated by the equation. The high reliability of this dating is suggested by the t-ratio for the variable "Date." The value of 2.62 with three degrees of freedom results in a rejection of the null hypothesis that the true slope coefficient is 0 (that is, that the variable Y, or frequency of unique strings, does not depend on the variable X, or date) at an alpha-level of less than .05.[43]

Since the fit of our nonlinear data to the most descriptive quadratic equations is not as tight as it is for these two linear patterns, and since the number of poems in our sample is so low in any case, our approach to the words with quadratic equations (i.e., *ad, sed, nec, and ne*) is somewhat different. Instead of deriving a date from all the hexameters except the *Ars Poetica* and then determining the date of the poem by substituting the value of the dependent variable, we will use an exploratory modelling approach.[44] With this method, we increase the plausibility, if not probability, of our results by including the *Ars Poetica* in our regression analysis. Controlling for all the other poems, we run the regression seventeen times by varying the date of the *Ars Poetica* from its earliest to its latest possible year of composition (i.e., 24 to 8 B.C.). We then pick out the years that are most and least likely, as determined, respectively, by the greatest and lowest R^2 value of the regression. This procedure tells us which dates of the *Ars Poetica* are the most and least likely for these data. The results may be seen on TABLE XVI.

WORD	BEST DATE	R_1^2	WORST DATE	R_2^2	RATIO R_1^2/R_2^2
SED	24	.848	8	.257	3.3
PER	24	.687	8	.224	3.1
AD	20	.594	8	.457	1.3
NEC[45]	24	.620	8	.415	1.5

TABLE XVI: BEST AND WORST REGRESSION MODELS FOR DATING THE *ARS POETICA* BY MEANS OF FUNCTION WORDS

[43]When the t-ratio is 2.62 with three degrees of freedom, alpha is < .05 and >. 025.

[44]For the difference between an explanatory and exploratory use of regression, see A. Agresti and B. Finlay, op. cit. (*supra* n. 19) 379-80, especially the following: "in exploratory research...the goal is not to explain relationships among variables so much as it is to find a good set of predictors. Here we want to maximize R^2, and we do not worry so much about theoretical explanations."

[45]The principle of parsimonious model-building suggests that the anomalous *Epist.* II.2 be excluded from consideration.

R^2, as noted earlier, measures the strength of the association of the variables; here, R_1^2 is the correlation coefficient of the best model and R_2^2 that of the worst. Three of the function words *(sed; per; nec)* give us R_1^2 values superior to that found for the unique strings; one *(ad)* is quite similar. While these absolute values are sufficient to permit the conclusion that, on this basis, the *Ars Poetica* should more likely be dated to the period 24-20 B.C. than to Horace's last years, they do not give us a sense of the degree to which the earlier datings are preferable to the latter. For this, we need to consider the ratio R_1^2/R_2^2, which quantifies the advantage of the best model over the worst. Perusal of the table confirms that *sed* and *per* are very reliable chronometers indeed, both in absolute and relative terms.

The R^2 value expresses the fit of the observed frequencies of *ad, per, sed,* and *nec* to those that can be predicted by the appropriate quadratic equation. The closer the fit, the higher the value of R^2, which varies, as previously noted, from 0.0 to 1.0. The graphs in TABLES Q-T will help the reader visualize the fit of the data to the predictive equations. In examining them, the reader should bear in mind that a quadratic equation can be derived to fit any three points on a graph; thus, it is not surprising that two or three points always fall on or very near the prediction parabolas. Visualization of the goodness of fit (R^2 values) of the predicted to the observed values depends on developing a sense of the number of points off the parabolic line and their distance from their predicted values on the line. The graphs are presented in descending order of their R_1^2/R_2^2 ratios, beginning with *sed*.

Summary of Arguments for Dating the *Ars Poetica*

At this point, a summary of our statistical investigations and other arguments for dating the *Ars Poetica* is in order.

Of the three approaches to dating the poem, the first—comparing and contrasting ideas of the *Ars Poetica* with Horace's beliefs about poetry in his other, datable poems—was rejected because the ideas in the *Ars* are so different from what we find in his other poems that the poem cannot readily be fitted into a chronological scheme of Horace's ideas about poetry. We did, however, note that the only echoes in the *Ars Poetica* to other passages in Horace's poetry were to poems published in 23-20 B.C., thus suggesting that the *Ars* dates from the same period. The second approach—based on dating the work by reference to biographical information available from other sources about historical personages mentioned in the poem—provided a firm *post quem* (24/23 B.C.), but was only suggestive about a *terminus ante quem* (19 B.C.).

The third approach of stylometrics confirmed this *terminus post quem* and added better evidence for an *ante quem* of *c*. 20 B.C. Starting from a reexamination of Duckworth's metrical arguments for dating the *Ars Poetica*—which he adduced in favor of a late date—we found that, by his own "naive" statistical methodology, the evidence supported dating the poem in Horace's "middle" period, well before the late hexameters of *Epistles* II. Subjecting the data to standard statistical tests, we then found that his metrical tests did not give strong support to even this revised dating. Instead of looking further for metrical chronometers—something presently difficult to do in the absence of a commercially available metrical scanner for Latin—we shifted our evidentiary base from meter to vocabulary, treating the books of poetry as nominal variables that can be arranged according to a relative chronology. We then sought criteria for dating the poems by running tests on Horace's use of function words, on the average number of characters per word and of words per strong stop, and on the ratio of unique to non-unique strings in Horace. The studies of word-length and words per stop were inconclusive, since no development over time was noted. On the other hand, our examination of function words and ratio of unique to non-unique strings proved fruitful: here we discovered linear and non-linear patterns of development over Horace's career, and both batteries of tests suggested that the *Ars Poetica* fell into Horace's middle period of hexameters. Finally, converting the nominal variables into interval variables by assigning the various poems their generally accepted absolute dates, we ran tests of the ratio of unique to non-unique strings and of the changing frequency of function words. These tests agreed in indicating a date in the period 24-20 B.C. as most probable for the composition of the *Ars Poetica*. The tests of the function words also showed that, the later we attempted to date the *Ars Poetica* down to 8 B.C. (the year of Horace's death), the *less* likely the result in terms of statistical probability. Three of the four function words indicated a best dating of 24 B.C.; one dated the poem to 20 B.C.

Our conclusion is thus that the most likely date of the *Ars Poetica* is between 24 and 20 B.C.

CHAPTER 3

INTERPRETIVE IMPLICATIONS OF CHRONOLOGY: THE *ARS POETICA* IN ITS CULTURAL CONTEXT

The problems considered thus far will almost certainly never have definitive answers: we simply lack the kind of information we need to have in order to know what Horace himself called the *Ars Poetica* and when he wrote the poem. Our effort has been much more modest: to show that some possibilities have been overlooked by earlier scholars and to demonstrate that some of these possibilities are even—statistically speaking—probabilities. The poem's title and date are not merely of antiquarian interest. They have a direct and indirect impact on how we construct our reading of the poem.

At this point, then, we need to address three issues. First, what consequences would our dating have for the relationship of the poem to its historical milieu? Secondly, in view of those consequences, what effect can an early dating have on our interpretation and understanding of the *Ars Poetica*? Finally, to what extent are these external and internal implications of the date consistent with—or, indeed, supportive of—a parodic reading of the poem?

For the first issue, the identity of the Pisones to whom the work is dedicated is of paramount importance. In the past, scholars have thought themselves forced by a date in the late 20s to see Cn. Calpurnius Piso (cos. 23) as the senior dedicatee of the poem. This has been resisted because, from what we know about him and his family, they do not seem appropriate recipients of a work on poetics. On the other hand, the favored candidate, L. Calpurnius Piso Pontifex (cos. 15), was too young in the 20s to serve as the senior dedicatee.[1] Once we have offered a new solution to the problem of identifying Piso père, we will examine the implications of our candidate for interpretation of the poem, particularly in the light of Horace's relationship to contemporary literary critics. We will see that by aligning the speaker of the *Ars Poetica* with such critics as

---

[1]Cf., with admirable succinctness, Brink, I, 239-240.

Piso and Sp. Maecius Tarpa, Horace undermines the speaker's authority in a way suggestive of parody.

Similarly, the dating proposed here invites us to examine the relationship between the poem and contemporary painting and art criticism, which, from the very first lines of the poem, play a prominent part in the *Ars Poetica*. A close reading of the opening lines of the poem will show that, right from the start, Horace portrays the speaker of the poem as a pedant and an ignoramus. This characterization, like the attack on his authority, is consistent with a parodic reading of the work.

Finally, dating the *Ars Poetica* to the 20s, and seeing it as a separate work in the corpus unrelated to the *Epistles* and replete with parodic elements should naturally make us wonder about the genre of the poem. In tackling this matter in *Chapter 4*, we will try both to put the Renaissance epistle-theory to rest once and for all and to link the *Ars Poetica* to the traditions of Horatian *sermo*.

The Identity of the Pisones

Foremost among the ten historical personages mentioned in the *Ars Poetica* are the Pisones, who are the addressees of the poem. Since their identification is closely connected to the poem's chronology and tone, I will have to delve into the matter here.

A full account of the extensive scholarship on the identity of the Pisones is no longer necessary after the thorough recent contributions of Brink and Syme, on which we can safely try to build. In particular, the claims of the unpoetical Cn. Calpurnius Piso (cos. 23) need no longer be rehearsed and refuted.[2] As mentioned above, Cn. Calpurnius Piso has, since the nineteenth century, been the Piso to whom scholars dating the poem to the 20s have had to turn, since L. Calpurnius Piso (cos. 15) was too young in the 20s to have had children old enough to be called *iuvenes* (cf. *Ars Poetica* 366). Our task here, then, is to find someone other than Cn. Calpurnius Piso who can serve as senior addressee in the late 20s.

Horace addresses his poem to Pisones (6, *credite, Pisones*...). Although there were several important late-republican families with this cognomen, it is at

---

[2]Brink, I, 239-243; III, 446-448, 554; R. Syme, "The Sons of Piso the Pontifex," *AJP* 101 (1980) 333-341 (= *Roman Papers*, vol. 3, ed. A. R. Birley [Oxford 1984] 1226-1232); *History in Ovid* (Oxford 1978) 115, 178. That the addressee in Horace normally has some connection to the topic of the poem is a commonplace; cf., e.g., R. G. M. Nisbet and M. Hubbard, *A Commentary on Horace: Odes Book II* (Oxford 1978) 2.

least clear that we have to do with Calpurnii Pisones,[3] because lines 291-292 (*vos, o / Pompilius sanguis*) imply that our family descends from Calpus, the son of King Numa.[4] Moreover, verse 366 (*o maior iuvenum*) tells us that our family consists of a father and two children, who must range in age somewhere between about 16 and 45 years of age.[5] Lines 385-388[6] suggest that the elder child is (or, plans to be) a poet and that his father is (or, considers himself to be) an authority on literary criticism. So much for the internal evidence.

The late-antique commentator, Porphyrio, in a note on the first line of the poem, identifies Piso père as L. Calpurnius Piso (cos. 15; *RE* Calpurnius 99): *hunc librum, qui inscribitur de Arte Poetica, ad Lucium Pisonem, qui postea urbis custos fuit, eiusque liberos misit, nam et ipse Piso poeta fuit et studiorum liberalium antistes*. This notice may, however, be incorrect because this Piso is not known to have had any children. Syme, presenting some possible sons of this Piso, must admit a lack of certainty about his candidates, though he sensibly points out that the silence of the ancient sources anent children may be the result of any number of good reasons, e.g., adoptions, early deaths, or political inactivity.[7]

However, even if children are postulated, one problem remains with Porphyrio's Piso père. The text of the poem presumes that the father is primarily a critic, not a poet: he is mentioned as such (388), and Horace says nothing about his poetry, which is strange if he has written anything of note. We are told by Porphyrio that the consul of 15 was a poet (*nam et ipse poeta fuit*....), and we may even have some of his poetry in the *Greek Anthology*.[8] Moreover, Por-

---

[3]And not, e.g., Domitii Pisones (Pliny, *NH praef.* 17), or Pupii Pisones (cf. *RE* Pupius 10-12; M. H. Crawford, *Roman Republican Coinage*, vol. 1 [Cambridge 1974] 87, 442-443, with bibliography).

[4]On whom see Münzer in *RE* III s.v. Calpurnius, col. 1365. For an updated account, see E. Champlin, "The Life and Times of Calpurnius Piso," *MH* 46 (1989) 101-124, at pp. 119-123. On the alleged descent of the family from Calpus see, in general, T. P. Wiseman, "Legendary Genealogies in Late-Republican Rome," *Greece & Rome* 21 (1974) 153-164, especially pp. 154-155.

[5]Cf. *OLD* s.v. *iuvenis* I.

[6]"Tu nihil invita dices faciesve Minerva: | id tibi iudicium est, ea mens. si quid tamen olim | scripseris, in Maeci descendat iudicis auris | et patris et nostras...."

[7]Syme, "The Sons of Piso," op. cit. (*supra* n. 2) 334-341. For a concrete case of how an early death may account for the absence of a famous man's brother from the historical record, see L. E. Reams, "The Strange Case of Sulla's Brother," *CJ* 82 (1987) 301-305.

[8]Cf. C. Cichorius, *Römische Studien* (Leipzig 1922) 325-327, 338-341; E. Groag, *PIR*[2] (Berlin 1936) Calpurnius 289 (p. 66). Because Porphyrio tells us that his Piso père was a poet, *AP* 11.424, attributed to a certain Piso, has been thought to be by this man. That Piso père is presented in the poem largely as a critic and the

phyrio's candidate was born in 48; any children he may have had would accordingly have become *iuvenes* only in the very last years of Horace's life—say after 12, if Piso married young and had his first child early on (e.g., born in 48; married in 29; first child born in 28 and Horace's *maior iuvenum* at age 16 in 12).[9]

If the period 24-20 is considered the likeliest for the composition of the *Ars Poetica*, then we must face the instant repercussion that Porphyrio must be wrong about the identity of Piso père.[10] Or, perhaps, partly wrong.

It is quite possible that Porphyrio has the right family, but the wrong generation.[11] If Piso père is more a critic than a poet and if his elder child is a poet, not a critic, then these requirements are better met by assigning to L. Calpurnius Piso Caesoninus (cos. 58; *RE* Calpurnius 90) the role of père and to his son, L. Calpurnius Piso Pontifex (cos. 15; *RE* Calpurnius 99), the part of *maior iuvenum* (25-28 years old in 23-20 B.C., since he was born in *c.* 48 B.C., according to Tac. *Ann.* 6.10). The consul of 15 was, as has been noted, a poet, according to Porphyrio; he is *maior iuvenum,* despite his famous elder sister Calpurnia (Caesar's last wife; *RE* Calpurnia 126), because she—betrothed to Caesar in 59, before her brother was even born—was too old in the 20s to be called *iuvenis*, assuming she was even alive (we hear no mention of her after 44). Their father was facetiously called a critic (*grammaticus*) by Cicero.[12] The implication behind Cicero's invective (on which, see pp. 57-59) is that the consul of 58 prided himself on being a literary critic—not unexpected in a man who we know was a patron of poets, including the poet-philosopher Philodemus.

---

elder child as a budding poet was noted by E. C. Wickham, *Quinti Horatii Flacci, Opera Omnia*, vol. 2, (Oxford 1891) 383-384.

[9]Cf. R. Syme, "The Sons of Piso," op. cit. (*supra* n. 2) 338-339, for speculation along these lines. Note that a *iuvenis* is "technically, any adult male up to the age of 45" (*OLD*). The *toga virilis* was assumed, in this period, at *c.* 16 years of age (cf. J. P. V. D. Balsdon, *Life and Leisure in Ancient Rome* [New York 1969] 120). Thus, in a technical sense, the senior dedicatee of the *Ars Poetica* must have children aged 16-45. To be sure, the term *iuvenis* could also be used more loosely, but the technical sense at least gives us guidance as to what Horace means.

[10]That a date in the 20s B.C. rules out Porphyrio's candidate has been seen since J. H. van Reenen's *Disputatio philologico-critica de Horatii Epistola ad Pisones* (Amsterdam 1806). As noted, Van Reenen and his followers have recourse to Cn. Calpurnius Piso (cos. 23). *Ars Poetica* 306, "nil scribens ipse," has sometimes been connected with the so-called *intervallum lyricum* of 23-18 B.C., when Horace wrote no lyric poetry. Equally possible is an interpretation based on persona-theory: the *Ars Poetica* speaker is presented as a typical *grammaticus*, who has never written poetry and has no plans to do so.

[11]Similar prosopographical confusions in Porphyrio are collected by A. Michaelis, op. cit. (*supra* n. 10) 421.

[12]*In Pisonem* 73.

Although the identifications of Caesoninus and Pontifex fit quite well with the evidence of the *Ars Poetica*, there still remain two potential difficulties that should be explored now. In his influential *RE* article on Caesoninus, Münzer suggested that Caesoninus died shortly after the Battle of Mutina, for he is no longer mentioned in the literary sources after 43 B.C.[13] This is, of course, a speculative argument from silence, but it has apparently been powerful enough to discourage earlier students of the problem from proposing Caesoninus as the senior dedicatee of the *Ars Poetica*. Let us note, first of all, that other speculations about Caesoninus after 43 are possible: we may, for example, just as easily imagine that the conciliatory and Epicurean Piso withdrew in disgust from politics into the pleasures of retirement, or semi-retirement, after 43.[14] In favor of this, we may recall Piso's reluctance to hold the office of censor in 50.[15]

We do not have to content ourselves with guesses that Caesoninus lived on after 43. After Münzer wrote, three inscriptions in Pola mentioning L. Calpurnius L.f. Piso Caesoninus have gradually been published. Here are the texts:

L·CASSIUS·C·F·LONGIN(US) | L·CALPURNIUS·L·F·PISO·| IIVIR(I)...

[*CIL* V 54 = *ILLRP* 639 = *Inscr. Ital.* X.i.81 (with photo), from the Porta Herculea]

L·CALP[URNIUS·L·F] | PISO·CA[ESONINUS]·| CO[S]

[= *Fig. I*; *CIL* I².2512 = *ILLRP* 423 = *Inscr. Ital.* X.i.65 (with drawing); found in v. Castropola (= M. Gupca Street); A. Gnirs, *JÖAI* 13 (1910) 196; P. Sticotti, *AMSI* 30 (1914) 114; A. Gnirs, *Pola* (Vienna 1915) 53; museum, inv. nr. 316]

[L·CAL]PURN[IUS·L·F·]
[CAE]SON[INUS]

[*ILLRP* 424 = *Inscr. Ital.* X.i.708 (with photo); now missing, formerly on a wall of the duomo; see M. Mirabella Roberti, *Il Duomo di Pola* (Pola 1943) 31n1]

---

[13]So, e.g., Münzer, *RE* III s.v. Calpurnius 90 (Stuttgart 1897) cols. 1387-1390; C. L. Neudling, *A Prosopography to Catullus, Iowa Studies in Classical Philology* 12 (1955) 42-45. According to A. Fraschetti, "La 'Pietas' di Cesare e la colonia di Pola," *AION* 5 (1983) 77-102, at p. 97n85, this was originally Münzer's suggestion. I have not attempted to trace the idea beyond Münzer.

[14]So E. Scuotto, "Realtà umana e atteggiamenti politici e culturali di Lucio Calpurnio Pisone Cesonino," *RAAN* 47 (1972) 149-166, at p. 162.

[15]Dio 40.63.2.

In an article published in an out-of-the-way journal, seventeen years after Münzer's article, Sticotti convincingly identified the Piso mentioned in these inscriptions as our man, the consul of 58. Since the first of the three can be dated as contemporary with Pola's first permanent wall (i.e., to *c.* 33 B.C.; see Appendix III for details), Pola provides important evidence of Piso's survival into the triumviral period.[16] In 23-20, he would have been about 80 (77-85 is the probable range),[17] and in this connection we should note that his son lived to be 80.

The second difficulty with our identifications of Piso père et fils is that we still lack a younger child. This will be held against my theory by any adherents of the claims of the family of Cn. Calpurnius Piso (cos. 23), who is known to have had two sons. However, one attested son is better than none (a disadvantage taken in stride by such recent supporters of Porphyrio as Brink and Syme). In addition to the reasons given by Syme for the absence of sons from the historical record, we might note that it is not even clear from the text of the *Ars Poetica* that we have to do with two sons, as has always been assumed: the words *iuvenes* (24, 366) and *liberi* (Porphyrio on verse 1) do not rule out the possibility that one of the children was, in fact, a daughter.[18] The odds of a daughter being mentioned in an independent historical source are not very high.

Two final points, this time in favor of my identification of the Pisones. First, we ought to bear in mind that the problem we are trying to solve has another aspect. Thus far, we have been concentrating on whom Horace intended by Piso père and the *maior iuvenum*. Equally important is who Horace's educated reader would have understood these people to be. There is obviously a relationship between these two problems: Horace reveals his intentions to the reader by the information he provides in the poem. That information indicates, as we have seen, Calpurnii Pisones (291-292). Of the two possible families—the Cnaei and Lucii Calpurnii Pisones—only the Lucii have a connection with

---

[16]See P. Sticotti, "Nuova rassegna di epigrafi romane," *AMSI* 30 (1914) 113-114; A. Degrassi, *Il confine nord-orientale dell'Italia romana, Diss. Bern.* ser. I, fasc. 6 (Bern 1954) 65-66 (= *Scritti vari di antichità,* II [Rome 1962] 918); J. Sasel, "Calpurnia L. Pisonis Auguris Filia," *ZAnt* 12 (1962-1963) 387-390; J. Sasel, "Probleme und Möglichkeiten onomastischer Forschung," *Acta CIEGR* 4 (1964) 352-368 at pp. 363-367; J. J. Wilkes, *Dalmatia* (London 1969) 331; L. Keppie, *Colonisation and Veteran Settlement in Italy, 47-14 B.C.* (London 1983) 204; A. Fraschetti, op. cit. (*supra* n. 13) 90-91.

[17]For his birth year, see R. G. M. Nisbet, *Cicero, In Pisonem* (Oxford 1961) v (*c.* 105-101 B.C.); A. Degrassi, ibid., *Il confine,* 66 (=*Scritti vari,* p. 918).

[18]For examples, see *OLD* s.vv. *iuvenis* 2 ("a young person of either sex") and *liberi* ("sons and daughters, children"). Young women did, of course, write poetry in the first century: cf. the cases of Sempronia, whose works do not survive (Sallust, *Cat.* 25), and Sulpicia, on whose poems see D. Roessel, "The Significance of the Name Cerinthus in the Poems of Sulpicia," *TAPA* 120 (1990) 243-250.

literature that is knowable, not only by us, but very likely also by Horace's contemporaries. For Horace's reader, then, the question was simply *which* Lucius, the consul of 58 (Caesoninus) or of 15 (Pontifex).

From the reader's point of view, I do not think that there could have been much hesitation in identifying Piso père as the consul of 58, only assuming that Caesoninus was still alive or very recently deceased when the poem was circulated—something, as we have seen, that we have no grounds for doubting. The reason for this is obvious: Piso Caesoninus was famously connected to literature and to literary criticism. Philodemus dedicated epigrams and at least one philosophical work to him; Catullus wrote two poems about him;[19] and, most importantly, Cicero branded him a cruel "Phalaris of literary critics" in an oration (the *In Pisonem*) that Cicero tells us (doubtless with some exaggeration) quickly became a school text.[20] On the other hand, his son, though rising politically in the period 23-20 B.C., was at best tangentially associated with poetry throughout his career. Tacitus, in his famous obituary, does not even mention this facet of his personality.[21] Once we view the problem of the addressee from the vantage point of the reader instead of the author, then the choice of Caesoninus as Piso père becomes stronger still. He is the literary Piso who would prob-

---

[19]Cf. Philodemus, *On the Good King According to Homer* and epigram 23 Gow-Page, and cf. Cic. *In Pisonem* 70-71 about other lost poems ("multa ad istum [scil. Pisonem] de ipso quoque scripsit [scil. Philodemus], ut omnis hominis libidines, omnia stupra, omnia cenarum conviviorumque genera, adulteria denique eius delicatissimis versibus expresserit..."). Some of these poems may be among the new epigrams of Philodemus whose incipits are in P. Oxy. 3724 (ed. P. Parsons in *P. Oxy.* LIV [1987] 65-82; cf. especially p. 67 on Philodemean authorship of some of the epigrams, and see now also M. Gigante, "Filodemo tra poesia e prosa," *SIFC* 82 [1989] 129-151; D. Sider, "Looking for Philodemus in P. Oxy. 54.3724," *ZPE* 76 [1989] 229-236). Cf. Catullus 28, 47, and on Piso in Catullus see C. L. Neudling, op. cit. (*supra* n. 13) 42-45. T. P. Wiseman's efforts to deny that Caesoninus was Catullus' Piso have so far failed to persuade; see *Catullus and His World* (Cambridge 1985) 2 with n2; T. R. S. Broughton, *MRR*, vol. 3 (Atlanta, Ga. 1986) 47.

[20]On the sense of "Phalaris grammaticus" see P. Grimal, *Cicéron, Discours, Contre L. Pison,* Tome XVI, 1º Partie (Paris 1966) 186-187. On the *In Pisonem*, see Cicero's remarks in *Ad Q. fr.* 3.1.11 ("meam [scil. orationem] in illum [scil. Pisonem] pueri omnes tamquam dictata perdiscant"); cf. J. Crawford, *M. Tullius Cicero: The Lost and Unpublished Orations*, Hypomnemata 80 (1984) 8; and J. Zetzel, *Latin Textual Criticism in Antiquity* (New York 1981; reprinted Salem, N.H. 1984) 27. On Piso's fame as a man of culture and learning—and the rarity of such qualities among Roman aristocrats of the first century—see E. Rawson, *Intellectual Life in the Late Roman Republic* (Baltimore 1985) 97.

[21]Tacitus, *Ann.* 6.10.

ably have leapt to the mind of Horace's average reader, especially in the absence of any strong counterindications from Horace that someone else was meant.[22]

Our second point is this: we have evidence that Horace knew the works in which Cicero attacked the consul of 58 and his literary pretensions. Keller-Holder give the following *loci similes* between Cicero's *In Pisonem* and *Pro Sestio*[23] and works of Horace. I put them in order of their cogency as evidence that Horace was familiar with the Ciceronian text:[24]

[1]	*In Pisonem* 37:	Confer nunc, Epicure noster ex hara producte non ex schola...
		~
	Epist. I.4.15-16:	me...Epicuri de grege porcum
[2]	*In Pisonem* 73:	te non Aristarchum sed Phalarin grammaticum habemus....
		~
	Ars Poetica 450-51:	fiet Aristarchus, nec dicet 'cur ego amicum offendam in nugis?'
[3]	*In Pisonem* 20:	supercilium tuum...fugi...frontis tuae nubeculam pertimescerem...
		~
	Epist. I.18.94:	deme supercilio nubem....[25]
[4]	*Pro Sestio* 42:	ut aliquo praesidio caput...tutetur...
		~
	Epist. I.18.81:	tuterisque tuo fidenter praesidio....

The first piece of evidence is doubtless the most important and persuasive: Horace applies to himself in a jocular vein the same kind of striking animal comparison that Cicero had used in his bitter invective against the consul

---

[22]Cf. now E. Champlin, op. cit. (*supra* n. 4) 122: "no other branch of the [Calpurnii Pisones] family comes near to rivalling this pair [viz., the coss. of 58 and 15] in war and the patronage of literature."

[23]Where Piso is attacked in 19-24.

[24]Two cases that I consider fortuitous I omit: Cic. *In Pis.* 47, "furiosum...dementiorem" ~ Hor. *Sat.* II.3.303 (sic: should be 133?) "demens"; and Cic. *Ad Q. fr.* 3.1.11, "meam in illum [scil. orationem] pueri omnes tamquam dictata perdiscant" ~ Hor. *Epist.* I.18.13-14, "ut puerum saevo credas dictata magistro reddere...."

[25]Nisbet (ad *Pis.* 20) points out the Horatian reminiscence but also presents Greek parallels which show that the background of Horace's text may not be Cicero's.

of 58. Moreover, in both cases it is their allegiance to Epicureanism (which, according to its ancient opponents, debased man to the level of beast because it defined pleasure as the highest good) that justifies the comparison. However natural the metaphor might seem to us, the ancient evidence does not suggest that it was commonplace. So here, as I will argue elsewhere, we have the same humorous association of Horace with Piso that we find in the *Ars Poetica*.[26] If these *loci similes* suggest that Horace had read works in which Piso is attacked, then they also suggest when he did so: during the period in which he was composing *Epistles* I and the nearly contemporaneous *Ars Poetica*.

To conclude the discussion thus far: the *Ars Poetica* was probably written in 24-20 B.C. and dedicated to L. Calpurnius Piso Caesoninus (cos. 58) and his two children, the elder of whom may have been the politician (and amateur poet?) L. Calpurnius Piso Pontifex (cos. 15), the younger of whom is unknown. Our next concern is why Horace should have dedicated the poem to Caesoninus. This raises the question of Horace's relationship to contemporary literary critics.

The *Ars Poetica* and *Epistles* I.19: Horace and his Critics

As Carl Becker noted, dating the *Ars Poetica* with respect to Horace's other poetry is a "Kardinalfrage."[27] Assigning the poem to the late 20s raises the questions of its relationship to the themes of *Epistles* I, especially as contained in poems like I.19 that deal in a humorous, but ultimately bitter, way with contemporary poets and critics.

If our suggested date of the *Ars Poetica* is correct, then the work was composed at a time when Horace was not yet the grand old man of Latin letters he may have been considered by the end of his life. To the contrary, *Epistles* I.19 suggests that—despite protestations of indifference to his reputation as a poet[28]—Horace was still rather insecure about his place in the literary firma-

---

[26]This association is most explicit in lines 386-89: "si quid tamen olim | scripseris, in Maeci descendat iudicis auris | et patris et nostras...." See, in general, for animal language used of scholars and philosophers I. Opelt, *Die lateinischen Schimpfwörter und verwandte sprachliche Erscheinungen* (Heidelberg 1965) 233-235.

[27]C. Becker, *Das Spätwerk des Horaz* (Göttingen 1963) 67.

[28]*Epistles* I.19.35-40: "scire velis, mea cur ingratus opuscula lector | laudet ametque domi, premat extra limen iniquus: | non ego ventosae plebis suffragia venor | impensis cenarum et tritae munere vestis; | non ego, nobilium scriptorum auditor et ultor, | grammaticas ambire tribus et pulpita dignor."

ment.[29] Like Virgil, he had his *obtrectatores* and was annoyed, too, by imitative poetasters, as the poem makes clear.

In the first part of the poem (lines 1-20), Horace complains about how bad poets mimic him and naively follow any advice that falls from his lips, so that if, for example, he writes that wine is essential to poetic inspiration, legions of poetasters spend their nights in wine-drinking competitions (cf. lines 1-11). Similarly, if Horace appears pale, his piteous imitators eat cumin to make their skin whiter (cf. 17-18). Horace exclaims that the servile herd of imitators stirs him to anger, but also to laughter (19-20). In the poem's second section (lines 21-34), Horace says that his achievement has been to find an untrodden path for Roman poetry: the implication is that the poetasters are behaving illogically in trying to equal Horace by copying him. In the last section of the poem (35-49), Horace vents his spleen against hypocritical readers, particularly the "tribes of grammarians," who praise Horace's poetry at home but condemn him before the public because Horace does not kowtow to them (35-41). It is important, in this connection, to note how often and how bitterly Horace, in his early and middle periods, expresses his dismay with the contemporary critical reception of his work[30] and how unreceptive the *grammatici* generally were to new poetry, according to Suetonius.[31] We need to think away Horace's millennial status as a classic author and recall that in his lifetime Horace's ultimate reputation was not clear, least of all to the poet himself (*Odes* II.20 and III.30 notwithstanding). Horace concludes *Epistles* I.19 with a testy exchange with a *grammaticus*—the kind of imaginary conversation that we would like to have when we find someone particularly galling.[32] That he should write, in this

---

[29]For bibliography, see R. S. Kilpatrick, *The Poetry of Friendship. Horace, Epistles I* (Edmonton, Alberta 1986) 169-170.

[30]Cf. *Sat.* I.10.74-91, II.1.1-4, *Epist.* I.19.35-49, II.1 passim, II.2.55-64. N. Horsfall, "Poets and Patron Reconsidered," *Ancient Society* (Macquarie) 13 (1983) 161-166, writes suggestively that "I am driven increasingly to conclude that Horace was a controversial or an actually unpopular figure." Cf. Kilpatrick, op. cit. (*supra* n. 29) 22: "Horace's views on both originality and public response [scil., in *Epistles* I.19] are consistent with those expressed earlier in the *Satires*, and are not those of a poet to whom a bad press is either a new or an intolerable experience." For a valuable recent survey of the *obtrectatores* of Virgil, with some pertinent information about ancient critics of Horace, see W. Görler, *Enc. Virg.* III s.v. *obtrectatores* (Rome 1987) 807-813. For a still useful study of Horace's ancient critics, see A. Weichert, "Commentatio de Q. Horatii Flacci Obtrectatoribus," in *Memoriam Anniversariam Dedicatae ante hos CCLXXI Annos Regiae Scholae Grimensis* (Grimae 1821).

[31]Thus, Suetonius (*De gramm.* 16) singles out Caecilius Epirota for the innovation of reciting in class the works of Virgil and other contemporary poets.

[32]Cf. Kilpatrick, op. cit. (*supra* n. 29) 22; W. S. Smith, Jr., "Horace Directs a Carouse: *Epistle* I.19," *TAPA* 114 (1984) 255-271, at pp. 266-269.

troubled period, a poem like the *Ars Poetica* as a parody of pedantic critics and as an intentionally misleading "instruction booklet" for poetasters on how to write good poetry is thus psychologically comprehensible.

Read as the parody of a pedantic member of the grammarian tribe, the *Ars Poetica* gives the reins to Horace's anger and sense of humor toward the annoying poetasters and critics. To the poetasters, Horace seems to give, in the *Ars Poetica*, not only a "secret ingredient" like wine or cumin, but the very recipe book for great poetry. In reality, the recipes are not so much tried and tested as trite and bland, and so the unwitting imitator, eagerly following Horace's instructions, ends up with very little poetic sustenance. By aping the grammarians Horace shows that, much like Nabokov, David Lodge, or Malcolm Bradbury in their satires (or like Horace himself in *Sat.* II.3 and 4), he can transmute the leaden utterances of dull academics into brilliantly amusing fiction.

If we read the *Ars Poetica*, not as Horace's sincere declaration of poetic belief but as the monologue of a fictional *grammaticus*, unsympathetic to contemporary poets and talented at composing, not poems, but only tedious ramblings on poetics; then we expect that Horace somewhere in the poem will give us a clue dissociating himself from his speaker, who is linked to critics and poetic doctrines with which Horace himself disagrees. That is, we would expect Horace to undermine the authority of the speaker of the *Ars Poetica*.

Critics in the *Ars Poetica:* Maecius, Piso, and Quintilius

The speaker's authority is an issue implicitly raised in lines 385-390:

> tu nihil invita dices faciesve Minerva;   385
> id tibi iudicium est, ea mens. si quid tamen olim
> scripseris, in Maeci descendat iudicis auris
> et patris et nostras nonumque prematur in annum
> membranis intus positis. delere licebit
> quod non edideris; nescit vox missa reverti.   390

In this passage, the elder son of Piso is urged to submit anything he may write to Maecius, his father, and the speaker—"a trio of formidable critics," writes Brink.[33] But how formidable were Maecius and Piso père as critics? The advice given in 388-389 is absurd—as Horace himself tells us in *Epistles* II.1.34-35: *si meliora dies, ut vina, poemata reddit, / scire velim chartis pretium quotus arroget annus*. Poetry does not improve simply by aging. Horace never practiced what he might naively be taken to be preaching here. The fatuousness

---
[33]Brink, II, 509.

of the speaker's advice ought to have alerted readers that our critical trio habitually plays out of tune. Investigation of its other two members reinforces the interpretation that, in verses 385-390, Horace not only undermines the speaker by putting words of dubious wisdom into his mouth but also by putting him into some very dubious literary-critical company.

Maecius, all agree, is Sp. Maecius Tarpa, the man who chose the plays performed at the opening of Pompey's theater in 55. Maecius' old-fashioned taste on that occasion was belittled by Cicero in a letter written just after the opening.[34] Cicero's opinion was, of course, privately expressed in a collection of letters probably not published for quite a few years. However, its importance for us lies not in its influence but in its reflection of what literati of Cicero's caliber thought of the man and his taste in the 50s. We do not have to guess about Horace's opinion of Maecius some twenty years later, for in *Sat.* I.10.36-39 he writes that Tarpa would hardly approve of what he was composing:[35]

> Turgidus Alpinus iugulat dum Memnona dumque
> diffindit Rheni luteum caput, haec ego ludo,
> quae nec in aede sonent certantia iudice Tarpa
> nec redeant iterum atque iterum spectanda theatris.

The implication is that Horace and Tarpa disagreed on the crucial question of what sort of poetry was worth writing: for Tarpa, it was drama; for Horace, satire. If the speaker of the *Ars Poetica*, a promoter of dramatic literature (cf. verses 86-127, 153-294), thinks highly of Tarpa (and he obviously does), then that is only one sign, among many, of his questionable and old-fashioned taste; and it is a strong indication that he is to be distinguished from Horace. As the passage just quoted from *Sat.* I.10 indicates, Horace was little inclined to write for the theater, and he never wrote a play. This attitude Horace explains in detail in *Epistles* II.1, from which it emerges that in rejecting the dramatic genres,

---

[34]Cic. *Ad Fam.* 7.1.1: "nobis autem erant ea perpetienda, quae Sp. Maecius probavisset."

[35]For the background to his critical activity in approving works for the Roman stage see N. B. Crowther, "The Collegium Poetarum," *Latomus* 32 (1973) 575-580 and N. Horsfall, "The Collegium Poetarum," *BICS* 23 (1976) 83. Crowther and Horsfall are correct in claiming that in *Sat.* I.10 Horace does not ridicule Tarpa (Crowther, p. 578; Horsfall, p. 93n38), yet Tarpa is clearly mentioned as the kind of critic who is not sympathetic to Horace's poetry. The justified opposition of these two scholars to wild speculation about the *collegium poetarum* has led them to misinterpret the tone of this section of *Sat.* I.10 and to forget that Horace could disagree with Maecius' taste in literature even if Maecius was not the *magister* of the college. On the *collegium*, see now E. Gruen, *Studies in Greek Culture and Roman Policy, Cincinnati Classical Studies* 7 (Leiden 1990) 87-91.

Horace felt weighed down by the dual burdens of the literary past (Plautus, Terence, Pacuvius, Accius, etc.) and of the debased taste of the contemporary audience.

The striking portrayal of the speaker here as a conservative in literary taste complements his ignorance of the contemporary scene in poetry. This comes across in small ways—for example, in his neglect of love elegy in lines 75-76,[36] where the speaker mentions only funerary and votive uses for the elegiac meter. It also comes across in larger ways—for example, the speaker's emphasis throughout the *Ars* on the genres of tragedy, comedy, and epic—departments of literature most important in Roman literature fifty to one hundred years before the Augustan age.[37] Even more surprising than his omission of love elegy is, in this context, the speaker's failure to mention contemporary plays written by acquaintances of Horace such as Varius' *Thyestes* and the *fabula trabeata* of C. Melissus, a freedman of Maecenas and librarian of the Porticus Octaviae library.[38] The latter might have served various purposes in the *Ars Poetica*, e.g., as an example of how Roman writers can succeed by writing drama on national themes (cf. 285-288). This is not to say that the speaker is depicted as the kind of Varronian archaizer attacked by Horace in the *Letter to Augustus*.[39] The speaker is, characteristically, inconsistent in his attitude toward the past: after he praises the audience and music of the early Roman theater in

---

[36]See M. E. Clark, "Horace, *Ars Poetica* 75-78. The Origin and Worth of Elegy," *CW* 77 (1983) 1-5. On Horace's attitude toward erotic elegy, see Rudd, 7-8.

[37]Accius (†ca. 85 B.C.) was "the last of the professional playwrights" (E. Fantham, *Seneca's Troades* [Princeton 1982] 5); in the decades after his death—with few notable exceptions—little new tragedy was written (cf. Fantham, pp. 4-7, and for a similar ancient perspective see Velleius Paterculus 1.17; for a different view cf. Rudd, 30). On comedy, see H. D. Jocelyn, "Studies in the Indirect Tradition of Plautus' *Pseudolus*," *BICS* Suppl. 51 (1988), 57-72, at pp. 57-60. As C. Segre noted, "the *Ars Poetica*...ends up being astonishingly anachronistic...unless we wish to regard it as the manifesto of a classical revival which never took effect" (*Introduction to the Analysis of the Literary Text*, trans. J. Meddemmen [Bloomington 1988] 202).

[38]On C. Melissus, see Schanz-Hosius, VIII.2, 176-177; H. Bardon, *La littérature latine inconnue*, vol. II (Paris 1956) 49-50. As Maecenas' freedman, he was doubtless known to Horace; cf. L. Müller, "Die Trabeatae des Gaius Melissus," *PhW* 13 (1893) col. 1468f.

[39]See the excellent analysis of Varronian criticism and its possible influence on *Epist.* II.1.50-59 in Brink, III, 83-92. Also important, we might note, was the quarrel over Sallust's archaizing, which was attacked by Asinius Pollio; see Suetonius, *De gramm.* 10 ("....Sallustii scripta reprehendit ut nimia priscorum verborum affectatione oblita...."). For literature and discussion, see L. Duret, "Dans l'ombre des plus grands," *ANRW* II.30.3 (Berlin 1983) 1507.

verses 202-207, we find him criticizing Plautus' wit and metrics and accusing Plautus' audience of stupidity and a lack of sophistication in lines 270-274.[40]

Piso père is an even more famous, or infamous, literary critic. Whatever Horace may privately have thought of Piso as a man of letters (and earlier in his career, he probably thought very highly, indeed, of Piso and his Epicurean circle), Cicero unforgettably branded him *non Aristarchus sed Phalaris grammaticus* (*In Pis.* 73) in a speech that quickly became popular in the schools.[41] Cicero's immediate motivation for so labelling Piso was Piso's charge, in a speech given in the senate in 55, that Cicero had meant to belittle Pompey's military accomplishments in his poem, *De consulatu suo*.[42] As evidence, Piso cited the line: *cedant arma togae, concedat laurea laudi*.[43] Cicero claimed that Piso had missed the point that *arma* and *toga* were meant figuratively, not literally, and that he had been speaking generally, without specific reference to Pompey.[44]

This must have been a rare, if not unique, instance in which a senator's literary criticism of a colleague's poem became the subject of a published exchange of speeches. Cicero's characterization of Piso as *Phalaris grammaticus*[45] must have been all the more effective if Piso prided himself on being something of a literary critic. That he did is suggested by the fact that he was patron of the poet-philosopher Philodemus, one of whose epigrams to Piso is

---

[40]To be sure, music is the topic in the earlier passage and meter and wit in the later, so that radically different appraisals of the historical development of the Roman theater can be defended. Harder to defend or explain, however, is the opposite opinion of the taste of early Roman audiences in the two passages. First, the speaker sounds like a "soft primitivist," then like a "hard primitivist" (for the concepts, see A. O. Lovejoy and G. Boas, *Primitivism and Related Ideas in Antiquity* [Baltimore 1935]). At no point does he praise a specific Roman dramatist; he remains ever the carping critic, able to find fault with—but seldom willing to express admiration for— Roman poets. I will treat elsewhere the speaker's habitual hostility toward writers.

[41]See above, n. 20. On Horace's connections with the Philodemus circle, patronized by Piso, see the discussion and secondary literary in B. Frischer, *At Tu Aureus Esto. Eine Interpretation von Vergils 7. Ekloge* (Bonn 1975) 168-171 (note that the supplements of Horace's name in the Philodemus passages cited in 171n29 now appear to be incorrect: see M. Gigante and M. Capasso, "Il ritorno di Virgilio a Ercolano," *SIFC* 7 [1989] 3-6).

[42]Remains in Morel-Büchner, *FPL*, M. Tullius Cicero, frr. 5-13; for discussion of the date and related problems see K. Büchner in *RE* s.v. M. Tullius Cicero (Stuttgart 1939) cols. 1245-1250.

[43]Morel-Büchner, *FPL* fr. 11, with the text of W. Allen, Jr., "O fortunatam natam...," *TAPA* 87 (1956) 130-146, at p. 133.

[44]*In Pis.* 73-75.

[45]On which see Nisbet ad *Pis.* 73.7 and Grimal, loc. cit. (*supra* n. 20).

preserved.⁴⁶ This also helps explain Catullus' obvious gall at being passed over by Piso for political and poetical patronage. It is amusing to suppose that Horace's source of inspiration in writing this mock didactic poem about poetics and in dedicating it to the Pisones was Cicero's barbed rhetorical question directed at Piso: *quid nunc te, asine, litteras doceam?* (73). That the work dedicated to Piso consists largely of a versification of the poetic theories of Neoptolemus of Parium (cf. Porphyrio on line 1 and Brink, I, 43ff.), must have intensified the fun, since Neoptolemus' poetics had been savagely attacked by Piso's client Philodemus in Book V of his Περὶ ποιημάτων (cf. Brink, I, 48ff.).

A parallel for Horace's ironic invocation of critical authority in verses 385-390 may not be far to seek. It has been noted that line 387 (*in [Maeci] descendat ...aures*) contains an allusion to a line in Book XXVI of Lucilius: *haec tu si voles per auris pectus inrigarier* (610 Marx).⁴⁷ Now it is interesting to note that in this, his earliest book of satires—and possibly in the first satire of the book⁴⁸—Lucilius expresses the wish that his poem be read, not by learned critics like C. Persius, but by such undistinguished and perhaps even dull readers as M. Iunius Congus, Decimus Laelius and the people of Tarentum, Cosentia, and Sicily (592-596 Marx). Here we may have the source of a second Horatian allusion to the same Lucilian satire. As Erich Gruen notes, "these passages [in Lucilius] have usually been taken seriously by moderns, but they are surely ironic....That is unquestionably true of Cic. *De Fin.* 1.3.7 (592 Marx) and, I believe, for the other lines as well."⁴⁹ To be sure, in Lucilius' case, the poet speaks of his own poetry and the readers he desires to find for it; whereas in the *Ars Poetica,* Horace has the speaker recommend proper readers—not for the speaker's own works—but for those that Piso's elder son, the speaker's addressee,

⁴⁶*AP* 11.44 (= 23 Gow-Page); Cicero states that Philodemus wrote much other poetry to and about Piso (*In Pis.* 70-71); cf. above, n. 19, for possible new epigram incipits of Philodemus.

⁴⁷Cf. Brink, ad loc. On the overall relationship of the *Ars Poetica* to Lucilius, Book XXVI, it is still useful to read G. C. Fiske, *Lucilius and Horace. A Study in the Classical Theory of Imitation* (Madison 1920) 425-475.

⁴⁸On the problem of reconstructing Book XXVI, see J. Christes, *Der frühe Lucilius. Rekonstruktion und Interpretation des XXVI. Buches sowie von Teilen des XXX. Buches* (Heidelberg 1971).

⁴⁹Personal communication of February 7, 1990. Prof. Gruen will treat the Lucilius passage in more detail in his forthcoming Townsend Lectures. The passage in *De Fin.* runs as follows: "nec vero ut noster Lucilius recusabo quominus omnes mea legant. utinam esset ille Persius! Scipio vero et Rutilius multo etiam magis; quorum ille iudicium reformidans Tarentinis ait se et Consentinis et Siculis scribere." For earlier interpretations of fragments 592-596, see Christes, op. cit. (*supra* n. 48) 87-92. From Christes' discussion, it appears that Gruen's interpretation may have been anticipated by J. Heurgon, *Lucilius* (Paris 1959) 44 (not available to me).

may someday write. Aside from this minor difference between the first and second person, however, the passages are similar in that both ironically advert to the authority of readers whose criticism cannot be accorded much respect.

In view of Horace's longstanding connections with the circle of Piso and Philodemus, we naturally wish to know why Horace dedicated the *Ars Poetica* to L. Calpurnius Piso Caesoninus, of all people. Of course, our answer can only be guesswork. My motivation in presenting a speculative explanation is simply to show that we are not necessarily forced into either of two extreme positions: [1] that for our identification of the senior dedicatee and for our interpretation of his role in the poem to be right, we must posit a strain or, indeed, break in Horace's relationship with Piso. Or, [2], if we have the right Piso, we cannot be correctly interpreting his role in the poem—or, indeed, the tone of the poem. Horace may have been treading a fine line between angering and amusing Piso: on the one hand, adverting tacitly to Piso's notorious reputation as a critic, he utilizes the public stereotypes of Piso and Maecius as critics in order to alert readers to his send-up of academic criticism in the *Ars Poetica*. On the other hand, by associating Piso with a poetic theory condemned so vehemently by Philodemus, and with which the Epicurean Piso will not have agreed, he winks at the old man and suggests that he not take the whole thing too seriously. In any case, Roman grandees of the first century B.C. had—or, at least, affected—a self-deprecating sense of humor in the face of poetic abuse. Catullus' raillery against Piso for his *lauta convivia* (47.5) was apparently echoed in poems by Piso's friend, Philodemus (cf. Cicero, *In Pis.* 70).[50] Horace made bold to convict Maecenas of guilt by association for attending the infamous *Nasidieni cena* of *Sat.* II.8. If Maecenas or Piso felt hurt by Horace's treatment, the poet could have pointed out that in poems like *Sat.* II.3 (cf. lines 305-326) and II.7 he gave himself a much rougher time.

If the two critics mentioned in lines 387-388 of the *Ars Poetica* represent dullness and dubious taste, then the same cannot be said about a third and last critic whose company the speaker seems to keep. The words on poetics of a certain Quintilius are quoted near the end of the poem in verses 438-444:

> Quintilio si quid recitares, 'corrige, sodes,
> hoc' aiebat 'et hoc.' melius te posse negares,
> bis terque expertum frustra delere iubebat   440
> et male tornatos incudi reddere versus.
> si defendere delictum quam vertere malles,
> nullum ultra verbum aut operam insumebat inanem,
> quin sine rivali teque et tua solus amares.

---

[50]Cf. L. Landolfi, "Tracce filodemee di estetica e di epigrammatica simpotica in Catullo," *CronErc* 12 (1982) 137-143, at p. 139.

Quintilius is probably, as Porphyrio says, Quintilius Varus Cremonensis, the Epicurean friend of Virgil, Horace, and Philodemus, who died in *c.* 24/23.[51] Horace consoled Virgil for his death in *Odes* 1.24, a poem combining traditional paramythetic motifs[52] with Epicurean ideas about the value of friendship, the inevitability and finality of death, and the survivor's need for self-control.[53]

The premise of the ode, then, is Horace's desire to mourn with Virgil for their departed friend in the proper Epicurean manner—a desire that is perhaps not so much appropriate because Horace and Virgil are still Epicureans (a doubtful assumption at this advanced stage in their intellectual development) as because Quintilius was.

Quintilius' Epicurean background is important for understanding his role in the *Ars Poetica*. He is the only critic quoted in the poem, and so we need to ask why Horace has presented him to us in this way. To the speaker, Quintilius embodied the same sort of arrogance toward poets that the speaker himself displays throughout the *Ars Poetica*. Quintilius' laconic words, *corrige, sodes, / hoc...et hoc* (438-439), and his icy silence in the face of a poet's defense of a criticized passage (442-444) are, for the speaker, indicative of an attitude of admirable toughness toward self-indulgent and self-enamored poetasters (444).

The speaker may accurately quote Quintilius and relate his silence in lines 438-444, but another interpretation of his behavior toward poets and his theory of poetics is possible. As an Epicurean and student of Philodemus, Quintilius must have believed that poetics is not a rational science that can be articulated and taught, but is instead an intuitive art, the practice of which depends to a large extent on natural ability.[54] Quintilius' polite words of criticism (*sodes*, 438) and his habitual unwillingnesss to debate with defensive poets understandably reflect just such an Epicurean view of poetry. For

---

[51]Philodemus mentions Quintilius two times in his Περὶ κολακείας and Περὶ φιλαργυρίας; see A. Koerte, "Augusteer bei Philodem," *RhM* 45 (1890) 172-177. For discussion of the ancient sources on Quintilius see C. L. Neudling, op. cit. (*supra* n. 13) 151-153; Nisbet-Hubbard, p. 279.

[52]Cf. Nisbet-Hubbard, pp. 279-281.

[53]On death in Epicurean thought see M. Gigante, "La chiusa del quarto libro 'Della morte' di Filodemo," in *Ricerche filodemee* (Naples 1983[2]) 163-234.

[54]On the Epicurean critique of the "sciences," see, in general, M. Gigante, *Scetticismo e epicureismo* (Naples 1981) 179-224; for a recent survey of Philodemus' poetics see E. Asmis, "Philodemus' Epicureanism," *ANRW* II.36.4 (Berlin 1990) 2400-2406. Possibly also relevant to Quintilius' poetics was the intuitive approach of Ser. Clodius, who, according to Cicero, could speak as laconically as Horace's Quintilius when separating authentic from false Plautine verses; cf. Cic. *Ad Fam.* 9.16.4: "facile diceret 'hic versus Plauti non est, hic est' quod tritas aures haberet notandis generibus poetarum et consuetudine legendi...." Cf., in general, J. Zetzel, op. cit. (*supra* n. 20) 18-21; E. Rawson, op. cit. (*supra* n. 20) 278.

Quintilius the Epicurean the appreciation of poetry is a matter of taste, not science. While he is quite willing to express an opinion about a poem, he is utterly unwilling to debate or to defend his views. This is because, in contrast to the Peripatetic speaker of the *Ars Poetica*, Quintilius' views do not derive from a set of "scientific" principles but from good taste alone.

How different is the speaker's approach to poetics! Quintilius' politeness toward the poets contrasts sharply with the speaker's pathological hatred of them, an attitude most clearly expressed in the very next section of the poem (lines 453-476). Quintilius' five words (three of them monosyllabic) of "literary criticism" contrast even more markedly with the speaker's analogous performance, viz., the *Ars Poetica* itself, Horace's longest poem by far and one filled with advice and rules as useless as they are dull and jejune. The appearance of Quintilius near the climactic end of the poem thus functions in two ways which enhance Horace's parody. First of all, the speaker is made to discredit himself by invoking Quintilius as his critical ideal because the appearance of Quintilius allows us to see how far short of Quintilius the speaker falls and how badly the speaker misinterprets Quintilius' behavior and words. Secondly, Quintilius can emerge from the speaker's mistreatment of him with his reputation as the ideal critic intact, because the speaker cites his *ipsissima verba*. As a result, we are not dependent upon the speaker for what we know about him. Thus, Horace has it both ways: the speaker's critical authority is debased by his misunderstanding of Quintilius; but Quintilius remains the standard by which critical excellence can be assessed. By Quintilius' standard, obtusely invoked by the speaker, the speaker's whole enterprise of an *ars poetica* is called into question.

These thoughts are consistent with a dating of the *Ars Poetica* in the period 24-20. If Quintilius has just died, this helps us understand why Horace gives him—of all possible candidates—such prominent notice near the end of the poem. Much evidence suggests that he was by no means the "inevitable" choice for the role of ideal critic: for example, in Horace's long list of ideal readers of his poetry in *Sat.* I.10.78-88, Quintilius is not mentioned. If Maecius and Piso Caesoninus are still alive, as they may well have been in the late 20s, then this helps explain Horace's strategy of making the speaker proclaim his own poetological guilt by association with these two notoriously old-fashioned and censorious critics.

The Parodic Introduction: The *Ars Poetica* and Contemporary Painting

But we do not have to wait until verses 385-90, let alone till the end of the poem, to sense that Horace was sending up his speaker as a tiresome and old-fashioned pedant. Although it is by no means a requirement of the parodic mode that hints of the parody be given at the very beginning of the work, such indications are to be found in the very first lines of the *Ars Poetica*:

> Humano capiti cervicem pictor equinam
> iungere si velit et varias inducere plumas
> undique collatis membris, ut turpiter atrum
> desinat in piscem mulier formosa superne,
> spectatum admissi risum teneatis, amici?   5

The speaker begins his *ars poetica* in a seemingly strange way: with the description of the painting of a monster with a woman's head, the neck of a horse, the feathers of a bird, and the tail of a fish. He claims that such a painting would be so absurd as to cause its viewers to laugh. In lines 6-9 the speaker provides his own gloss on the meaning of these lines and their relevance to what follows: *ut pictura, poesis*. The painting described in lines 1-4 is comparable to a book lacking unity, with no beginning and end, and filled with the empty imaginings of a sick man's dreams.[55] The speaker thus would appear to find two things wrong with such a monstrous figure or book: formally, it lacks unity in the sense of a clearcut division between beginning, middle (we may presume), and end.[56] Substantively, it lacks verisimilitude.[57] The background is clearly Peripatetic: in the *Poetics*, Aristotle stresses the importance of unity of plot, which must have a beginning, middle, and end. Interestingly, he compares such well-made plots to animals, just as the *Ars Poetica* speaker compares disunity to a monster.[58] Next, the speaker confronts the only possible excuse for such a creation: poetic license.[59] Licenses are, to be sure, permissible, he tells us, but not if the result is an *adynaton*: "sed non ut placidis coeant immitia, non ut | serpentes avibus geminentur, tigribus agni" (12-13).

---

[55]"Credite, Pisones, isti tabulae fore librum | persimilem cuius, velut aegri somnia, vanae | fingentur species, ut nec pes nec caput uni | reddatur formae."

[56]Cf. lines 8-9: "ut nec pes nec caput uni | reddatur formae." Unity is, of course, a touchstone of poetic virtue in the Peripatetic tradition; cf. Aristotle, *Poetics* 1450b23 and see also Brink, II, 77-85; M. Heath, *Unity in Greek Poetics* (Oxford 1989).

[57]Cf. lines 7-8: "velut aegri somnia, vanae | fingentur species...."

[58]Cf. Aristotle, *Poetics* 1450b24ff. As J. Pigeaud aptly puts it, "dis-moi ta biologie, je te dirai ton esthétique"; see "La greffe du monstre," *REL* 66 (1988) 197-218, at p. 217.

[59]Lines 9-13: "'pictoribus atque poetis | quidlibet audendi semper fuit aequa potestas.' | scimus, et hanc veniam petimusque damusque vicissim; | sed non ut placidis coeant immitia, non ut | serpentes avibus geminentur, tigribus agni."

Despite their obvious importance, these lines have rarely been subjected to close analysis.[60] The most important problem in lines 1-13 for our purposes is what kind of unity the speaker means by the phrase, "uni...formae" (8-9). The precedent of the *Poetics* would lead us to expect that the speaker refers to unity of plot or, more generally, structure. This interpretation is firmly rejected by Brink,[61] and since antiquity other readings have been proposed. In Ps.-Acro, the monster represents a violation of *dispositio et convenientia;* in Porphyrio, of ἀκολουθία, or inconsequentiality. Porphyrio elaborates what he means, saying that the painter of the monster "valde ridebitur, quod contra naturam omnia faciat: ita poetice, si ornatus causa plus, quam exigit materia, aliquid institutum ornetur, meretur contempni." Porphyrio combines the two faults into something composite: a poem that has formal qualities inappropriate to its subject matter is contrary to nature, that is, lacks verisimilitude. Ps.-Acro's interpretation stresses the shift in subject matter from beginning to end of the work: "unde in primordio dicit, deridendum eum, qui de una re disputare inchoans diversitatem materiarum conponit ...." For Ps.-Acro, then, a book is monstrous if it lacks unity of subject. If we ask what has motivated ancient and modern commentators to propose these different explanations of the first lines of the *Ars Poetica*, then the answer must be that verses 1-13 are not self-contained but must be read in the context of the first section of the poem, which ends at line 40. The range of subjects touched on in this section is so broad as to make it necessary to interpret the monster of lines 1-5 and the disunity she represents in a way that transcends structure alone.

Perhaps the most interesting interpretation of the passage is to be found in Quintilian. For him, too, the issue is not disunified structure; instead he sees in the monster a symbol of inappropriately mixed *dilectus verborum,* the fault he called Σαρδισμός, or, in Latin, the infelicitous combination of different kinds of vocabulary (poetic and vulgar, elevated and humble, archaisms and neologisms, etc.).[62] How did Quintilian arrive at such a relatively restricted view of the

[60]The most detailed treatments to date are by J. D. Meerwaldt, "Adnotationes in Epistulam ad Pisones ad picturam praesertim collatam pertinentes," *Mnemosyne* 4 (1936-37) 151-163, at pp. 151-155; K. Gantar, "Die Anfangsverse und die Komposition der horazischen Epistel über die Dichtkunst," *SO* 39 (1964) 89-98.

[61]Brink, II, 80-81: "Horace too talks largely of tragedy and epic. Aristotle's confrontation of the whole and its parts appeals to him. But the unity that these forms evince to him is not simply unity of plot. It is the unity of a work of poetry seen by a poet."

[62]Quintilian 8.3.59-60: "Σαρδισμός quoque appellatur quaedam mixta ex varia ratione linguarum oratio, ut si Atticis Dorica, Ionica, Aeolica etiam dicta confundas. Cui simile vitium est apud nos, si quis sublimia humilibus, vetera novis, poetica vulgaribus misceat. Id enim tale monstrum, quale Horatius in prima parte libri

monster's meaning? I would suggest that he did so, not by trying to subsume all the artistic faults discussed in the first section of the poem, but by focussing specifically on lines 11-13 where poetic license is mentioned.

Poetic license was an aspect of poetics about which the ancient theoreticians—including the speaker of the *Ars Poetica*—had definite ideas. Licenses include any unusual use of words, such as neologisms, metrical anomalies (e.g., systole and diastole), and the rhetorical device of metaphor. According to Aristotle and later ancient literary critics, poetic license, as such, can be either good or bad. Speaking of what later came to be called ποιητικὴ ἐξουσία or ἄδεια[63] (he himself used no technical term for the phenomenon), Aristotle wrote:

> The merit of diction is to be clear and not commonplace. The clearest diction is that made up of ordinary words, but it is commonplace. An example is the poetry of Cleophon and of Sthenelus. That which employs unfamiliar words is dignified and outside the common usage. By 'unfamiliar' I mean a rare word, a metaphor, a lengthening, and anything beyond the ordinary use. But if a poet writes entirely in such words, the result will be either a riddle or jargon; if made up of metaphors, a riddle, and if of rare words, jargon.[64]

So, unusual words are the spice of good poetry. Without them, literature seems too bland; with too many, it becomes distasteful and obscure. A little later, Aristotle says that the effect of excessive use of metrical, verbal, or rhetorical license is unintentionally comic.[65] The speaker of the *Ars Poetica* obviously agrees.[66]

---

de arte poetica fingit: 'humano capiti cervicem pictor equinam | iungere si velit,' et cetera ex diversis naturis subiciat." It is odd that Brink, II, 85, should write that "the *wider* context was discerned by Quintilian" (my emphasis); in fact, Quintilian's interpretation is the narrowest on record. On this passage, see the critical and interpretive remarks of J. Cousin, *Quintilien, Institution Oratoire*, vol. 5 (Paris 1978) 285-286.

[63]Illustrated by J. E. B. Mayor, "On Licentia Poetica," *Journal of Philology* 8 (1879) 260-262.

[64]*Poetics* 1458a.18-26 (translation by W. Hamilton Fyfe).

[65]*Poetics* 1458b.11-13. Among Roman writings, we might compare *Rhet. ad Heren.* 4.10.15, where archaism and bad metaphors are condemned as elements of the "swollen" style, the perversion of the grand style of oratory: "Nam ita ut corporis bonam habitudinem tumor imitatur saepe, item gravis oratio saepe inperitis videtur ea quae turget et inflata est, cum aut novis aut priscis verbis aut duriter aliunde translatis aut gravioribus quam res postulat aliquid dicitur...." W. Lebek, *Verba Prisca, Hypomnemata* 25 (1970), reasonably notes that the author of the *Rhet.* probably did not

It is important to note that in the poetic tradition prior to Horace, poetic license is limited to meter, vocabulary, and the use of rhetoric. Nowhere is plot, or, more generally, structure, included among the elements of poetry through which a poet can achieve a special effect by violating normal usage. Given Aristotle's stress on the importance of a unified plot, this is hardly surprising.[67] It is doubtless for this reason that Quintilian "misinterpreted" the sense of the first five lines of the *Ars Poetica* by limiting the application of disunity to *dilectus verborum* alone. Quintilian's error is an intelligent one: this is what the poetic tradition on license would lead one to expect. Brink, on the other hand, perceiving that for Horace "unity...is not simply unity of plot," must argue that lines 1-13 pertain—in some vague way he does not specify—to unity of all the elements of poetry, including structure, something which, if true, he acknowledges to be an Horatian contribution to poetic theory.[68]

Quintilian's overly precise and Brink's overly broad interpretation of the monster of lines 1-3 results from the fact that, even after two millennia of trying,[69] we still cannot be certain we understand what the speaker intends to say in the opening lines of the poem. If the monster represents poetic license carried too far (implied by verses 11-13), then we expect the monster to represent (as Quintilian saw) a misuse of vocabulary, meter or figures of rhetoric. It should not symbolize a work with little or no structure, for we have no evidence that

---

intend to condemn all archaism, just "an excessive use of such idioms." (p. 23; my translation). However, it should be noted that the quality of clarity (*explanatio*) is said to be derived, in part, from the use of "current vocabulary" (*usitata verba*, defined as *sunt ea quae versantur in consuetudine cotidiana, Rhet. ad Heren.* 4.12.17). It would be nice to be able to include the pertinent parallels that must have been present in Q. Laelius' "De vitiis virtutibusque poematorum" (see Charisius, p. 179.18-20 Barwick); if this is Laelius Archelaus (cf. Suetonius, *De gramm.* 2), the expounder of Lucilius (as Münzer thinks: *RE* s.v. Laelius [13]), then Horace must surely have known his writings. After Horace, we find Aristotle's view on the necessary balance of common and unusual words in, e.g., Seneca, *Epist.* 114.13-14.

[66]Cf. lines 9-13 (general limits of license); 48-51 (limited use of neologism approved); and 263-268 (critics give poets too much metrical license). On excessive license as risible, cf. lines 1-5 (especially 5: "spectatum admissi *risum* teneatis, amici?").

[67]Cf. *Poetics*, 1450b24ff.

[68]Cf. Brink II, 81: "But the unity that these forms evince to him [i.e., to Horace] is not simply unity of plot. It is the unity of a work of poetry seen by a poet. It lacks Aristotle's clarity of concept and coherence of argument. It cannot ultimately be resolved into a series of propositions."

[69]For the medieval interpretations, see C. Villa, "'Ut Poesis Pictura': Appunti iconografici sui codici dell'*Ars Poetica*," *Aevum* 62 (1988) 186-197, at pp. 187-189.

the ancient theorists were willing to bend their firm rules about the necessity of structural unity. On the other hand, the speaker's comparison of a monster to a book ("isti tabulae fore librum | persimilem," 6-7) would seem better adapted to express problems of relating parts to a whole (i.e., structure) than those of style. Moreover, the simile comparing the contents of such a book to the "dreams of a sick man" ("velut aegri somnia," 7) raises an entirely different matter: the verisimilitude of an artistic representation. Could the subject of a poem or painting really exist, or is it the feverish product of a demented mind (cf. "vanae | fingentur species," 7-8)? That the simile ends with the metaphor "nec pes nec caput" obfuscates rather than clarifies the speaker's meaning because the metaphor must apply simultaneously to four realms—the book, the sick dreams, the idle imaginings, and the monster. The fact that this phrase was proverbial does not diminish its literal force here, which simply cannot bear the weight put on it by the speaker's multiply mixed metaphor. What does it mean for a book to have "caput et pes," and while the monster has a woman's head, it has a fish's tail, not "pes"; etc.[70]

Brink has rightly observed that the speaker, who condemns a *descriptio* in verses 14-19, himself begins with a *descriptio* in lines 1-4. This inconsistency is typical of the speaker and can be seen elsewhere: he does not practice what he preaches. I would suggest that an even greater inconsistency can be found in the whole introduction (1-13): roundly condemning the abuse of poetic license, the speaker hypocritically falls into the error of taking the license of metaphor too far in lines 1-9 as evidenced by the fact that we have no way of understanding how he wants us to apply the monster simile to poetry. Later in the poem, he will likewise botch the simile comparing painting to poetry because, while he tells us a good deal about painting, he says absolutely nothing about poetry (361-365). The literal defectiveness of the simile (it lacks a *sic*-clause) makes it impossible to know in what way poetry is similar to painting. In the *Poetics* (1459a1ff) Aristotle said that metaphor (by which he also meant simile)[71] is the "most important" form of poetic diction because it cannot be acquired from someone else and is a "sign of genius." The speaker's clumsy use of metaphor (or simile) can be attested so frequently in the *Ars Poetica* that we may view the botched metaphor as the speaker's typical rhetorical figure. If

---

[70]Cf. G. Lakoff and M. Turner, *More than Cool Reason. A Field Guide to Poetic Metaphor* (Chicago and London 1989) 203: "Though wide-ranging metaphorical interpretations are possible, they are far from arbitrary. A metaphor, after all, is not a linguistic expression. It is a mapping from one conceptual domain to another, and as such it has a three-part structure: two endpoints (the source and target schemas) and a bridge between them (the detailed mapping). Such structures are highly constrained. It is not the case that anything can be anything."

[71]Cf. R. Janko, *Aristotle, Poetics* (Indianapolis and Cambridge 1987) 130.

proper use of metaphor is a sign of genius, then consistent misuse of metaphor is not only an example of the abuse of poetic license but also an indication of a lack of genius.

The introduction throws the speaker's authority on poetry into doubt in two other ways. Even so apologetic a critic as Brink has noted that the speaker begins his speech with no formal introduction: "there are no preliminaries. The poem, as it were, jumps into a subject."[72] Similarly, the poem is open-ended, lacking a conventional conclusion.[73] The middle is the most problematic section of all: for centuries, the greatest scholarly issue about the *Ars Poetica* is whether it has a clearcut structure.[74] The monstrous book decried by the speaker and the monstrous image used to represent it, we may conclude, are exemplified by the *Ars Poetica* itself. One might, to be sure, excuse the speaker for these faults by recalling that with mock modesty he does not claim to be a poet,[75] so that the *Ars Poetica* ought not to be judged as a poem. Yet, this actually weakens the case for clemency, since, according to the speaker, poetic licenses such as lack of a proper introduction and ending are granted only to writers of poetry, not prose. As Quintilian put it, "meminerimus tamen, non per omnia poetas esse oratori sequendos nec libertate verborum nec licentia figurarum...." (10.1.28).

There is another way—even more important—in which these key introductory lines discredit the speaker. Since the eighteenth century it has been commonplace to connect the speaker's outburst against monsters in painting to Vitruvius' polemic against contemporary art:[76]

Sed haec, quae ex veris rebus exempla sumebantur, nunc iniquis moribus inprobantur. <Nam pinguntur> tectoriis monstra potius quam ex rebus finitis imagines certae: pro columnis enim struuntur calami striati, pro fastigiis appagineculi cum crispis foliis et volutis, item candelabra aedicularum sustinentia figuras, supra fastigia eorum surgentes ex radicibus cum volutis teneri plures habentes in se sine ratione sedentia sigilla, non minus coliculi dimidiata habentes sigilla alia humanis, alia bestiarum capitibus.

[72]Brink, I, 85.
[73]Cf. below, p. 94.
[74]I will elsewhere discuss the structural issues and show that the poem also exemplifies the fault of Σαρδισμός.
[75]Lines 301-305: "o ego laevus, | qui purgor bilem sub verni temporis horam; | non alius faceret meliora poemata. verum | nil tanti est. ergo fungar vice cotis, acutum | reddere quae ferrum valet exsors ipsa secandi...."
[76]The first reference to the passage in a commentary on the *Ars Poetica* appears to be in R. P. Sanadon, *Les poesies d'Horace, traduites en françois*, tome septième (Amsterdam, Leipzig 1756²) 57.

Haec autem nec sunt nec fieri possunt nec fuerunt. Ergo ita novi mores coegerunt, uti inertiae mali iudices convincerent artium virtutes: quemadmodum enim potest calamus vere sustinere tectum aut candelabrum ornamenta fastigii, seu coliculus tam tenuis et mollis sustinere sedens sigillum, aut de radicibus et coliculis ex parte flores dimidiataque sigilla procreari? At haec falsa videntes homines non reprehendunt sed delectantur, neque animadvertunt, si quid eorum fieri potest necne...Neque enim picturae probari debent, quae non sunt similes veritati, nec, si factae sunt elegantes ab arte, ideo de his statim debet 'recte' iudicari, nisi argumentationes certas rationes habuerint sine offensionibus explicatas.[77]

The relationship of Vitruvius' passage with the introduction of the *Ars Poetica* has never been explored in detail.[78] The context is Vitruvius' account of the development of wall painting in homes. Painting should represent "quod est seu potest esse, uti homines, aedificia, naves, reliquarumque rerum" (7.5.1), and in the earlier phases of wall painting, this was the case. First, painters imitated marble (this is equivalent to what, since the last century, we have called the First Pompeian Style; Vitruvius, 7.5.1); then they imitated buildings, columns, gardens, scenery, etc. (the Second Pompeian Style; Vitruvius, 7.5.2). In the passage quoted, Vitruvius recounts the latest developments, the final phase of the Second Style, in which realism has given way to fantastic creatures and architectural constructions.[79] In such works may be seen monsters, stalks functioning as

---

[77] Vitruvius 7.5.3-4. For a recent philological and archaeological commentary on the passage see W. Ehrhardt, *Stilgeschichtliche Untersuchungen an römischen Wandmalereien von der späten bis zur Zeit Neros* (Mainz 1987) 152-162.

[78] Commentators on the *Ars Poetica* simply note the Vitruvian passage and its polemic against monsters in painting without further analysis; Vitruvian scholars, too, have failed to pursue the relationship in any depth. See, most recently, W. Ehrhardt, op. cit. (*supra* n. 77) 162: "Eine Untersuchung dieser Fragen unter Berücksichtigung der historischen und literarischen Quellen geht über den Rahmen einer stilgeschichtlichen Analyse ebenso hinaus wie der Vergleich der von Vitruv angewendeten moralisch-ästhetischen Kriterien mit denen, wie sie z.b. Horaz in seiner Ars poetica und Augustus nach der Überlieferung Suetons [Augustus 86] gegenüber Marc Anton auf literarisch-rhetorischem Gebiet erhebt."

[79] The classic work on the Second Style is by H. G. Beyen, *Die Pompejanische Wandedekoration vom zweitem bis zum vierten Stil*, 2 vols. (The Hague 1938, 1960). Beyen divides the Second Style into Phase I and Phase II; each phase has two sub-phases (Phase Ia, Ib, etc.; cf. vol. II, 20; cf. also his article on "Pompeiani, Stili" in *EAA* 6 [Rome 1965] 356-366, at pp. 358-362). The beginning of Phase II Beyen dates to the years 50-30. Beyen's classification has recently been criticized as too elaborate by A. Barbet, *La peinture murale romaine: Les styles décoratifs pompéiens*

columns, men and animals growing up out of plants, etc. (7.5.3). Since such fantasies violate the principle of realism and verisimilitude[80] ("haec autem nec sunt nec fieri possunt nec fuerunt"; 7.5.4), Vitruvius roundly condemns them and the debased taste that approves of them. Telling the anecdote of how Licymnius the mathematician forced the scenery painter Apaturius to replace some overly imaginative sets with more conventionally realistic designs (7.5.5-6), he longingly recalls the good old days when such violations of nature were not permitted and were felt to be signs of bad taste and dullness ("quod enim antiqui insumentes laborem ad industriam probare contendebant artibus, id nunc coloribus et eorum alleganti specie consecuntur"; 7.5.7).

The passage in Vitruvius is important to readers of the *Ars Poetica* for several reasons. First of all, Vitruvius' polemic is roughly contemporary with the *Ars Poetica*, if we date the poem to the late twenties, since 22 B.C. is the last possible date for the composition or revision of the *De Architectura*.[81] Vitruvius' vocal rejection of contemporary tendencies in wall painting is thus consistent with our dating of the *Ars Poetica* to the same period because it shows that, in a period of dramatic change in painting, such reactions as we find in Horace and Vitruvius were understandably topical. Secondly, Vitruvius shows us that Classicizing theorists were just as outspoken and influential in the fine arts as we know they were in literary criticism.[82] Although Vitruvius' condemnation of what we might call the "fantasy-style" was, in the end, to be ignored by painters and patrons, he does seem to have had a restraining influence for several decades.[83] We can only imagine how closely twentieth-century characterizations of him as a pedantic conservative[84] correspond to what artists and

---

(Paris 1985) 36-37. Problems of Beyen's dating of Phase II of the Second Style are discussed by Ehrhardt, op. cit. (*supra* n. 77) xiv-xv.

[80]Brink, II, 85, errs in saying that Vitruvius is concerned only about the truth of the representations, not their verisimilitude. Verisimilitude is implied by the words "seu potest esse."

[81]For literature on the date of Vitruvius' publication of *De Architectura* in 22 B.C. at the latest, see W. Ehrhardt, op. cit. (*supra* n. 77) 153n1330; B. Baldwin, "The Date, Identity, and Career of Vitruvius," *Latomus* 49 (1990) 425-434.

[82]See, e.g., E. Gabba, "Political and Cultural Aspects of the Classicistic Revival in the Augustan Age," *CA* 1 (1982) 43-65; P. Zanker, *Augustus und die Macht der Bilder* (Munich 1987); E. Simon, *Augustus. Kunst und Leben in Rom um die Zeitenwende* (Munich 1986) 188: "Die hier wiedergegebene Stelle (Vit. 7.5.3) läßt etwas von der Lebendigkeit der damals geführten Kunstdiskussionen spüren, auch von der Beschränktheit der Ästhetik Vitruvs, die in der Imitation der Natur befangen bleibt."

[83]Cf W. Ehrhardt, op. cit. (*supra* n. 77) 157-162.

[84]See the examples from the older art-historical literature collected by W. Ehrhardt, op. cit. (*supra* n. 77) 155n1343 and add, more recently, J.-M. Roddaz, *Marcus Agrippa, BEFAR* 253 (1984) 252.

architects of his day thought of him. In any case, his fulminations against contemporary "avant-garde" painting give us a taste of what an equally avant-garde poet like Horace must have had to hear from his critics.

Besides serving these purposes, the Vitruvius passage can also help us to see the most important way that Horace undermines the authority of his speaker and hence clues the reader into his parody in the very first lines of the poem. Interestingly enough for our purposes, where Vitruvius seems to have had least success was in suppressing paintings of monsters, which, as Ehrhardt notes, were quite common during and just after the period when he was writing.[85] We should note that, whereas Vitruvius condemns actually existing paintings for an excess of imagination, the *Ars Poetica* speaker talks as if no contemporary painter—unless mad—would actually paint the monster described in verses 1-4. So right from the start, the speaker (who elsewhere shows himself to be ignorant of contemporary poetry) shows himself equally uninformed about contemporary painting. In fact, archaeological evidence—which, oddly enough, has hitherto been neglected by commentators on the poem—shows that from the late thirties to the late twenties B.C., Roman painters were experimenting with monsters and other unreal subjects condemned by Vitruvius.[86] So, to any reader knowledgeable about the state of contemporary Roman painting, the speaker's character emerges clearly from his first words: he is not only a pedant of old-fashioned taste like Vitruvius, but—unlike Vitruvius—he is also an ignoramus.

We will soon see which of Horace's readers would have been able to appreciate this clue. The evidence for monsters in Roman painting and from sculpted and stucco friezes of the 30s and 20s has not yet been assembled. The following list of monsters from the city of Rome in the period of ca. 40-20 B.C. will let us see how common *Mischwesen* were in this period and which patrons encouraged their artists to work in the fantasy-style condemned by Vitruvius.[87]

---

[85]See W. Ehrhardt, op. cit. (*supra* n. 77) 157.

[86]Gantar, op. cit. (*supra* n. 59) perceptively notes the frequency of monsters in contemporary literature (pp. 90-91) but thinks the pertinent *comparandum* in painting comes not from contemporary Roman works of art (which he does not mention) but from Zeuxis' hippocentaur (pp. 91-92). Rudd, 36, writes: "why should an artist not produce grotesques? Granted, Vitruvius disliked them (7.5.3-4), but *medieval stone-masons and illuminators* thought otherwise" (my emphasis). E. Leach, in *The Rhetoric of Space. Literary and Artistic Representations of Landscape in Republican and Augustan Rome* (Princeton 1988) 6n8, perceptively notes that Horace's monster "may well refer to specific examples of contemporary art."

[87]The best collection of the visual material is to be found in I. Bragantini and M. De Vos, *Le decorazioni della villa romana della Farnesina, Museo Nazionale Romano: Le Pitture,* II.1 (Rome 1982) 32-35, 52-55, 60 (figs. 3-14; 29-35; 60), with examples from the House of Livia, the Villa of the Farnesina, and Pompeii.

Nr./DATE	BLDG	M/C[88]	FIGURES
(1) 42-29	Temple of J. Caesar	S	Winged Victory terminating in shoots (fig. 2)[89]
(2) 36-27	House of Augustus	P/5	Winged females growing from plants[90]
(3)		P/13	Winged females growing from plants[91]
(4)		P/14	Marine centaurs atop frieze[92]
(5)		P/15	Walls: Winged griffins with shoot tails on sides of a floral obelisk[93]
(6)		P/15	Ceiling: Winged male and female figures growing from plants[94]

TABLE XVII: MONSTERS IN WALL PAINTING, STUCCOES, AND SCULPTED FRIEZES FROM THE CITY OF ROME, C. 35-20 B.C.

[88]M/C=Medium/Context. **P**=painting; **St**=stucco; **S**=sculpture (including sculpted frieze); numbers and letters given under "C" correspond to standard spatial denominations in the referenced archaeological publications.

[89]See M. Montagna Pasquinucci, "La decorazione architettonica del tempio del Divo Giulio nel Foro Romano," *Monumenti Antichi* 48 (1973); M. Floriani Squarciapino, "Il fregio del tempio del divo Giulio," *RAL* 12 (1957) 270-284; H. v. Rohden and H. Winnefeld, *Architektonische römische Tonreliefs der Kaiserzeit* (Stuttgart 1911) 200ff. For a history of the motif, see J. M. C. Toynbee and J. B. Ward Perkins, "Peopled Scrolls: A Hellenistic Motif in Imperial Art," *PBSR* 18 (1950) 1-43.

[90]See G. Carettoni, "La decorazione pittorica della Casa di Augusto sul Palatino," *MDAI(R)* 90 (1983) 373-419 at p. 378 (= Carettoni I). For the date, see G. Carettoni, *Das Haus des Augustus auf dem Palatin* (Mainz 1983) 23-27 (= Carettoni II).

[91]Carettoni I, 396; Carettoni II, 56.

[92]Carettoni I, 400; Carettoni II, 60-66.

[93]Carettoni I, 405; Carettoni II, 74. For griffins in this period and in ancient art generally, see C. Delplace, *Le griffon de l'archaïsme à l'époque impériale, Études de philologie, d'archéologie et d'histoire anciennes, l'Institut Historique Belge de Rome* 20 (1980), especially pp. 346-353.

[94]Carettoni I, 409; Carettoni II, 83.

Nr./DATE	BLDG	M/C	FIGURES
(7) 36-30	House of Livia	P	Left *Ala*: Winged male and female figures with *kalathiskos*[95]
(8)		P	Left *Ala:* Griffins on shoots (*fig. 3*)[96]
(9)		P	Left *Ala:* Winged victories seated on shoots[97]
(10)		P	Triclinium: Griffins with shoot tails[98]
(11) 30-20?	Villa of the Farnesina	P	Fauces: Griffins with shoot tails[99]
(12)		S t	Cubic. B: Winged griffin with human head and shoot tail[100]
(13) *c.* 20	Aula Isiaca	P/B	Birds ending in shoots[101]

TABLE XVII (CONTINUED)

[95]See G.E. Rizzo, *Le pitture della 'Casa di Livia,' Monumenti della pittura antica*, III.3 (Rome 1937) 9ff., figures 8-10; Bragantini and De Vos, op. cit. (*supra* n. 87) fig. 12. Note that it is possible that the House of Augustus and House of Livia were part and parcel of the same palace complex, not two separate dwellings as they appear today; see W. Ehrhardt, op. cit. (*supra* n. 77) 3n74. On the date, see F. Coarelli, *Roma* (Bari 1980) 131.

[96]See Bragantini and De Vos, op. cit. (*supra* n. 87) fig. 10; Rizzo, op. cit. (*supra* n. 95) fig. 10.

[97]Bragantini and De Vos, op. cit. (*supra* n. 87) fig. 13; Rizzo, op. cit. (*supra* n. 95) fig. 9.

[98]See Bragantini and De Vos, op. cit. (*supra* n. 87) fig. 3.

[99]See Bragantini and De Vos, op. cit. (*supra* n. 87) fig. 11, tav. E. See Bragantini and De Vos, ibid., with literature speculating on the identification and date reported on p. 23 and their own view (20s B.C.) suggested on p. 40. W. Ehrhardt, op. cit. (*supra* n. 77) 3, implies a similar dating, as does A. Bartet, op. cit. (*supra* n. 79) 96-97. E. Leach, "Patrons, Painters, and Patterns," in *Literary and Artistic Patronage in Ancient Rome*, ed. B. Gold (Austin 1982) 135-173, at p. 164 suggests that the owner was the equestrian A. Crispinus Caepio. Roddaz, op. cit. (*supra* n. 84) accepts the identification as the Villa of Agrippa (passim; cf. 249n108, 321n55).

[100]See Bragantini and De Vos, op. cit. (*supra* n. 87) fig. 14.

[101]See G. E. Rizzo, *Pitture dell'Aula Isiaca di Caligola, Monumenti della pittura antica* III.2.2 (Rome 1936) tav. A. On the date of the building, see A. Barbet, op. cit. (*supra* n. 79) 97.

I stress that the examples on TABLE XVII are from the city of Rome and date to this limited period. Later, monsters become even more common, as Roman painting moves into the Third and Fourth Styles. This means that our need to interpret the discrepancy between the opening lines of the *Ars Poetica* and trends in Roman painting is not dependent on dating the poem to the period 24-20 B.C. but arises even if we date the poem to the last years of Horace's life.

Late Second-Style monsters are also to be found in Campania at, e.g., the House of Obellius Firmus in Pompeii, the wall from Portici in the Naples National Museum (inv. 8593), the Caserma of the Gladiators at Pompeii,[102] and at the villa in Boscotrecase.[103] Outside of Campania, we find painting reminiscent of this style at a villa in Sabine country north of Rome near Licenza (ancient Digentia), where, amid fragments of wall painting, we find a griffin, two sphinxes, and fragments of a wing and the hind parts of creatures that are perhaps also remains of monsters. The villa seems also to have had a mosaic with griffins, now vanished.[104]

---

[102]For these examples from the first century B.C. and others from the first century A.D., see Bragantini and De Vos, op. cit. (*supra* n. 87) 50-61; W. Ehrhardt, op. cit. (*supra* n. 77) 17-31.

[103]See P. H. von Blanckenhagen and C. Alexander, *The Paintings from Boscotrecase, MDAI(R)* Ergänzungsheft 6 (1962) 58.

[104]Only the griffin (from *riquadro* 31) is published; see G. Lugli, "La villa sabina di Orazio," *Monumenti Antichi* 31 (1926) cols. 456-598, at col. 570 (with fig. 52). The sphinxes are from *riquadri* 3 and 20; the hind parts of an animal and a wing (?) are from *riquadro* 15.

The griffin mosaic is known only from a literary source: like most of the mosaics of the villa, it has vanished. In 1828 Filippo Alessandro Sebastiani, in *Viaggio a Tivoli* (Fuligno 1828) wrote: "mi aveva assicurato il sig. cav. Gell gentiluomo inglese, persona di vastissima erudizione, e già nota per le sue produzioni geografiche, che vi aveva rilevato un altro pezzo di mosaico ornato di piccoli grifi, ma o fosse, che il guidatore non lo conoscesse, o che quest'avanzo venisse distrutto, io non fui così fortunato da poterlo vedere" (395-396).

Gell is Sir William Gell (1777-1836), "Resident Plenipotentiary" of the Society of Dilettanti in Italy; see *The Dictionary of National Biography*, vol. 7 (Oxford 1963-1964) 994-996. He was, indeed, known for his erudition and accuracy; cf. E. Clay (ed.), *Sir William Gell in Italy. Letters to the Society of Dilettanti* (London 1976) 18-36, especially p. 30. Gell himself appears to corroborate Sebastiani's report when he writes in *The Topography of Rome and Its Vicinity* (London 1834[1], 1846[2]) vol. 2, p. 350: "The ruins of this famous villa consist only of a Mosaic pavement, and of two capitals and two fragments of Doric columns lying among the bushes....The pavement has been much ruined by the planting of a vineyard, and can only be seen on removing the earth which covers it. The groundwork is white, with a border of animals in black."

The Interpretive Implications of Chronology   81

We can now see what kinds of persons patronized the late Second-Style and Third-Style painters condemned by Vitruvius and the *Ars Poetica* speaker: in the first instance, Livia, Augustus, and the powerful owners of the Villa of the Farnesina and the Villa in Boscotrecase.[105] It is even remotely possible that the same workshop of artists was active at all four projects.[106] Be that as it may,

---

The fact that Sebastiani saw only one mosaic on his visit and not the griffin mosaic reported to him by Gell is typical of the period. Different visitors saw different remains, doubtless depending on the knowledge, vigor, and mood of their guides. Thus, some travellers reported seeing two or more mosaics—see Andrea Manazzale, *Viaggio da Roma a Tivoli, Palestrina, Frascati, ed altri contorni di Roma* (Roma 1817) 31 ("in una vigna situata a' piedi del monte Lucretile, si vede qualche vestigio di questa Villa, consistente in differenti camere pavimentate di mosaico...."); Giuseppe Antonio Guattani, *Monumenti Sabini*, tom. 3 (Rome 1830) 16 ("concludiamo che da questi campi Oraziani ore gran parte della sua vita menò il genio delle muse latine non devi partir lettor cortese senza osservare, in mancanza di significanti rovine, i pochi rimasugli de' pavimenti a mosaico della sua casa...."); Fabio Gori, *Viaggio pittorico-antiquario da Roma a Tivoli e Subiaco* (Rome 1855), parte seconda, pp. 22-23 ("il Garzone che n'è custode, alla tua richiesta rompe con la marra la terra e mostra un bel frammento di musaico. Fattagli la domanda, se vi è altro da vedere, ei ti risponde che scavando profondamente il suolo, si trovano altri pezzi di pavimento di musaico, e resti di antico edifizio, gli stessi che vi scoprì il Baron di Santedille"). Other visitors saw just one (in addition to Gell and Sebastiani, cf. A. Nibby, "Viaggio antiquario alla Villa di Orazio, a Subiaco, a Trevi, presso le sorgenti dell'Aniene," *Memorie Romane di Antichità e di Belle Arti* [Pesaro 1827] 37 [=*Analisi storico-topografico-antiquaria della carta de' dintorni di Roma*, tomo 3 (Rome 1849²) 720) or even none (cf. J. H. Westphal, *Die römische Kampagne* [Berlin und Stettin 1829] 115: "Trümmer derselben sind nicht mehr vorhanden"). Knowledge of the various mosaics probably goes back to the amateur excavations carried out on the site over a thirty-year period from 1755-1783 by the Scottish artist Allan Ramsay; see J. Holloway, "Two Projects to Illustrate Allan Ramsay's Treatise on Horace's Sabine Villa," *Master Drawings* 14 (1976) 280-286. On Ramsay (1713-1784) see *DNB* vol. 16 (London 1909) 676-677.

[105] The Villa at Boscotrecase is the latest of the group and represents the Third Style; see von Blanckenhagen and Alexander, op. cit. (*supra* n. 103). For speculation about the owners of these villas see Bragantini and De Vos, op. cit. (*supra* n. 87) 22-24; von Blanckenhagen and Alexander, ibid., 59; Simon, op. cit. (*supra* n. 82) 182; Zanker, op. cit. (*supra* n. 82) 279-284.

[106] Cf. von Blanckenhagen and Alexander, op. cit. (*supra* n. 103) 58-59, on the similarity of the Farnesina and the villa in Boscotrecase; for the similarity of the Farnesina and the House of Livia and House of Augustus, see Bragantini and De Vos, op. cit. (*supra* n. 87) 30; Carettoni I, p. 408. Both Carettoni and Bragantini—De Vos think the workshop was of Alexandrian origin. R. E. Ling, "Studius and the Beginnings of Roman Landscape Painting," *JRS* 67 (1977) 1-16, at pp. 11-12, sees no need to invoke a non-Roman origin for motifs that are vaguely Egyptian.

the evidence from Campania suggests that once given this powerful impetus, the new style caught on rather quickly and spread to households much lower down the socio-economic ladder.[107] These were certainly some of the readers who would have noted, right from the start, that something is quite odd about the *Ars Poetica*.

The material from the Sabine villa is particularly interesting because it was very possibly Horace's own. Its site and characteristics correspond well to the literary evidence from Horace's own poetry, and so it has been identified by twentieth-century Roman topographers and archaeologists.[108] The monster paintings and griffin mosaic—the one lost, the others hidden away in an ill-lit museum of difficult access—have never been the subject of a detailed scholarly study, and the villa as we have it is the result of several building phases, so we cannot be certain that we have here evidence dating from Horace's own lifetime. The extant mosaics of the villa find their closest parallels with mosaics found in the House of Livia on the Palatine and in the Villa of Livia ad Gallinas Albas.[109] The vanished griffin mosaic may have come from a later phase of the building—a possible candidate would be the bath complex on the west—since such creatures are common enough in bath contexts, particularly from the Antonine period. On the other hand, there is a chance that the work was contemporary with the other four preserved mosaics in the villa, which like it, were black and white.[110] As for the wall paintings, these fall into different groups

---

[107]Cf. Zanker, op. cit. (*supra* n. 82) 282; Roddaz, op. cit. (supra n. 84) 250-251; a similar diffusion has been observed for the so-called sacral-idyllic landscape; see S. R. Silberberg, *A Corpus of the Sacral-Idyllic Landscape Paintings in Roman Art* (Diss. UCLA 1980) xx, 35. E. Leach, op. cit. (supra n. 99) 164-167, has perceptive remarks on the reasons for the revolutionary change from the middle to late Second Style. See also her book, op. cit. (*supra* n. 86) 373-377.

[108]See Lugli, op. cit. (*supra* n. 104) cols. 462-492; M. E. Blake, *Pavements of Roman Buildings, MAAR* 8 (1930) 89; F. Coarelli, *Lazio* (Bari 1982) 112-113; H. Mielsch, *Die römische Villa* (Munich 1987) 61. In a stimulating recent article, A. Bradshaw makes a strong case against reports in Porphyrio (on *Epod.* 1.31 and *Carm.* II.18.12-14) and Ps-Acro (on *Carm* II.18.12) that Maecenas gave the villa as a gift to Horace; see "Horace *in Sabinis*," *Collection Latomus* 206 (1986) 160-186.

[109]For similarities in the mosaics, see M. E. Blake, *Ancient Roman Construction in Italy from the Prehistoric Period to Augustus* (Washington 1947) 253; M. L. Morricone Matini, *Roma: Reg. X Palatium, Mosaici Antichi in Italia* (Rome 1967) 6.

[110]That the mosaic was black and white is indicated by Gell's description; see n. 104 above. The earliest griffins of which I am aware are those on a pavement (now vanished) from the Casa del Cinghiale in Pompeii (VIII, 3, 8). The mosaic is described by M. E. Blake, op. cit. (*supra* n. 108) 99 as follows: "sea griffins and dolphins were swimming about between a meander center and a border representing a

stylistically, and we thus far have no records of their original location in the villa which would help us establish a chronology. Pasqui—who, according to the Soprintendenza Archeologica per il Lazio, did not leave behind such records—made later study of the fragments harder than it had to be by attaching them to thirty-eight *riquadri* according to subject and color. Thus we have a group of *riquadri* with yellow ground (R.1, 2, 3, 4, 6, 9, 10, 11, 12, 15, 16, 19, 20, 21, 22, 24, 26, 27, 28, 37); white ground (R. 7, 8, 14, 17, 19, 23, 25, 30, 31, 32, 33, 34, 38); red ground (R. 5, 13); and mouldings from cornices (R. 5, 8, 20, 26, 34, 35, 36). Some fragments may well be from one of the later building/remodelling phases of the villa. Published scholarly opinion on the painting is scarce and quite divergent: Lugli thought they were mostly "secondo stile pompeiano"; Borda, in brief remarks about the fragments, claimed that they were an academic revival of the Second Style during the Flavian or Trajanic period.[111] Borda's position is not so surprisingly different from Lugli's as it might, at first, appear to be: the Fourth Style involves, among other things, a revival of late Second-Style motifs.[112] Though this is not the place to decide the dispute between Lugli and Borda, I can report that Roman painting experts Volker Strocka and Irene Bragantini have informed me in personal communications that they exclude an Augustan date, assigning the paintings to the Fourth Style.

Of course, if the villa is Horace's and if the monster paintings or at least the griffin mosaic are Augustan, then we have striking evidence that Horace and the *Ars Poetica* speaker must be strictly distinguished from one another, for it would mean that Horace, in his beloved Sabine villa, which was completed in the late 30s or early 20s before the *Ars Poetica* was written, chose to decorate his walls and floors with precisely the kind of creatures condemned without qualification by the *Ars Poetica* speaker. As we have seen, the material from Licenza

---

turreted wall." E. La Rocca, et al., *Guida archeologica di Pompeii* (Verona 1976) 139, date the mosaic to the first half of the first century A.D.; Blake states that it is "pre-earthquake" (p. 99). For monster designs in general, see Blake, ibid., 123. The fact that a griffin design would be an "advanced" trait for a villa of the late 30s B.C. should not necessarily deter us from considering such a dating since, for example, the mosaic in room B of the villa also has a design only popular in the next century; cf. M. E. Blake, ibid., 90. We need to keep in mind that our corpus of domestic mosaic designs is biassed against the first century B.C. and earlier, since most of our Roman houses are later.

[111]Lugli, op. cit. (*supra* n. 104) col. 571; M. Borda, *La pittura romana* (Milan 1958) 90, 266.

[112]Cf. W. C. Archer, "The Paintings in the Alae of the Casa dei Vettii and a Definition of the Fourth Pompeian Style," *AJA* 94 (1990) 95-123, especially p. 121: "as has been noted in other studies, each of the principal compositional possibilities comprising the Fourth Style...can be found directly previewed in the Second or Third Style...."

must be subjected to further investigation before it can safely be used in this discussion. In any case, it can only have been known to a select few of Horace's readers. Much more important is the fact that, on the basis of the examples of the fantasy-style known from Rome, we can already say that the taste condemned by the speaker in lines 1-5 closely reflects that attested for the imperial circle in which Horace moved.

Is there any way to spare the speaker our unequivocally negative interpretation of his introductory lines? Ehrhardt attempted to moderate Vitruvius' critique and thus make him appear less distastefully extreme by suggesting that Vitruvius did not condemn standard mythological monsters like griffins, but only new-fangled monsters, like the many *Mischwesen* in our list that belong to both the animal and plant kingdoms.[113] If this were the case, then Vitruvius' harsh condemnation of monster painters would apply to a much more restricted set of *Mischwesen*, but Ehrhardt's suggestion is merely a hypothesis and an unlikely one at that. While it is true that griffins, for example, are encountered (albeit rarely) in early Second-Style painting[114]—a fact that might make it appear less likely that Vitruvius could object to them in "decadent" late Second-Style paintings—it is probably not their existence in a painting per se but their verisimilitude that mattered to Vitruvius. In an early Second-Style painting like that in the House of the Labyrinth, griffins are represented as part of the realistic scene: they decorate corbels holding up a construction that could really exist and could really have corbels with griffins. In the late Second-Style examples, they are not integrated into a realistic scene as decorative elements of objects that might actually exist; rather, they are paratactically isolated within a purely whimsical and painterly fancy.[115]

However we understand Vitruvius, the *Ars Poetica* speaker condemns, not (as has sometimes been thought) a painting of a Scylla—that is, a standard mythological creature—but a unique *Mischwesen* that has no exact parallel in

---

[113]See W. Ehrhardt, op. cit. (*supra* n. 77) 157: "Mythische Mischwesen, wie z.B. Sphingen und Kentauren, sind von vornherein von dieser Kritik [scil. of Vitruvius] auszunehmen...."

[114]See Beyen, op. cit. (*supra* n. 79), vol. I, p. 261 with 261n3 on the difference between the griffins in the early Second-Style House of the Labyrinth and those in the House of Livia.

[115]Cf. Beyen, loc. cit. (*supra* n. 79). E. Leach, op. cit. (*supra* n. 99) 162-167, has attractive suggestions about the overall decorative scheme. The primary object, she thinks, is to create a *pinacotheca* and "the unreal structures and impossible ornaments deplored by Vitruvius, however fantastic they may sound in the abstract, explain themselves perfectly in context as the elements of an appropriately rich setting for the display of pictures" (p. 162).

literature or art.[116] While the speaker's creature with a woman's head, birds' feathers, and a fish's tail resembles a Scylla in many respects, it lacks the crucial component of dog protomes at the waist.[117] To this extent, at least, the speaker might be compared to Vitruvius, as interpreted by Ehrhardt. Such an interpretation might spare the speaker our harshest criticism, but it still leaves him open to criticism enough, for by concocting and ridiculing a new *Mischwesen*, the speaker, like Vitruvius, expresses his hostility toward the very skill in inventing monsters in which contemporary Roman painters revelled. As is clear from the material cited in TABLE XVII, this was a period in which painters tried to devise uniquely original monsters, and so we find few, if any, exact correspondences between the monsters found at the different sites. The lack of any exact correspondence between the *Ars Poetica* monster and the monsters of TABLE XVII is thus no surprise and, far from being problematic, is just what we would expect: Horace's monster painter is very à la mode in creating a type that, as far as we can tell, is new. Of course, we should not neglect to notice the *similarity* of Horace's monster to many of the extant examples: they often involve a fusion between the animal and vegetable realms (e.g., nrr. 1, 2, 3, 5, 6) or between sea, land, and air creatures (e.g., nrr. 4, 5, 12). The *Ars Poetica* monster is also such a fusion, with characteristics of the the sea (the fish-tail), land (the human head and horse's neck) and sky (the bird feathers).

The most important point of all is that, unlike Vitruvius, the *Ars Poetica* speaker seems totally unaware of the fact that such a painting was not only conceivable but, indeed, common, particularly in works commissioned by members of the imperial circle. And so, in the end we laugh, not at the painter of verses 1-4, but at the hapless speaker, whose pretentious claims to expertise on the arts are undermined by his eccentric taste, his inept way of expressing himself, and his ignorance of the subject. Right from the start of the poem Horace gives us and his contemporary reader ample reason to suspect that the *Ars Poetica* is to be the inept ramble of an unreliable narrator.

---

[116]On the *Ars Poetica* monster as a Scylla, cf. Ps.-Acro and later commentators such as Dillenburger and Orelli. Brink, II, 85, following Rostagni ad loc., writes more accurately: "inevitably the painting resembles the hybrid monsters of Classical art...—scyllas, sirens, centaurs, goat-stags, etc."

[117]On the iconography of the Scylla, see E. Paribeni in *EAA* 7 s.v. Scilla (Rome 1966) 109-110.

CHAPTER 4

GENRE OF THE *ARS POETICA:* EPISTLE, DIDACTIC POEM, OR TERTIUM QUID?

An interpretation of the *Ars Poetica* based on the assumption that the work contains the speech of a very unauthoritative dullard, holding forth *ad nauseam* about a subject about which he is poorly informed and can only mouth trite truisms, raises important generic questions: how can such a parody be classified and can it be paralleled within the Horatian corpus?

If, as we saw earlier in this study, the *Ars Poetica* is not to be associated with *Epistles* II, what kind of work is it? A debate has continued for centuries over classifying the *Ars Poetica* as a letter or as a didactic poem. Much labor was spent in this century and the last tracing the alleged derivation of the *Ars Poetica* from the genre of the technical handbook—the revival of an idea driven from the field by the epistle-thesis in the sixteenth century.[1] Is the *Ars Poetica* a letter, didactic poem, or technical handbook (or, at least, essay)? The issue is important: classification by genre is not simply a matter of defining a literary work; it concerns the very essence of the communcative act joining author and reader.[2]

---

[1] Cf. the works of Vahlen, Wecklein, Birt, Cauer, Norden, and others discussed by Brink, I, 18-40. For the sixteenth-century literature, see below, n. 3.

[2] Cf. J. Culler, *Structuralist Poetics* (Ithaca, New York 1975) 147-148 (cf. p. 147: "the function of genre conventions is essentially to establish a contract between writer and reader so as to make certain relevant expectations operative and thus to permit both compliance with and deviation from accepted modes of intelligibility"); A. Fowler, *Kinds of Literature. An Introduction to the Theory of Genres and Modes* (Oxford 1982) 37-53 (cf. p. 22: "of all the codes of our literary *langue*, I have no hesitation in proposing genre as the most important, not least because it incorporates and organizes many others. Just how many other codes are generically articulated remains uncertain....At any rate there is no doubt that genre primarily has to do with communication. It is an instrument not of classification or prescription,

Of commentators working on the poem in recent decades, C. O. Brink has perhaps devoted the most attention to this matter. He has persuasively discredited the view that the *Ars Poetica* is a technical handbook on poetics, noting that although it may share certain structural features that come from the technical tradition of literary criticism, the poem is not to be reduced to a handbook.³

---

but of meaning"). For a critical survey of contemporary theoretical views on the dialectic of genre and interpretation, see J. Reichert, "More Than Kin and Less Than Kind: The Limits of Genre Theory," in *Yearbook of Comparative Criticism* 8 (1978) 57-79; T. Kent, *Interpretation and Genre* (London and Toronto 1986) 147-150.

³See Brink, I, 15-40. As I plan to show elsewhere, the debate about whether the poem is an *ars* or merely something loosely derived from the technical tradition of poetics may be traced back to the sixteenth century, particularly the polemics of Antonio Riccoboni and Nicolaus Colonius. See (in chronological order): *Antonii Riccoboni a quodam viro docto dissensio de epistola Horatii ad Pisones: quae nullam quidem methodum habere: sed ad methodum redigi posse ostenditur,* printed at the end of *Compendium Artis Poeticae Aristotelis ad usum conficiendorum poematum ab Antonio Riccobono ordinatum et quibusdam scholiis explanatum* (Padua 1591); *Nicolai Colonii responsio adversus absurdissimam sententiam Antonii Riccoboni de Horatij libello ad Pisones de poetica* (Bergamo 1591); *Antonii Riccoboni I.C. humanitatem in Patavino gymnasio profitentis defensor seu pro eius opinione de Horatii epistola ad Pisones in Nicolaum Colonium ad Ethica Aristotelis in eodem gymnasio interpretanda designatum* (Ferrara 1591); *Epistola Nicolai Colonii Ad Antonium Riccobonum* (n. p. 1591); *Conciliatio Antonii Riccoboni cum Nicolao Colonio ad Illustriss. et Excellentissimum Principem, Alexandrum Estensem* (Padua 1591). Riccoboni's first contribution to the quarrel was written in reaction to Colonius' earlier treatise, *Q. Horatii Flacci Methodus De Arte Poetica: Per Nicolaum Colonium Exposita Quomodo antehac ab alio nemine* (Bergamo 1587).

In their debate, Colonius (*c*. 1520-1602) represented the view that the *Ars Poetica* had a "method," or plan, and that the plan was based on a technical treatment of all the literary genres, which, according to Colonius, numbered four (epic, tragedy, comedy, satyr drama). Riccoboni (1541-1599) maintained the thesis of Robortello, his predecessor as professor of Humanities at Padua, and of his friend and colleague De Nores (Colonius' predecessor as professor of Moral Philosophy at Padua) that the *Ars Poetica* was not a technical treatise but a loosely written letter. He may be said to be partly responsible for attempts, over the next three centuries, to transpose hundreds of lines of the *Ars Poetica* in a vain attempt to restore order to the poem because, in arguing against Colonius' assertion that the poem had a plan, Riccoboni showed how the poem would have to be rearranged to correspond to the plan of Aristotle's *Poetics*. In contrast to D. Heinsius (*Q. Horati Flacci Opera cum Animadversionibus et Notis Danielis Heinsi* [Leiden 1612] 295-307), a student of Riccoboni's adversary Joseph Scaliger, Riccoboni did not believe that his wholesale transpositions were to be taken seriously: they were merely illustrative of the informality with which Horace re-worked the Aristotelian technical tradition. Incidentally, Heinsius rewrote through transposition, not only the *Ars Poetica*, but also—a fact rarely mentioned—the *Letter*

Brink does not go on to define the genre of the *Ars Poetica* in any detail, simply asserting baldly that "of course, the *Ars* is a letter."[4] Be that as it may, it should by now be clear that determination of the genre of the *Ars* cannot proceed from any assumption about its title and alleged inclusion in *Epistles* II.

Once we see that the *Ars* is most likely an independent work in the corpus, three possible ways of classifying it as something other than a handbook come to mind, of which the second two have rarely, if ever, been raised in this century: a verse letter, a didactic poem, or some *tertium quid*. The first two possibilities generally stand for distinct categories of writing: a letter is usually informal in spirit and supplies or requests information of some sort from or to a friend. As Ps.-Acro and Porphyrio sensibly remark on *Sat.* I.1.1, a letter presumes an absent recipient: "epistulis enim ad absentes loquimur, sermone cum praesentibus" (Ps.-Acro); "in sermonum autem libris vult intellegi, quasi apud praesentem se loqui, epistolas vero quasi ad absentes missas" (Porphyrio). In a didactic work like Lucretius' *De Rerum Natura* or Virgil's *Georgics*, formal instruction in moral, technical, and like matters is offered to an interlocutor who is imagined to be present listening to the speaker and with whom the speaker has some social bond.[5]

Now, this clearcut distinction between the formal instructive genre of didactic literature and the informal reportorial genre of the letter can and does break down, for it is, of course, possible for a letter to be didactic, and, indeed, in the Augustan age such letters, in prose form, are known to have existed. Interestingly enough, the ones we happen to hear about all resemble the *Ars*

---

to *Florus* (pp. 289-294). His methodological model was undoubtedly Joseph Scaliger's edition of Propertius and Tibullus in *Catulli, Tibulli, Propertii Nova Editio* (Paris 1577), on which see A. Grafton, *Joseph Scaliger. A Study in the History of Classical Scholarship,* vol. 1 (Oxford 1983) 177-179. The first scholar seriously to propose large transpositions of the *Ars Poetica* was Francisco Sanchez, explicitly stating that Scaliger's Propertius was his inspiration; cf. *Francisci Sanctii Brocensis...In Artem Poeticam Horatii Annotationes* (Salamanca 1591) fol. 6r (transposing 136-152 to follow 38-45, with reference to Scaliger's Propertius) and fol. 9r (putting 251-274 after 73-85).

[4]Brink, III, 556. The poem has recently been categorized as epistolary—without detailed argument—by W. Hering, *Die Dialektik von Form und Inhalt bei Horaz* (Berlin 1979) 78-85; and by R. S. Kilpatrick, *The Poetry of Criticism. Horace Epistles II and Ars Poetica* (Edmonton, Alberta 1990) 34-35. Brink (II, 518) and Kilpatrick (p. 54) also (rightly, in my opinion) connect the work to *sermo*.

[5]E.g., Perses is Hesiod's brother; Maecenas is Virgil's benefactor. Lucretius' exact relationship with Memmius is not known, but he appears to have been on "intimate terms" with Memmius, as Bailey puts it (vol. I, p. 6).

Poetica in concerning grammatical and literary topics.[6] Adding to the difficulty of distinguishing the two genres from each other is the fact that, since Hesiod, it had been conventional for a didactic poem, like a letter, to have an addressee (cf. Hesiod's Perses, Lucretius' Memmius, etc.).[7] Moreover, the conventions (if any) of the verse letter could only have been loose indeed when Horace wrote the *Ars Poetica,* since the genre, as far as we can tell, was still in its infancy.[8]

It is strange that the case for categorizing the *Ars* as a didactic poem has not, to my knowledge, been made in a serious way during this century: Lucretius' *De Rerum Natura* and Virgil's *Georgics* certainly show how popular and prestigious was the genre in the mid- to late first century.[9] The question of genre

[6]Such letters are known from the testimonia of lost works by M. Valerius Messalla Corvinus, M. Verrius Flaccus, Sinnius Capito, Livy, C. Valgius Rufus, and Asinius Pollio: see Schanz-Hosius, *Geschichte der römischen Literatur, HdA* VIII.2 (Munich 1935) 408-409. On the *genos didaktikon,* see K. Berger, "Hellenistische Gattungen in Neuen Testament," *ANRW* II.25.2 (Berlin 1984) 1031-1432, at pp. 1295-1325.

[7]For a useful survey of the conventions and examples of wisdom literature from around the world see M. L. West, *Hesiod. Works and Days* (Oxford 1978) 3-25 (with sensible comments about the addressee on pp. 23-25). On the addressee in the Roman didactic poem, see E. Pöhlmann, "Charakteristika des römischen Lehrgedichts," *ANRW* I.3 (Berlin 1973) 850, 900.

[8]The earliest verse letters on record are those of Sp. Mummius in 146 B.C.; see Cicero *Ad Att.* 13.4 and cf. P. Cugusi, *Evoluzione e forme dell'epistolografia latina nella tarda repubblica e nei primi due secoli dell'impero con cenni sull'epistolografia preciceroniana* (Rome 1983) 129-130.

[9]The *Ars Poetica* has occasionally been classified as a didactic poem in previous centuries; cf., e.g., *Petri Nannii Alcmani Commentarius in Q. Horatii Flacci de arte poetica librum,* bound with Laevinus Torrentius, *In Q. Horatii Flacci Satyras et Epistolas Commentarius* (Antwerp 1608) 783: "hoc porro poema Horatii nostri versatur in genere didactico. Docet quippe Poeta, qua ratione tractanda sint poemata"; R. Hurde, *Q. Horatii Flacci Epistolae ad Pisones et Augustum,* 2 vols. (Cambridge 1757) vol. 1, xiii; F. Dorighello, *Q. Horatius Flaccu⸗ Illustratus* (Padua 1774) 3-7; W. Scherer, *Poetik,* ed. G. Reiss (Tübingen 1977; originally published in 1888) 41: "Horaz gehört in weiterem Sinn selbst zur Schule des Aristoteles; die aristotelischen Grundsätze von Nachahmung, Handlung, Führerrolle der Tragödie u.s.w. finden sich bei ihm wieder. Aber er hat doch eine besondere Strömung begründet: *das Lehrgedicht über die Poesie hat er eingeführt.* Den Brief an die Pisonen, Epist. 2,3..., nennt schon Quintilian *Ars poetica:* und damit that man eigentlich wohl Horaz Unrecht, denn er hat gewiß nicht die Absicht gehabt, hiermit eine vollständige Poetik zu liefern, obgleich man die Schrift oft so angesehn hat" (my emphasis). See also Orelli-Baiter-Mewes, *Q. Horatius Flaccus* (Berlin 1892) vol. 2, 566: "Quod ad ipsam poematis formam attinet, illi tantummodo interpretes verum viderunt, qui 'epistulam didacticosatiricam' esse contenderunt, non poema didascalicum universae poesis leges ac regul-

does matter: if we read the poem as a normal letter, then we expect and gladly tolerate a good deal of informality in tone, content, and structure;[10] and, taken as

---

as proponens, ut olim plerique rati sunt, non animadvertentes praecepta paene omnia referri ad genus dramaticum, ea vero genera, in quibus ipse excellebat, lyricum (quod leviter dumtaxat attingit vv. 83-85), satiras, epistulas, epigramma, poema didascalicum, quamquam ipse Lucretium suspiciebat, prorsus praeteriri."

[10]This point was already made by De Nores in 1553 (App. I [3]), who wrote, "amat enim epistola familiaritatem quandam. At nimis accuratus ordo ad severitatem potius, quam ad familiaritatem propendet." For an amusing statement of the effect our generic expectations have upon our interpretation of the *Ars Poetica,* see R. K. Hack, "The Doctrine of Literary Forms," *HSCP* 27 (1916) 1-65, at p. 14. Cf. also l'Abbé Batteux, *Les quatre poétiques d'Aristote, d'Horace, de Vida, de Despréaux* (Paris 1771), vol. I, II° Partie, pp. 1-4: "le Poète n'a pas toute fois eu dessein dans cet Ouvrage, de nous donner un traité complet de Poétique....C'est un Epître qu'il addresse à Lucius Pison, homme de goût, l'un des plus grands Seigneurs de Rome....D'après cette idée, on sent que l'ouvrage d'Horace ne devoit pas être une suite systématique de précepts, rangé par ordre dans des articles séparés. Ce ne pouvoit être qu'une sorte de Recueil de maximes de goût, d'axiomes presque isolé, renfermans tout leur sens sous une forme sentencieuse, et applicables chacun à leur object, indépendamment de ce qui pouvoit les précéder ou les suivre....On ne pouvoit guères en demander davantage, sur-tout à un Poete, qui aux privilèges de la Poesie, déjà très-étendus, avoit joint ceux du Genre épistolaire, dont le premier est la liberté. Il est donc inutile de nous fatiguer, avec Daniel Heinsius, pour remettre dans l'Art Poetique d'Horace, un ordre qui, selon toute apparence, n'y fut jamais." See also Orelli-Baiter-Mewes, op. cit. (*supra* n. 9) vol. 2, 567: "Sententiarum ordo atque mutuus nexus a multis reprehensus, a pluribus etiam parum perspectus, mihi quidem semper admirabilis visus est et talis profecto, qualis debet esse in epistula, vera sermonis familiaris imagine, id est occultior et laxior quam qui requiritur in poemate mere didascalico"; H. Schütz, *Q. Horatius Flaccus, Episteln* (Berlin 1883) 238: "Die Stellung nach den Episteln...ist die naturgemäße....Nur wenn man einen anderen Maßstab anlegt, nämlich den eines wirklichen Lehrbuches der Dichtkunst...verdient das Werk den Tadel, den man über die Lückenhaftigkeit, mangelhafte Anordnung, einseitige Hervorhebung einzelner Teile u.a.m. ausgesprochen hat."

In ancient theory, the looser structure of the letter was noted; cf. Demetrius 229. In recent research on epistolography, the structural conventions of the genre have been emphasized; see the literature cited by K. Berger, op. cit. (*supra* n. 6) 1326-1327; and cf. J. L. White, "New Testament Epistolary Literature in the Framework of Ancient Epistolography," *ANRW* II.25.2 (Berlin 1984) 1730-1756, especially pp. 1733-38. Pietro-Antonio Petrini, *La poetica di Orazio restituita all'ordine suo* (Rome 1777) 9, noted that the argument from genre was a red herring since "costoro per difendere il componimento, fanno manifesta ingiuria all'Autore, il quale era uomo troppo illuminato per non comprendere, che un tal qual metodo è necessario anche in una Lettera, quando è dottrinale, ed instruttiva, e che i documenti perdono assai di vigore, e di efficacia, se sono confusamente proposti."

a letter, then a necessary but not sufficient condition for including it in the second book of *Epistles* is satisfied. After all—despite what we know about the title and place of the text in the Horatian corpus in antiquity—the ancient scribes may have erred in separating the *Ars Poetica* from the *Epistles*. Horace could clearly write verse letters of the normal type but also of the didactic variety (for the first, cf. *Epist*. I.11; for a moralizing letter, cf. *Epist*. I.12 or I.14).

There are perhaps one or two indications that Horace was thinking of the *Ars Poetica* more as a didactic poem than as a conventional epistolary poem, or at least that he did not consider the poem a letter, whatever else he did consider it. In all but one of Horace's poems that are indisputably epistles, the addressee is named, or referred to by some form of *tu* or a verb in the second person singular, in the first sentence and usually in the very first line.[11] The *Ars Poetica* does not begin in this typically epistolary way. In it, the first sentence proceeds through clauses in the third person singular about a hypothetical painter and grotesque figure (lines 1-4) before ending with a clause in the second person plural, the subject of which appears, on a first reading, to be generic, not specific (*amici*, the last word of line 5). The addressees of the poem, the Pisones, are first mentioned in line 6. In having multiple addressees, the *Ars Poetica* also departs from the indisputable epistles. Moreover, nothing about the way they are spoken to in this part of the poem indicates that the Pisones are absent, as the addressee of a letter normally would be. Indeed, in lines 9-10, as if they are present, Horace gives us the response of his addressees to what he has just said—something he frequently does in the *Satires* (especially in Book II) but rarely, if ever, in the first or second book of *Epistles*.[12]

The subject of the first lines—painting, or proper artistic representation in general—is, of course, not a standard *introductory* topic of a letter. Virtually all of the indisputable letters treat topics—at least in the opening section—appropriate to that genre and are strongly motivated *as letters*. They convey information and/or greetings (*Epist*. I.1, 2, 8, 10, 16), request information or

---

[11]Cf. *Epist*. I.1 (*quaeris / Maecenas*, 2-3); 2 (*Maxime Lolli*, 1); 3 (*Iuli Flori*, 1); 4 (*Albi*, 1); 5 (*potes...Torquate*, 1-3); 6 (*Numici*, 1); 8 (*Celso...Albinovano*, 1); 9 (*Claudi*, 1); 10 (*Fuscum*, 1); 11 (*Bullati*, 1); 12 (*Icci*, 1); 13 (*te...Vini*, 1-2); 14 (*Vilice*, 1); 15 (*Vala*, 1); 16 (*Quinti*, 1); 17 (*Scaeva*, 1); 18 (*Lolli*, 1); 19 (*Maecenas*, 1); 20 (*liber*, 1); *Epist*. II.1 (*sustineas...Caesar*, 1-4); 2 (*Flore*, 1). The exception is *Epist*. I.7, where Maecenas is not adddressed until the second sentence, beginning at the end of the second line of the poem; he is actually named in line 5.

[12]For examples, cf. *Sat*. I.9.1-8; II.1.1-12; II.3.1-18; II.4.1-3; II.5.1-8; II.7.1-5; II.8.1-5. In the *Epistles*, Horace often quotes the typical or imaginary saying or statement of a stock (usually unnamed) character (cf., e.g., *Epist*. I.1.82 ["nullus in orbe sinus Bais praelucet amoenis"]), but Horace is not imagining himself actually conversing with such persons in the same way he, say, exchanges words with Davus in *Sat*. II.7.1-5.

news (*Epist.* I.3, 4, 11, 15), issue an invitation (*Epist.* I.5), moralize (*Epist.* I.6, 12, 14, 17, 18), seek forgiveness (*Epist.* I.7), or commend one friend to another (*Epist.* I.9). The five literary letters (*Epist.* I.13, 19, 20; II.1, 2) have different points of departure. *Epist.* I.20 is written like a conventional letter of farewell; the wit of the poem lies in the fact that the departing "person" is Horace's book of letters. *Epist.* II.1 begins with Horace telling Augustus that he writes so as not to waste Augustus' precious time with idle conversation. *Epist.* I.19 and II.2 begin in a more round-about manner. *Epist.* II.2 tells a moralizing tale in lines 1-24, the point of which becomes clear in verses 24-25: Horace has not answered some letters Florus has sent him from abroad and, in particular, has not responded to Florus' request for new lyric poems. Although it is slow to get to the point, the poem thus concerns a typical epistolary topic.

Epist. I.19, addressed to Maecenas, is less ostensibly epistolary; Horace seems, rather, to use the letter format as a mere excuse for publishing a defense of his poetry. Before considering the piece an exception to the epistolary nature of this group of poems, we might note that the addressee has not been chosen accidentally, however small a role he plays in the text itself, for Horace offers his poetic apology to none other than his most illustrious friend.[13] Thus, even this poem has an epistolary occasion—sending someone a letter "accidentally on purpose" in order to be sure that he is apprised of a matter of mutual concern. In this case, Horace wants Maecenas to know that he does have something to say for himself and his poetry in the face of recent critical attacks—attacks that might conceivably make his friend think twice about continuing his support. *Epistles* I.13 is another matter; we will return to it in a moment.

The *Ars Poetica* also stands out from Horace's poetic letters because of its ending—or, better, lack of ending. As Berger has noted, the topics appropriate to the closing section of a letter are: summation; general *sententia*; threats; self-commentary; "epistolaria" (e.g., "I leave here in a week"); demand to pay heed.[14] In Horace's undisputed letters we can readily find such standard endings, as the table on the next page shows.

In contrast to Horace's verse letters, the *Ars Poetica* has no conventional conclusion. As Brink observes (*ad* 453-476), "like many poems of Horace the *Ars* is open-ended. No attempt is made to bring to a close the conceptual schema of his literary theory." Instead, the poem ends as the speaker of the *Ars Poetica* compares the mad poet to a bear or leech (472-476), who must be avoided lest he "read you to death." While it is true that many Horatian poems are open-ended, this is not true, as we have seen, of his epistles. Open-endedness is, however, a

---

[13]On the friendship of Maecenas and Horace see E. Lefèvre, "Horaz und Maecenas," *ANRW* II.31.3 (Berlin 1981) 1987-2029; M. S. Santirocco, *Unity and Design in Horace's Odes* (Chapel Hill and London 1986) 153-168.

[14]Op. cit. (*supra* n. 6) 1348-1350. I omit the "Ketzerschluß."

typical feature of the *Satires*, which frequently conclude abruptly with the end of a story (*Sat.* I.5, I.7, I.8, I.9, II.5, II.6, II.8) or a conversation (II.1, II.3, II.4, II.7). More rarely, they finish with a moment of self-reflection (I.1, I.3, I.4, I.6) or with a general *sententia* (I.2) and thus have a more substantial sense of an ending. Indeed, as Griffin has noted, "given the special decorum of satire—an aroused or merely a chatty speaker, a virtually unlimited subject matter—endings present a problem which satirists have historically had difficulty solving."[15] In having a "non-ending," the *Ars Poetica* resembles more a *sermo* than an epistle.

If it is a letter, then the *Ars Poetica* stands out from the indisputably "normal" epistles in not having a typically epistolary motivation, topic, situa-

Epist.	Lines	Su	S	T	C	E	H	Key Words
I.1	106-08	x						Ad summam
I.2	67-71						x	adbibe...verba
I.3	30-36				x			vestrum reditum
I.4	12-16	x						omnem crede diem
I.5	30-31					x		tu...rescribe
I.6	67-68	x						si quid novistis
I.7	96-98	x						metiri se quemque
I.8	15-17			x				ut tu fortunam....
I.9	11-13	x						scribe tui gregis hunc
I.10	49-50				x			dictabam post fanum
I.11	28-30	x						quod petis hic est
I.12	25-29				x			ne tamen ignores....
I.13	19						x	cave ne titubes....
I.14	44	x						...exerceat artem
I.15	42-46				x			nimirum hic ego sum
I.16	79	x						mors ultima linea
I.17	43-62	x						coram rege sua....
I.18	104-112				x			me quotiens....
I.19	48-49	x						ludus enim genuit...
I.20	19-28				x			me libertino natum....
II.1	250-270				x			nec sermones ego....
II.2	205-216	x						non es avarus? abi....

Su=Summary; S=Sententia; T=Threats;
C=Commentary; E=Epistolaria; H= Heed

TABLE XVIII. CONCLUDING TOPICS IN HORACE'S EPISTLES

[15]D. Griffin, "Satiric Closure," *Genre* 18 (1985) 173-189, at p. 173.

tion, or ending. To see the poem as epistolary, one would have to imagine that the elder son of Piso is thinking of writing a poem and has asked Horace for advice—a situation that has, in fact, been proposed since the Middle Ages.[16] However, in contrast to all the other poems that are definitely letters, this situation becomes clear, not in the very first few lines, but only toward the end of the poem, in verses 385-390. Moreover, the point is made (if it is made at all) only by implication, not explicitly.[17] Thus, as correspondents, the Pisones are

---

[16] Many commentators since the early Middle Ages have imagined just this—or some such similar—background to the poem. The most recent (and, perhaps, original) example is T. P. Wiseman, "Satyrs in Rome? The Background to Horace's *Ars Poetica*," *JRS* 78 (1988) 1-13, at p. 1: "Horace's poem quite clearly presupposes a Calpurnius Piso, the older son of a morally exemplary Roman aristocrat, proposing to write a satyr-play...." For examples in medieval scholia, see C. Villa, "'Ut Poesis Pictura': Appunti iconografici sui codici dell'*Ars Poetica*," *Aevum* 62 (1988) 187-189. For example, the anonymous author of the Scholia Vindobonensia wrote: "Facit autem hunc librum amicis suis, patri ac filiis quorum maior erat scriptor comoediarum; ideo istis facit, quia volebant scribere, ut Romano populo placerent et eorum fama tali modo crescerent et quoniam multi scriptores reprehendebantur non habentes certam regulam dictandi, rogaverunt Pisones Horatium, ut certas poeticae artis daret praeceptiones...." (*apud* Villa, p.187). Cf. also Kiessling-Heinze, *Q. Horatius Flaccus, Briefe* (Berlin 1959[6]) 283: "irgend ein Anlaß des Schreibens wird nicht einmal entfernt angedeutet, und der Leser muß sich bei der Möglichkeit beruhigen, daß die Pisonen...dem Dichter den Wunsch geäußert haben mögen, über Fragen der Dichtkunst...unterrichtet zu werden."

The poet Christoph Martin Wieland, in his 1782 translation of the poem, proposed an interesting variation on the epistle-theory: Horace's motivation was to do a favor to Piso père by implicitly warning off his elder son from becoming a poet by showing, in the *Ars*, how few really great poets there are and how many ridiculous poetasters. Cf. *Horaz, Über die Dichtkunst,* in *Christoph Martin Wieland Werke*, 5. Band, ed. H. W. Seiffert (Munich 1968) 586-604, especially p. 591: "Dies vorausgesetzt, stelle ich mir di Veranlassung zu dieser Epistel so vor. Der junge Piso zeigte im Lauf seiner Schulstudien eine besondre Liebe zur Poesie, und einen so starken Hang zum Versemachen, daß der Vater endlich unruhig darüber wurde...." Note that Seiffert, in his excellent *Nachwort* to the edition, errs in claiming (p. 885) that Wieland was the first to explain Horace's lack of "Methode" because the poem is supposedly not a technical treatise on poetics but an informal letter: exactly this explanation was set forth in 1591 by Antonio Riccoboni in the works mentioned above in n. 3.

[17] Here are the lines: "Tu nihil invita dices faciesve Minerva: | id tibi iudicium est, ea mens. si quid tamen olim | scripseris, in Maeci descendat iudicis aures | et patris et nostras, nonumque prematur in annum, | membranis intus positis; delere licebit | quod non edideris, nescit vox missa reverti." The *tu* addressed is the *maior iuvenum*, previously addressed in verse 366; the conditional clause in 385-86 ("si quid tamen olim | scripseris") shows that the posited epistolary situation is, at best, implied.

rather puzzling. On the other hand, their role becomes more comprehensible as the addressees of a didactic poem. Although it must be granted that no other known didactic poem has multiple addressees, in such a poem the addressee is imagined to be present listening to the speaker and need only have a tangential relationship to the topic under discussion. This is, for example, the case with Lucretius' Memmius, whose relevance to the *De rerum natura* is quite problematic.[18] As for Hesiod's *Erga*, West has well observed that "it is apparent that Perses is a changeable figure that Hesiod stations in his poem as he chooses."[19] The same might be said of the Pisones: unlike the addressees of the poems that are clearly letters, the Pisones change identity to suit Horace's didactic intent: they seem to be critics of poetry in vv.6 and 292; poets in v.24; one a critic (the father) and one a poet (366-369, 385-388); and it is even possible to see their number change from plural (16, 235, 291) to singular (102, 119, etc.). If we may say that, generally, the addressee of an epistle determines the writing and contents of a letter and that the needs of instruction dictate the mutable nature of the addressee in a didactic work, then for this reason, too, the *Ars Poetica* more closely resembles a didactic than an epistolary poem.

Nevertheless, at least two technical points, one minor and one major, militate against taking the *Ars* as a didactic work: first, Horace twice uses the word *iste*, which had been avoided by Lucretius and Virgil in their didactic poetry.[20] This is, to be sure, a minor point, but given what we know about the tendencies of Golden Latin poets to associate vocabulary with genre, it may, nevertheless, be telling.[21] Perhaps what Brink rightly calls the word's "derisory nuance"[22] explains the apparent exception: if this is in some sense a mock didactic poem, then *iste* helps make the speaker look unsympathetically supercilious. This is consistent with the speaker's lack of any positive social bond with his addressees. The second point is more telling: a didactic poem generally begins with an invocation to a god, which the *Ars*, of course, does not. Hence, even the apparently anomalous case of the invocation of Tiberius at the beginning of the *Astronomica* is not, in fact, exceptional at all since Manilius calls Tiberius a god (*deus ipse mereris*, I.9).

So, if the simple alternatives of letter or didactic poem are not wholly convincing, then some *tertium quid* solution to the problem of genre is worth consideration. At this point we encounter some complications that may make us

---

[18] See C. Bailey on Lucretius I.26 (*Memmiadae*).

[19] West, op. cit. (*supra* n. 7) 40; E. Pöhlmann, op. cit. (*supra* n. 7) 900, with useful comments on the addressee in Greek and Roman didactic poems.

[20] *Ars Poetica* 6, 376, and see P. Watson, "Axelson Revisited: The Selection of Vocabulary in Latin Poetry," *CQ* 35 (1985) 430-448, at p. 438.

[21] See Watson, loc. cit.

[22] Brink, II, *ad* 376.

want to throw our hands up in despair. Some poems in *Epistles* I are either only weakly motivated as letters[23] or else do not seem to be letters at all but conversations. This is particularly true of *Epist.* I.13, the poem in which Horace gives Vinnius instructions on how to deliver his poetry to Augustus.[24] Support for blurring the hard and fast distinction we have up to now been observing between the epistolary and didactic genres comes from Horace himself, who in *Epist.* II.1.250 (and, implicitly, in *Epist.* II.1.4) refers to both his *Sermones* and *Epistulae* as *sermones*.[25] Now, the *Sermones* contain two clearcut paraenetic poems: *Sat.* II.2, Ofellus' discourse on the virtues of simple living; and II.4, the lessons of Catius the cook on correct preparations for a dinner party. So there is nothing generically inconsistent about a didactic *sermo*. Nor is it surprising that the second poem is mock didactic, since *Sat.* II contains several other extended parodies: II.3, the philosophical parody of Damasippus and the Stoic philosopher Stertinius; II.5, the epic parody of Odysseus' *katabasis* in *Odyssey* XI;[26] and II.7, the philosophical parody of the Stoic philosopher Crispinus. In the didactic satires, Horace sets the scene with an exposition which, however brief (that of II.2 is only a parenthetical aside in lines 2-3) does make it plain that the precepts being offered are not Horace's own. Given Horace's own hints that the *Sermones* descend from the traditions of literary moralizing to be found in Old and New Comedy and Platonic philosophy,[27] it is not surprising that the collection should contain didactic poems like these. On the other hand, the *Satires* also contain poems that are not conversations but monologues addressed to no one in

---

[23]*Epist.* I.1 and I.2, on which see M. J. McGann, *Studies in Horace's First Book of Epistles*, Collection Latomus 100 (1969) 39.

[24]A whole list of such examples is given by N. M. Horsfall, "Horace, *Sermones* 3: Epilegomena," *LCM* 4.8 (1979) 169-171. Of the poems cited there, the best is *Epist.* I.13.

[25]See N. Rudd, "The Names in Horace's Satires," *CQ* 10 (1960) 161-178, at pp. 175-176. Rudd is correct, I think, to see at *Epist.* I.4.1 a reference to the *Satires*, not *Epistles* (*pace* N. M. Horsfall, "Horace, *Sermones* 3?" *LCM* 4.6 [1979] 118). The similarity of the *Sermones* and *Epistulae* has been noted since antiquity and has frequently figured in discussions of genre in the last hundred years; cf. Porphyrio on *Epist.* I.1.1; G. L. Hendrickson, "Are the Letters of Horace Satire?" *AJP* 18 (1897) 313-324; C. A. Van Rooy, *Studies in Classical Satire and Related Literary Theory* (London 1965) 182n100; N. M. Horsfall, ibid.,117-119; H. D. Jocelyn, "Horace, *Epistles* I," *LCM* 4.7 (1979) 146; J. Moles, "Cynicism in Horace *Epistles* I," *PLLS* 5 (1985) 33-60, at p. 33. Kiessling-Heinze, *Q. Horatius Flaccus, Briefe* (Berlin 1959[6]) 283, see the *Ars Poetica* as a *sermo* with an epistolary form. On the relationship between *sermo* and diatribe, see K. Berger, op. cit. (*supra* n. 6) 1124-1132.

[26]*Sat.* I.7 also has striking elements of mock epic.

[27]Cf. *Sat.* I.4.1-8; I.10.14-19; II.3.9-14.

particular: cf. *Satires* I.2, I.3,[28] I.4, I.7, I.8, and II.6. True, all of these poems contain lively snatches of conversations, but they are conversations reported or imagined by the speaker, not acted out in the fictional present between the speaker and an interlocutor.[29] In one of these poems, the speaker is not Horace (*Sat.* I.8, whose speaker is Priapus). In others, the speaker is anonymous and could be almost anyone since Horace takes no pains to characterize him (*Sat.* I.2, I.7).[30] In similar fashion, Horace is absent from the mock epic dialogue between Ulysses and Tiresias in *Sat.* II.5, and there is no exposition whatsoever preparing us for the sudden switch from Horace's day and age to the world of epic.

These complications lead us to the following observations that are helpful in considering the genre of the *Ars Poetica* as some *tertium quid* between the epistolary and didactic genres. In accordance with his understanding of the genre of *sermo*, Horace could: [1] write a "letter" that is a conversation (*Epist.* I.13); [2] present a "conversation" that is a monologue or even soliloquy and which hence could easily be a letter if it had a salutation (*Sat.* I.2, I.3, I.4, I.8, II.6); [3] therefore subsume both the *Epistulae* and *Sermones* under the common generic rubric of *sermo* (*Epist.* II.1.4, 250); [4] present didactic monologues in this genre (*Sat.* II.3, II.4); [5] populate poems with dramatis personae other than himself (*Sat.* I.8, II.5)—even without an exposition (*Sat.* II.5)—or make his speaker nondescript (*Sat.* I.2, I.7, II.8); and [6] base poems on the parody of other genres (*Sat.* I.7, II.3, II.4, II.5, II.7). Clearly, then, if we seek a genre that is a *tertium quid* between didactic and epistolary poetry, we could do no better than choose Horace's version of *sermo*, a genre so obviously based on a very Hellenistic attempt at *Kreuzung der Gattungen*.

It would be sufficient to classify the *Ars Poetica* as a Horatian *sermo* on the basis of features [1]-[4], and such a classification is likely to be uncontroversial and greeted, I would hope, as a definite improvement over viewing the poem as a letter when it displays so few epistolary features. Even those who insist on classifying the poem as a letter can console themselves with point [3], just as those who would read the poem as didactic (or mock didactic) can take comfort in point [4]. That the *Ars* displays features [5]-[6] as well has emerged from our examination of the speaker's authority. Needless to say, much more can be—and needs to be—said before a reading of the poem along these lines may be called exhaustive. Lest the suggestion that the *Ars Poetica* be classified as exem-

---

[28] At *Sat.* I.3.63-64 Maecenas is addressed; but the poem as a whole is not presented as a conversation with Maecenas. It might more accurately be called a monologue directed at him in a way that recalls *Epist.* 1.19.

[29] Such "reported" or "imaginary" conversations are also frequent in the *Epistles*; cf., e.g., *Epistles* I.15.11-12, 39-41.

[30] *Sat.* I.3 belongs in this class but for the slight brush stroke in lines 63-5, where Horace personalizes the speaker's voice as his own by addressing Maecenas.

plifying the mixed genre of *sermo*—an *Aufhebung* of the simple forms of technical handbook, didactic poem, and letter—seem strange or unlikely, it may be well to point out that such portmanteau arrangements of genres-within-genres have been encountered in other periods and literatures, as the genre-theorists Dubrow and Fowler have noted.[31] Indeed, in a famous poetological statement in *Epistles* I.19, Horace claims that his achievement was due to his originality in mixing generic characteristics—for example, combining the meter of Archilochus with a content and tone different from cruel, Archilochean invective.[32]

Here we may simply conclude by noting that, in answer to the questions asked at the beginning of this chapter, Horatian precedents can be cited for some of the key features we have so far identified in the *Ars Poetica*—in particular, the Horatian version of *sermo* can easily accommodate a mock-didactic parody of a pedantic speaker not to be confused with Horace himself or his usual poetic persona. Moreover, finding features [5] and [6] in the *Ars Poetica*—otherwise attested in the *Satires* but not in the *Epistles*—accords well with dating the *Ars Poetica* to the period just after *Sat.* II, as was suggested in *Chapter 2*.

For now, having adumbrated several key features of how a new reading can result from this "paradigm shift" in the way we view the genre of the *Ars Poetica*, we can stop and summarize our efforts in this book as having mainly concerned the background and external features of the poem.[33] Its title was

---

[31]H. Dubrow, *Genre* (London and New York 1982) 28-30 (cf. p. 29: "often the Chinese-box arrangement of genre within genre that we observed in *The Jew of Malta* is a reflection of a pattern writ large in the literary system of the period: frequently when two forms assume the relationship of genre and counter-genre they enact their dialogue within poems of either genre as well as in the larger literary culture"); A. Fowler, op. cit. (*supra* n. 2) 179-188. At pp. 188-190, Fowler discusses how "many satiric works can be looked on as hybrid." See also the brilliant treatment of generic "inclusionism" in R. L. Colie, *The Resources of Kind. Genre-Theory in the Renaissance,* ed. by B. K. Lewalski (Berkeley and Los Angeles, 1973) 76-128.

[32]Lines 21-34, on which see E. Fraenkel, *Horace* (Oxford 1957) 341-348; W. S. Smith, Jr., "Horace Directs a Carouse," *TAPA* 114 (1984) 255-271, at pp. 263-266. On the σύμμικτον in the poetry of Horace, see L. Ferrero, *La 'Poetica' e le poetiche di Orazio, Univ. Torino Pubb. Fac. Lettere e Filosofia* 5, fasc. 1 (1953) 80-89; Nisbet and Hubbard, *Horace: Odes Book I* (Oxford 1970) xi-xxvi, discuss the mixed features of Horace's *Odes*; and see also J. E. G. Zetzel, "Re-creating the Canon: Augustan Poetry and the Alexandrian Past," *Critical Inquiry* 10 (1983) 83-105.

[33]The concept of a *paradigm shift* I borrow from T. S. Kuhn, *The Structure of Scientific Revolutions* (Chicago 1962^1, 1970^2). For an introduction to Kuhn and the reception of his work, see B. Barnes, *T. S. Kuhn and Social Science* (London 1982). On p. xiv Barnes discusses the terminological controversies surrounding the term paradigm, which he defines simply as "an accepted problem-solution in science, a particular concrete scientific achievement." Though devised by Kuhn with reference

probably something like *Ars Poetica*, not *Epistula ad Pisones*. It almost certainly has nothing to do with *Epistles* II but was an independent work in the corpus, written in the period 24-20 B.C. Generically, it resembles the parodic monologues of *Sat.* II and displays other characteristics of the genre of *sermo*. We have traced the imbroglios arising from these fundamental and intertwined problems back to their sources and have seen—at the very least—that our arguments do not have to keep moving in the same circles. By a variety of approaches we have certainly found new passages in. Whether they also lead out in the directions I have indicated is, of course, for others to determine.

The invocation of paradigm theory at this late point in our discussion is perhaps not unexpected in a work that began with a discussion of the importance of titles. A new paradigm for *Ars Poetica* interpretation such as that sketched here is, to be sure, very much in keeping with the aesthetics of postmodernism, a time aptly called by Malcolm Bradbury the "age of parody."[34] Yet this may just as easily be a case of the way in which anachrony can serve the ends of diachrony by sensitizing us to ancient precedents for seemingly modern developments, since, in the case at hand, "the parodic tone recently adopted in criticism"[35] can be traced back to ancient sceptics like Timon of Phlius. Moreover, the late Renaissance (or, better, Counter-Reformation) paradigm of "saving" the poem's authority as a poetic rulebook by inventing a generic excuse for its lack of method was itself no less anachronic.[36] Similarly the Romantics' indifference to the *Ars Poetica* was a consequence of their rebellion against a rule-based approach to artistic creativity.[37] The theologian, Hans Küng, has emphasized how paradigm shifts generally involve as much continuity as discontinuity.[38] Such is certainly true in the present case: the new parodic paradigm, far from invalidating earlier models of *Ars Poetica* interpretation, explains how they are possible. But that is another story.

---

to the physical sciences, the concept of paradigm has in the meantime been found useful in other branches of scholarship, including the humanities and theology.

[34]"An Age of Parody," *Encounter* 55 (1980) 44.

[35]The title of a stimulating article on recent trends in criticism by G. L. Ulmer in *New Literary History* 13 (1982) 543-560.

[36]For the impact of the Counter Reformation on critical theory see C. Dejob, *De l'influence du Concile de Trente sur la littérature et les beaux-arts chez les peuples catholiques* (Paris 1884); G. Toffanin, *La fine dell'umanesimo* (Milan 1920).

[37]Cf., e.g., F. Schlegel, "Von der Wiedergeburt der neuern Poesie," *Über das Studium der Griechischen Poesie. 1795-97,* vol. 1 in E. Behler (ed.), *Kritische Friedrich-Schlegel-Ausgabe* (Paderborn, Munich, Vienna 1979) 350: "Das Talent kann die Theorie nicht verleihn, und nie hat die Griechische Theorie den Zweck und das Ideal des Künstlers bestimmt...." On Romantic literary theory and its cultural context, see M. H. Abrams, *The Mirror and the Lamp* (New York 1953).

[38]"Paradigm Change in Theology," in *Paradigm Change in Theology,* ed. H. Küng and D. Tracy (Edinburgh 1989) 29-31.

APPENDIX I

Key Documents for the Renaissance Theory That the *Ars Poetica* Is an Epistle

Since the sixteenth-century texts referred to in *Chapter 1* are by no means available in the collections of even very good university libraries, I reprint the key passages here.

[1] *Marini Becichemi Scodrensis Epistolicarum Quaestionum Centuria* (Brescia 1504) (unpaginated; printer not indicated). Caput duodecimum (pp. 59-67):

...Opus est eum, qui diligenter scribere epistolas velit: simplicem et perspicuam materiam proponere. Et neque resscare neque producere supra quam oportere. Et exornare optima elocutione, non dictionibus turgidis et asperis sed attico more loqui et modice. Perspicuitas ornet literas: et gratia dictionum florida....Et Demetri Phalerii sententia: In tenui humilique dicendi genere epistolam versari; cuius dicendi modus, et stilus gracilis esse debet....Solutior epistolae compositio esse debet: unde Fabius: Est igitur ante omnia oratio alia iuncta atque contexta. Soluta alia qualis in sermone et epistolis: nisi cum aliquid supra naturam suam tractant: ut de philosophia, de republica, similibus....Proverbia sint in ea crebra: Quibus accepta congruaque de qua agitur materia ita sapienter scribi opinantur: Quod in epistolis utcunque versu custodit Horatius: quod epistola sicut proverbium, quiddam commune ac vulgare sit. Qui sententias scribit et adhortationes non similis videtur narranti per epistolam: sed per consilium. Qui decore sententiarum epistolam cupit implere non iam (dicit Demetrius) loquentis similitudinem gerit: sed struentis aliquid. Et Dionysius sententias non pertinere ad epistolas clamat. Quare Seneca olim insectati sunt: ut supra tetigi. Nec hodie incessere desinunt eruditorum plurimi: quod disputationes pro epistolis scripserit....

[2] *Francisci Robortelli Utinensis Paraphrasis in Libellum Horatii, Qui Vulgo De Arte Poetica Inscribitur,* 19 pages, printed after *Francisci Robortelli Utinensis, in Librum Aristotelis De Arte Poetica, Explicationes* (Florence, in officina Laurentii Torrentini Ducalis Typographi, 1548)[1] 1:

Etsi libellus hic de Arte poetica inscribitur, videturque ipsa inscriptio prae se ferre, methodo quadam certa et ordinata, praeceptiones tradi scribendorum poematum. Puto tamen ego inscriptionem illam a Poeta non fuisse appositam, neque cum ad Pisones scriberet, in animo habuisse artem ullam aut methodum praeclarae huius facultatis tradere. Nam si id efficere voluisset, ab initio omnia repetens, et naturae ordinem sequens, praeceptiones omnes singillatim esset persecutus, quae ad poema recte scribendum spectant: hac enim commodiore ratione potuisse artem poeticae facultatis describi ab Horatio satis patet. Nunc vero quis credat hominem doctissimum de arte tam confuse fuisse locutum. Sic igitur omnino sentiendum. Cum Romae sua aetate videret Horatius esse multos, qui poetae nomen sibi falso vindicabant, diesque totos in scribendo aliquo poemate ponebant, et ignorabant tamen quanto in versibus scribendis opus esset artificio, diutius illorum inscitiam, et insolentiam aequo animo cum ferre non posset, sermone hoc satis longo cum Pisonibus habito, eos reprehendere instituit, ac singillatim omnes illorum errores demonstrare: quibus patefactis, dat operam ut eos ad meliorem frugem reducat, praescribens rectam rationem scribendi poematis: in eo praesertim, in quo eos labi animadvertat. Quo fit, ut ego existimem, temere a multis libellum hunc in plurimas ac minutissimas praeceptiones fuisse dissectum, cum miro ordine totus liber sit contextus, perpetuamque prae se ferat et minime interpellatam de eadem re orationem, ut conabor ostendere, ac facile perspicient ii et probabunt, opinor, qui cognitam habent scribendi rationem, quam ubique secutus est Horatius in Epistulis.

[3] *In Epistulam Q. Horatii Flacci De Arte Poetica Jasonis de Nores Cyprii Ex Quotidianis Tryphonis Gabrielii Sermonibus Interpretatio.* (Venice, apud Aldi filios, 1553).[2] From the Preface to the reader; fol. 3v-4v:

Quare adductum me primum sciant ad inscriptionem operis immutandam non levioribus de causis, et quod formam epistolae, non autem libri, in quo praecepta

---

[1]This has been republished in the series *Poetiken des Cinquecento*, vol. 8, ed. B. Fabian (Munich 1968). In 1555, the work was reprinted in Basle, "per Ioannem Hervagium Iuniorem."

[2]There was a second Venetian edition, "apud A. Arrivabenum," in 1553, according to Mills, 15 (nr. 157). A Paris edition was published in 1554, "ex Typographia M. Dauidis."

tradantur, vel ex ipso principio prae se ferat, et quod in vetustis exemplaribus epistolarum libros subsequatur, et quod etiam summi, et praestantissimi homines ita sentiant, et quod minime nobis obstet Quintiliani testimonium, ut nonnullis videtur. Nam etsi librum appellat Quintilianus, non est cur non possit inter epistolas enumerari, cum et illae ab Horatio in libros digestae fuerint. Quod vero de arte poetica idem Quintilianus adiungat, nihil commoveor, cum et in epistolis praecepta de aliqua re tradi possint, ab eodemque in omnibus paene et in iis ad Scaevam et Lollium praecipue iam factum videatur, in quibus breviter eos instituit, qua ratione apud maiores facile versarentur....Quod autem attinet ad ea, quae ab iis, qui interpretantur, ante ipsam interpretationem afferi solent: ea propter eam causam omittemus, quia ordinem in arte poetica demonstranda non ita servatum ab Horatio videmus, ut ab aliis, qui de aliqua re documenta litteris tradiderunt. Est ille quidem peracutus et diligens in praecipiendi ratione, ordinem tamen, cum epistolam scribat, non ita custodit, ac tuetur ut si librum scriberet. Amat enim epistola familiaritatem quandam. At nimis accuratus ordo ad severitatem potius, quam ad familiaritatem propendet. Itaque non est alienum ab epistolae decoro non imitari rationem illam, quam ceteri servant in explicanda doctrina. Quo circa ne nos quidem operam non necessariam adhibebimus in ordine declarando.....

[4] *M. Antonii Mureti In Horatium Scholia* (Venice, apud P. Manutium, 1555), tom. 2, p. 967:

Poteram facile supersedere hoc labore annotandi quicquam in epistulam de arte poetica: tot enim eruditi homines in eam scripserunt scribuntque quotidie, ut ea brevi pauciores aliquanto versus, quam interpretes, habitura videatur.

[5] *Q. Horati Flacci Sermonum Libri Quattuor...a Dionysio Lambino Monstroliensi Ex Fide Novem Librorum Manu Scriptorum Emendati, Ab Eodemque Commentariis Copiosissimis Illustrati* (Lyons, apud Ioan. Tornaesium, 1561), 480. The second edition was published in Paris in 1568. Where the readings differ, the variant of the first edition is in parentheses. Angular brackets indicate my supplements.

De inscriptione autem huius libri, seu epistolae ad Pisones de arte poetica paucis tibi, lector, sententiam quorundam doctorum nostrae aetatis virorum, et meam aperiam. Illi igitur eam inter epistolas referendam, et ita inscribendam censent, *ad Pisones*: nihil praeterea: a quibus dissentire difficile est. Nam, quin ad Pisones scripta sit [est], quemadmodum aliae ad Maecenatem, aliae ad Iulium Florum: una, ad Augustum: aliae, ad alios, negari id quidem non potest. Neque est, quod quemquam vel longitudo, vel argumentum moveat. De longitudine facilis responsio est. Epistola ad Augustum, epistola ad Iulium Florum lib. 2 longae sunt. Platonis, et M. Tull<ii> epistolae quaedam sunt longissimae, quae tamen non idcirco epistolarum nomen amittunt. De argumento, suo quaeque epistola constat argumento: neque debent esse inanes epistolae. Exempli causa, in prima epistola lib. I hortatur ad studium philosophiae, eius utilitatem demonstrat, vulgi opinionem sequi vetat....Possem eodem modo singulas epistolas percurrere, et quodnam sit cuiusque argumentum indicare, nisi vererer, ne alieno loco haec videar inculcare. Sic igitur Horatius in hac ad Pisones epistola, cum de omni poeseos genere disputat, tum maxime de comoedia, et tragoedia utilissima praecepta dat, non ut philosophus, sed ut poeta. Haec me ratio adduxit, ut putem cum multis doctis, primum hanc esse epistolam, deinde simpliciter ita esse inscribendam *epistola ad Pisones*. Quod si quis volet, haec addi, *de arte poetica*, non reclamabo, modo idem facere licere in omnibus epistolis, fateatur. Ego interea tamen receptam consuetudinem, vulgique opinionem in eo secutus sum, quod hunc titulum *de arte poetica* retinui: in altero, quod epistolam appellavi, doctorum sententiam approbavi [probavi].

[6] Iulius Caesar Scaliger, *Poetices Libri Septem* (Lyons, apud A. Vincent, 1561).

(a) From Preface, p. iii (unpaginated):

Nam et Horatium Artem quum inscripsit, adeo sine ulla docet arte, ut Satyrae propius totum opus illud esse videatur.

(b) p. 336:

Age vero quando non solum Satyra ipsa, verum etiam quodvis opus scripturaque simplex esse debet et unum: neque in Satyris, neque in Epistulis, at ne in Poetica quidem, in qua hoc ipsum praecipit, observavit.

[c] p. 338:

Haec est Horatii ars: quam si praeceptores nostri nobis olim ad hunc modum partiti essent, eius sane facies nota fuisset, ita ut aliunde auxilium petendum esse intelligeremus.

Appendix I: Key Texts for the Epistle-Theory 105

[7] Henricus Stephanus, *Diatribae De Suae Editionis Horatianae Accuratione, et Variis in Eum Observationibus* (Paris, apud H. Stephanum, 1575) 31-32:

DE ARTE POETICA liber ad Pisones, item Carmen, item Epistula dicitur. Atque illorum in numero qui Epistulam vocant, est Charisius. Sed hic certe eam absque adiectione sic appellat: atque adeo quidam verba illa De Arte Poetica non esse addenda contendunt: nihilo magis videlicet quam aliis epistulis titulus argumentum earum ostendens praefigitur. Sed enim uno eodemque loco ille grammaticus inscriptam etiam fuisse *De Arte poetica* hunc librum, vel potius *Artem poeticam*, declarat, cum de adverbio Impariter loquens, et versum hunc afferens *Versibus impariter iunctis,* etc. Terentius Scaurus in Commentariis in Artem poeticam, libro 10, Adverbium, inquit, figuravit [Charisius 263.9-12 Barwick]. Quae cum ita sint, varie olim quoque inscriptum fuisse hunc librum existimo. Ad me certe quod attinet, si nominem Epistulam, non libenter addiderim *De arte poetica*: sed tantum *ad Pisones* adiungere Epistulae appellationi malim. Alioqui *De arte poetica librum* vel *libellum*, aut *carmen*, aut *poematium* dixerim. Nisi forte quispiam ignotam illis fuisse hanc vocem poematium existimet. Verum haec adeo parvi esse momenti iudico (quamvis longis aliorum disceptationibus agitata) ut mihi propemodum de lana caprina contentio haec esse videatur.

[8] *In Q. Horatii Flacci Venusini Librum De Arte Poetica Aldi Manutii Paulli F. Aldi N. Commentarius* (Venice, Apud Aldum, 1576), on p. i of the (unpaginated) Prolegomena:

Antequam Horatii librum de Arte poetica (sic enim a veteribus inscribitur, Quintiliano lib. VIII. cap. 3 Prisciano, Diomede lib. III. cap. 1., Donato in Ter. Ad. act. 5. sc.3, Servio in Virg. Aen. lib. I et Probo: quamquam Charisius inter epistulas referat lib. II) aggrediamur explanare; definiendum videtur, quid Poetica sit, et unum ne, an plura Poematum genera.

[9] *Commentarii In Artem Poeticam Horatii, confecti ex Scholis Io. Sturmii. Nunc primum editi, opera et studio Ioannis Lobarti Boruβi.* (Argentorati, Excudebat Nicolaus Vvyriot, 1576) 1-3:

...Quod autem quidam genus huius scripti, volunt esse ἐπιστολικὸν: quidam διδασκαλικὸν. Sciendum, si scripsit Horatius ad Pisones, fuisse epistolam, si vero recitavit praesentibus Pisonibus, non iam esse epistolam, sed διδασκαλικὸν. Quicquid tandem sit hoc scriptum Horatii, sive epistola, sive διδασκαλία: est ars poetica, docens quomodo faciendus sit λόγος ποιητικός:

ostendens qua ratione possis esse poeta, qua I ratione possis vultum poeticum repraesentare.

Qui scriptum hoc referunt inter epistolas, utuntur hac una ratione, quia scilicet missum sit ad Pisones. Quemadmodum enim illa Horatii, quae inscripta sunt ad viros illustres et amicos: ad Maecenatem, ad Numicium, ad Augustum, ad Julium Florum, et ad alios, epistolae dicuntur: ita et hoc epistolam dici volunt. Sed haec eorum ratio infirma est, Cicero libros de Oratore misit ad Q. fratrem, non tamen singuli libri sunt epistolae: et liber de Claris oratoribus, ad Brutum scriptus est, non tamen pro epistola habetur. Alia est ratio quae me movet, ut fere accedam ad illorum opinionem. Liber primus epistolarum Horatii, habet supra mille versus; liber secundus vix quingentos: si huic secundo addas hunc de arte poetica, qui est etiam quingentorum prope versuum, secundus erit par primo. Hac ratione puto hanc epistolam tertiam, esse partem secundi libri epistolarum. Ista sunt ingeniosa, sunt subacuta, studium habent novitatis. Est et tertia ratio, quamobrem possit haberi pro epistola. Illa ad Augustum libro 2. epistolarum est λογική, est sermonis, agit de poetis. Ad Iulium Florum epistola item magna ex parte est λογική, continet praecepta de poetis. Sic hoc opus totum est λογικὸν, plenum praeceptis poeticis, de oratione scil. poetarum. Si ergo epistolae dicuntur, quae inscriptae sunt. Augusto, et Iulio I Floro libro 2. epistolarum: cur non est et hoc scriptum, epistola diceretur. Hae duae posteriores meae sunt opiniones ut putem esse epistolam. Sed mihi antiquam retinere placet inscriptionem: HORATII DE ARTE POETICA LIBER et hanc libenter retineo (I) honoris et dignitatis caussa. Ostendit enim haec inscriptio, in hoc libro res maximas tradi. Non res parva est posse poetam facere. Inter omnes enim scriptores, perfectissimi et consummatissimi sunt poetae.....(II) Propter utilitatem, quia unum verbum habet argumentum totius operis. (III) Propter veritatem. Totus enim hic liber est τεχνικὸς: tradit artem poeticam integram.

[10] *Henrici Stephani Schediasmatum Variorum*, Liber Primus (Paris, apud H. Stephanum, 1578) 78-79:

Nec verbum verbo curabis reddere, fidus Interpres [*Ars Poetica* 133-134]. Quotusquisque est enim qui hunc versum Horatii statim in ore non habeat et auctoritate eius nitatur ut verbum verbo reddere, fidi interpretis non esse probet? At ego illis qui in ea sunt opinione non suffragari sed refragari hunc versum Horatii, et contrarium ei quod dicunt, illo probari, atque adeo quod illo probatur, verissimum esse, contendo: esse nimirum fidi interpretis, verbum verbo, quantum fieri potest, reddere. I Sed quoniam nunc satis est eam quam dico fuisse Horatii mentem ostendere, lectorem moneo subesse huic versui familiarem illi poetae ellipsin particulae Ceu vel Tanquam, aliusve huiusmodi: et intellegi debere, Nec verbum verbo reddere curabis, tanquam fidus interpres. Id est, Perinde acsi fidum interpretem agere velles. Vel, fidi interpretis officio fungi. Tantum enim abest ut Horatius ei quem compellat, et cui praecepta dat, neget fidi esse interpretis verbum verbo reddere, ut contra diligentiam hanc, seu diligentem operam, fido interpreti relinquendam esse dicat. Esse autem morem Horatii, relinquere subaudiendam illam vocabulam, multis exemplis docui in quaedam Diatriba ex iis quas operibus huius poetae in mea editione subiunxi. Atque hanc meam observationem ante multos annos Dionysio Lambino communicavi, cum Patavii degeremus....

APPENDIX II

Calculating the Odds of Finding Matched Pairs of Trend Lines in the Lyrics and Hexameters

Our fourth criterion for determining whether we have found a good chronometer for Horace's poetry is that the effect we are measuring is not the result of chance (see above, p. 27). In this Appendix, I will show that chance is probably not responsible for our discovery of four function words with similar trend lines in the hexameters and lyrics.

Since our sample consists of the sixteen function words satisfying the requirement of frequency, we have to do with a small sample, since n < 30. Four of the sixteen members of our sample display the categorical characteristic of similar trend lines in the lyrics and hexameters; twelve do not. We must thus determine whether finding a sample in which—at first glance—25% of the members may be classified as having the required characteristic is statistically significant or not. The test appropriate to making this determination is the binomial test.[1] The formula for this test is:

$$P(X) = \frac{n}{X!(n-X)!} \pi^X (1-\pi)^{n-X}$$

where **P** means probability, **X** the number of observations in sample-size **n** classified in the required way, and π is the proportion of **n** that we expect to be classified as **X**. To solve this equation with **n** = 16 and **X** ≤ 16, we need to know π.

The value of π is dependent on a typology of line types: to know the percentage of matched lyric-hexameter patterns that are theoretically possible—

[1] See A. Agresti and B. Finlay, *Statistical Methods for the Social Sciences* (San Francisco and London, 1986²) 142-146.

and hence to calculate how many we ought to find given sixteen chances—we need to determine how many combinations of lyric and hexameter trend lines can occur. To perform these calculations, we need a model of line-types.

The very simplest model of line-types is one that standardizes the interval values of the points constituting a line. The simple model is good enough for our purposes because, by standardizing intervallic values, it gives us a sharp reduction of line-types, hence simplifying the task of classification but also making it more difficult to achieve statistical significance. The simple model is thus quite practical for the case at hand. It gives us, as we will see in a moment, 9 three-point and 81 five-point line types (3^5), whereas a model only modestly more complex—one in which we distinguish two interval increments and decrements on the Y axis—yields an unworkable 125 three-point and 3,125 (5^5) five-point line types with 390,625 combinations of 3- and 5-point line types.

In the simple model, each point on a line may be followed by one of three new points: a point of greater value (+); a point of the same, or roughly the same, value (0); and a point of lesser value (-). Thus, from any existing point or line of x points, we may generate three new lines of $x + 1$ points. The simplest line has two points with three types (positive slope, no slope, and negative slope: Types I-III, not shown). From the two-point lines, we may generate nine three-point lines, as follows:

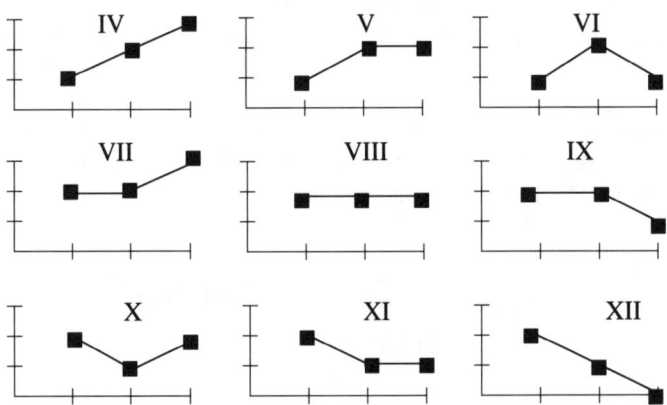

TABLE α: TYPES OF POTENTIAL PATTERNS IN HORACE'S USE OF FUNCTION WORDS IN THE LYRICS

Since in this study we are using three books of Horatian lyrics (*Epodes*, *Carm*. I-III, and *Carm*. IV), the shapes in TABLE α provide the typology for the lyrics. We begin our numeration with Type IV, because the complete typology of lines begins with the three two-point lines that generate our nine three-point lines. It may bear repeating that in designing this typology, we are not at all concerned with the

Appendix II: The Odds of Finding Matched Pairs of Trend Lines   111

values of actual points on the lines, simply in the mere quantitative relationship of successive points.

Horace's hexameters consist of five works (combining the *Satires* and placing the *Ars Poetica* after *Epistles* I, as implied above in TABLE VII and as seen in TABLE K), and so we move now to the five-point lines. These may be generated from the three-point lines by the same procedure, omitting, for the sake of space, an intermediary generation of twenty-seven four-point lines, from which we derive the 81 five-point line types, such as the following:

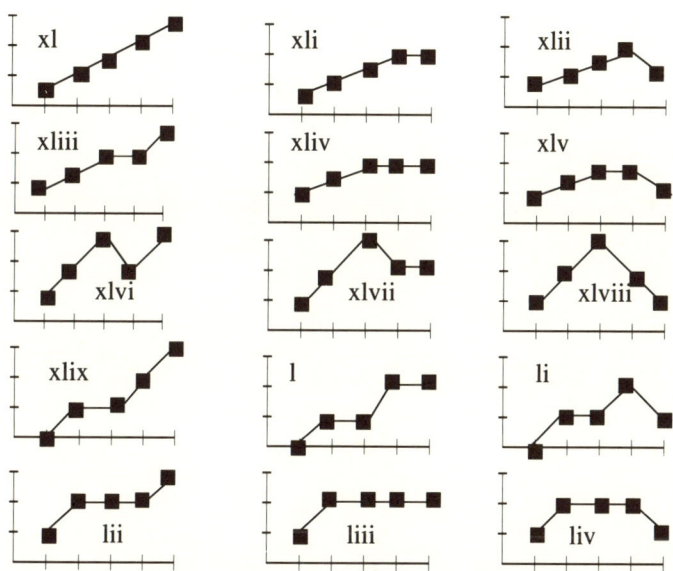

TABLE β: TYPES OF POTENTIAL PATTERNS IN HORACE'S USE OF FUNCTION WORDS IN THE HEXAMETERS

We begin numbering this set at xl and end at cxx, since there are altogether thirty-nine two-, three-, and four-point line ancestors to the five-point lines. From TABLE β, it it easy to see that five-point type xl can be considered equal to three-point type IV; five-point type xlviii can be equated to three-point type VI; etc. The generating principle of such equivalences is symmetry, which is achieved by the insertion of the fourth point between the first and second point of the three-point line and the addition of the fifth point between the second and third point of the three-point line. We will call these equivalences the set {centered}, or {C}.

Since we are disregarding interval values in this model, it is important to recognize another possible generating principle for equivalence: asymmetry. Two asymmetrical conversions are possible. The first, in which we may imagine the two new points to be added in between points one and two of the three-point line, we will call the set {left}, or {L}. In a second conversion, the two new points are added between the second and third points of the three-point line. This set, asymmetical to the right, we call {R}. Note that it makes no difference whether we visualize our two additional points as being inserted between the preexisting points of the three-point line (as we have done) or before/after the end-points of the three-point line.

From this it follows that there are nine five-point lines in each of the three sets that are exactly equivalent to the nine three-point lines. It also follows that, having converted each three-point type into a five-point equivalent, we can also establish three 81 x 81 matrices—one for each set {L}, {C}, and {R}—measuring the degree of similarity of all five-point lines to each other. The method of measurement is simply the subtraction of one type from another, absolutizing the remainder. If the remainder is 0, the lines are exactly equivalent; if the remainder is 1, they differ slightly at one point; etc. The smaller the remainder, the more similar the lines. Establishing an objective measurement of "similarity" is important, since in statistics, the similarity of line-types is potentially just as important as their exact equivalence.

For the 6,561 combinations of 5-point types in each set, we have the following histogram of equivalence/similarity:

REMAINDER	CASES	PERCENTAGE
0	81	.0123
1	432	.0658
2	1080	.1646
3	1632	.2487
4	1624	.2475
5	1088	.1658
6	480	.0731
7	128	.0195
8	16	.0024

TABLE γ: COMBINATIONS OF TWO 5-POINT LINE TYPES IN EACH SET

The "Percentage" column will help us determine the value of π in the formula of the binomial test. Since an equivalent or similar combination can be made by matching a given three-point line to a five-point line in any of the three sets, we must multiply the values in the "Percentage" column by three to establish the probability of finding a pair with these remainders. For example, given a three-point line and a five-point line, the odds of finding a exact match (i.e., remainder = 0) are .0123 x 3 = .0369. The odds of finding a similar pair with remainder 1 are much higher: .0658 x 3 = .1974. We can see immediately that similar pairs will prove nothing in our case, since .197 x 16 = 3.15: that is, all things being

Appendix II: The Odds of Finding Matched Pairs of Trend Lines 113

equal, we should expect at least 3 similar pairs among our 16 pairs of function words. We thus limit our search to exact pairs, of which we expect only .590 among our 16 words.

In looking through the five-point line sets for exact matches, we need the following table of the three- to five-point line-type conversions for each set:

TYPE =	{L}	{C}	{R}
IV	xl	xl	xl
V	xli	xliv	liii
VI	xlii	xlviii	lvii
VII	lxxix	lxxvi	lxvii
VIII	lxxx	lxxx	lxxx
IX	lxxxi	lxxxiv	xciii
X	cxviii	cxii	xciv
XI	cxix	cxvi	cvii
XII	cxx	cxx	cxx

TABLE δ: CONVERSION OF THREE-POINT LINE-TYPES TO THEIR EXACT FIVE-POINT EQUIVALENTS IN THE SETS {L}, {C}, AND {R}

The following table reports the remainders of the combinations of lyric and hexameter line-types for the function words with sufficient frequency to be investigated in this study. In boldface are the two words (*ad* and *sed*) with an exact correspondence; in capitals are the two words (*nec* and *per*) that are very similar (remainder = 1):

WORD	Lyric Pattern	Hex Pattern	(SET)	WORD	Lyric Pattern	Hex Pattern	(SET)
AD	X	xciv	{R}	non	IV	cii	
atque	IX	cxiv		nunc	II	lx	
aut	IX	cxiv		PER	X	xci	
cum	IX	cxv		**SED**	X	cxii	{C}
et	II	lxix		si	V	c	
iam	IV	lxiv		sic	VI	cvi	
in	VII	xlvi		ut	III	cxviii	
NEC	VI	lxix		vel	III	c	

TABLE ε: CLASSIFICATION OF FUNCTION WORD PATTERNS IN HORACE'S LYRICS AND HEXAMETERS

We now have all the information we need to determine the π-value and to run the binomial test. In testing the odds of calculating π on the basis of three 9 x 81 matrices of three-point and five-point combinations, we limit our calculation to the types of three-point lines that satisfy our third criterion of a potential chronometer (above, p. 27) that there be a trend in the variation of a word's frequency. Once we apply this requirement, fully five of our nine three-point types can be eliminated from consideration (Types V, VII, VIII, IX, and XI), for these types either imply no change in frequency at all (Type VIII) or else random variation. Two of the remaining four three-point types (IV and XII) are the same in all three five-point sets; we count them only once. The other two (VI, X) are different in all three sets, giving us six possible matches. Thus, out of a total of 729 possible combinations per set, we have globally 8 / 729, or .01097, possible combinations satisfying all our conditions. We can now solve the binomial test with a π-value of .01097 to see if our two exact equivalences are statistically significant:

	Prob. of X:	X or fewer:	X or more:
P(0)	0.838154	0.838154	1.000000
P(1)	0.148798	0.986952	0.161846
P(2)	0.012383	0.999335	0.013048
P(3)	0.000641	0.999976	0.000665
P(4)	0.000023	0.999999	0.000024
P(5)	0.000001	1.000000	0.000001
P(6)	0.000000	1.000000	0.000000
P(7)	0.000000	1.000000	0.000000
P(8-16)	0.000000	1.000000	0.000000

TABLE η: RESULTS OF BINOMIAL TEST, $N = 16$, $\pi = .01097$

In this test of the odds of finding two cases like *ad* and *sed*, the probability that chance alone is responsible is quite low—just 1.2%.

What about *per* and *nec*? It may be granted that chance alone may well have given us the similarity of their hexameter and lyric frequencies. However, when we see that the result of using all four of our function words as chronometers is a date for the *Ars Poetica* in a single period of Horace's life (24-20 B.C.), then the probability that mere randomness is at work is reduced—logically, if not statistically—for, if any or all of our four words were not valid chronometers, then we should expect them to indicate widely different dates for the *Ars Poetica*. This is not the case.

APPENDIX III

Piso in Pola. The Date of *Inscr. Ital.* X.I.81

As noted in the body of this study, three inscriptions from Pola mention a certain L. Calpurnius Piso Caesoninus, whom Sticotti recognized as the consul of 58 B.C. and father-in-law of Julius Caesar.[1] These monuments are of interest because, if datable, they permit us to determine the validity of Münzer's influential theory that Piso died shortly after the Battle of Mutina—a theory based on Piso's alleged absence from the historical record after April of 43 B.C.[2] Needless to say, Piso's survival well beyond Mutina is a necessary but not sufficient condition for my theory that he is the senior addressee of the *Ars Poetica*. *Inscr. Ital.* X.i.81, from a gate in the city wall, is the only inscription of the three found in a datable context. Neither it nor the other two inscriptions (cf. *fig. 1*) mentioning Piso were taken into account by Münzer. In this appendix, I will reargue the case that *Inscr. Ital.* X.i.81 is triumviral (42-31 B.C.),

---

[1] *Inscr. Ital.* X.i.65, 81, 708. See P. Sticotti, "Nuova rassegna di epigrafi romani," *AMSI* 30 (1914) 113-114. Sticotti's identification can be supported by the facts that the consul's family owned land in Illyria since the second century B.C. (cf. *infra*, n. 34), the inscription is late-Republican in style, and the city gate, contemporaneous with the city wall, can be dated to the 40s or 30s B.C. (cf. B. Forlati Tamaro *AMSI* 44 and 48, *infra*, n. 3) when the consul of 58 was the only known bearer of the name. On Sticotti, see A. Degrassi, "Pietro Sticotti," *AMSI* 55 (1954) 35-41 (= *Scritti vari*, vol. 4 [Trieste 1971] 187-192).

[2] *RE* III s.v. Calpurnius 90 (Stuttgart 1897) cols. 1387-1390. Münzer, of course, must himself be put into an historical context: the identification of the Piso of the three Pola inscriptions as the consul of 58 occurred almost two decades after Münzer was writing.

something necessitated by two recent studies by Fraschetti and Keppie that independently put the monument into the Caesarian period (46-44 B.C.).[3]

Dating the inscription is unfortunately not a straightforward matter, since it contains no explicit chronological indication. We must thus approach the problem by trying to find the most likely political and archaeological context into which the monument can be fitted. The political context at once supplies a solid *terminus post quem* and a somewhat more fluid *terminus ante quem*. In the inscription Piso and L. Cassius Longinus[4] are called *duoviri*, and the existence of this office in Pola presumes that the Roman colony, *Pietas Iulia*, also exists. Although this name, which is transmitted by Pliny,[5] may be incomplete or otherwise inaccurate, the epithet *Iulia* may be safely accepted as a constituent part of the colony's title. This gives us our *post quem*: after the three Caesarian colonies created at Capua in 59 B.C., no colony is known to have been called *Iulia* before Julius Caesar's foundations of the period 46-44.[6] A less firm *ante*

---

[3] A. Fraschetti, "La 'Pietas' di Cesare e la colonia di Pola," *AION* 5 (1983) 77-102; L. Keppie, *Colonisation and Veteran Settlement in Italy, 47-14 B.C.* (London 1983) 203-204.

Before 1983, it was long held that the colony at Pola was a triumviral foundation by Octavian: see T. Mommsen, "Die italischen Bürgercolonien von Sulla bis Vespasian," *Hermes* 18 (1883) 161-213, at p. 182; E. Pais, "Le colonie militari dedotte in Italia dai triumviri ad Augusto," *Museo italiano di antichità classica* 1 (1885) 56; E. Kornemann in *RE* IV s.v. Coloniae (Stuttgart 1900) col. 526; B. Forlati Tamaro, "Cenni preliminari sulle recenti scoperte archeologiche a Pola e Trieste," *AMSI* 44 (1932) 325; "La fondazione della colonia romana di Pola," *AMSI* 48 (1936) 243-246; A. Degrassi, "La data della fondazione della colonia romana di Pola," *AIV* 102 (1942-1943) 667-678 (= *Il confine nord-orientale dell'Italia Romana, Diss. Bernenses*, ser. I, fasc. 6 [1954] 60-68; *Scritti vari di antichità*, vol. 2 [Rome 1962] 913-924 [*N.B.* cited hereafter according to the *Diss. Bernenses* version]); E. Polaschek in *RE* XXI s.v. Pola (Stuttgart 1951) cols. 1219-1220; M. P. Charlesworth, *The Cambridge Ancient History*, vol. 10 (Cambridge 1966) 88; M. Zaninovic in *The Princeton Encyclopedia of Classical Sites* (Princeton 1976) 720. Degrassi specifically dated the founding of Pola to 42/41 and has been followed in this by B. Forlati Tamaro, *Pola* (Padua 1971) 14; E. Gabba, "Sulle colonie triumvirali di Antonio in Italia," *PP* 8 (1953) 101-110, at p. 110.

[4] On Longinus, see Münzer, *RE* III s.v. Cassius (65) (Stuttgart 1897) col. 1739; Longinus was identified as Cassius (65) by P. Sticotti, loc. cit. (*supra* n. 1), and this identification has been accepted by later scholars.

[5] *N.H.* 3.129 is our source for the name of the colony.

[6] Caesar's earlier colony at Capua came to be known as *Concordia Iulia Felix Augusta*, perhaps indicating that the earliest title was *Concordia Iulia*, as suggested by Mommsen, *CIL* X.1, p. 368. There is no reason to suppose the creation of any Caesarian colonies between 59 and 46. On the colonies of 46-44, see L. Keppie, op. cit. (*supra* n. 3) 49-58.

Appendix III: Piso in Pola 117

quem is provided by the bestowal of the title *Augustus* on Octavian in 27. After that date, Augustan colonies were generally, though not always, given the epithet *Augusta* or *Iulia Augusta*.[7] Although the absence of *Augusta* from Pola's name would seem to provide a solid enough *ante quem*, it is important to bear in mind that Pliny always omits *Augusta* from his references to colonies, unless the colony is founded at a new site with no preexisting name, leaving him no other recourse.[8] When we know that a *colonia Iulia* mentioned by Pliny is really a *colonia Iulia Augusta*, this is only because of local inscriptions giving a fuller title. In the case of Pola, we have no such inscriptions from the first century B.C. or A.D. so that we cannot be certain that Pola's full name did not contain the epithet *Augusta*. Thus—because such an inscription might someday turn up—in fixing our *ante quem* we cannot completely rule out the possibility of an Augustan (i.e., post-27 B.C.) foundation. For our purposes, this matters but little, since our main aim here is simply to show that Münzer's guess that Piso died just after the Battle of Mutina is likely to be wrong. However, if anyone someday makes the case for a *deductio* of Pola in the years just after 27 B.C., that will only help bolster our interpretation of the *Ars Poetica*.

Within the period 46-27 B.C. there are three moments at which we would expect a colony to have been planted at Pola; and, as might be expected, each possibility has found its scholarly advocate: (1) 46-44, by Julius Caesar[9]; (2) 42-41, by Octavian[10]; and (3) 41-31, by Octavian.[11] For purposes of refuting Münzer, it is not absolutely necessary to reject any of these dates: the context of *Inscr. Ital.* X.i.81 is a city gate known to be contemporary with the earliest city

---

[7]On the difficulties of interpreting colonial nomenclature see P. A. Brunt, *Italian Manpower 225 B.C.—A.D. 14* (Oxford 1971) 234-235; B. Galsterer-Kröll, "Untersuchungen zu den Beinamen der Städte des Imperium Romanum," *Epigraphische Studien* 9 (1972) 37-145, at pp. 65-66.

[8]Examples of the latter in Italy are Augusta Praetoria, Augusta Taurinorum, and Augusta Bagiennorum (for the archaeological evidence that these were not founded on preexisting sites, cf. *The Princeton Encyclopedia of Classical Sites* [Princeton 1976] 114, 116, 118). Outside Italy, Pliny's policy can be similar: cf. the case of *C(olonia) C(aesarina) A(ugusta) A(sido)* (*CIL* II.5407), called Asido Caesarina by Pliny in *N.H.* 3.30. Cf., in general, B. Galsterer-Kröll, op. cit. (*supra* n. 7) 57-59. This is an important point because in the period 46-27 B.C. Pola was not yet in reg. X Italia. Until *c.* 18-12 B.C., Pola and Istria formed part of Illyria; see Weiss in *RE* VIII s.v. Histria (Stuttgart 1913) cols. 2111-2112; E. Polaschek, op. cit. (*supra* n. 3) cols. 1219-1220; A. Degrassi, Review of Polaschek in *AMSI* n.s. 2 (1952) 226-227 (= *Scritti vari*, vol. 4 [Trieste 1971] 244-245).

[9]L. Keppie and A. Fraschetti, opp. citt. (*supra* n. 3).

[10]A. Degrassi, B. Forlati Tamaro, and E. Gabba, opp. citt. (*supra* n. 3).

[11]T. Mommsen, E. Pais, E. Kornemann, B. Forlati Tamaro (*AMSI* 44 and 48), M. P. Charlesworth, and M. Zaninovic, opp. citt. (*supra* n. 3).

walls of Pola.[12] These walls may be contemporaneous with the founding of the colony, or, as we will see, they may date from a few years later. Thus, even if the controversy over the founding of the colony at Pola should be settled in favor of 46-44, this does not necessarily mean that *Inscr. Ital.* X.i.81 cannot have been inscribed in the 30s. But does the colony date to the Caesarian period?

The odds are against such a date: Octavian/Augustus founded many more colonies that did Julius Caesar.[13] Caesar's colonies were concentrated in a few provinces—particularly in Africa and Spain[14] Augustus' were spread all over the empire.[15] Of the three kinds of colonies—civilian settlements, titular colonies, and veterans' settlements—Pola almost certainly falls into the first class. We know that, in provincial colonization, Caesar favored the last class, for he was, of course, mainly preoccupied with finding land for his veterans. Augustus was also heavily involved in settling veterans on the land.[16] He was, however, also more apt than Caesar to upgrade a *conventus civium Romanorum* into a *colonia*, reinforcing the Roman population with new settlers. Finally, Octavian was personally active in military campaigns on the Dalmatian coast, whereas Caesar did not live long enough to undertake his Balkan expedition. This puts Octavian, but not Caesar, in the immediate vicinity of Pola and makes an Octavian foundation more likely.

Against this background, we can appreciate why, before 1983, the consensus of scholars was that Pola became a colony under Octavian sometime between Philippi and Actium. What arguments did Keppie and Fraschetti bring forward in that year in favor of an earlier, Caesarian date?

Keppie begins by trying to disprove a triumviral date. He first claims that Degrassi probably erred in using the Arch of the Sergii in Pola as evidence of the settlement of military colonists in the town after Philippi. Granting that Piso would have been an excellent candidate to help either Caesar or Octavian organize the new colony because of his experience at Capua in 58, Keppie finds

---

[12]See B. Forlati Tamaro (*AMSI* 44 and 48), opp. citt. (*supra* n. 3).

[13]There are various scholarly estimates. The most conservative (i.e., pro-Caesarian) is perhaps that of F. Vittinghoff, *Römische Kolonisation und Bürgerrechtspolitik, Akad. Wiss. Mainz, Abh. Geistes- und Sozialwiss. Kl.* 14 (1951) 85, 125, who assigned thirty-one colonies to Caesar and seventy-five to Augustus (as counted by E. T. Salmon, *Roman Colonization Under the Republic* [London 1969] 193n264).

[14]Cf. P. A. Brunt, op. cit. (*supra* n. 7) 255-259; for Italy, see L. Keppie, op. cit. (*supra* n. 3) 43-58.

[15]See *Res Gestae* 16, referring only to the many provinces with Augustan military colonies and so understating the case for Augustus' overall colonizing (cf. G. Alföldy, "Caesarische und augusteische Kolonien in der Provinz Dalmatien," *Acta Antiqua* 10 [1962] 357-365, at p. 362).

[16]See P. A. Brunt, op. cit. (*supra* n. 7) 238.

a Caesarian date more likely "in that Piso is not known to have been alive after 43 B.C." Finally, the second duovir on *Inscr. Ital.* X.i.81, L. Cassius Longinus, as brother of the tyrannicide C. Cassius, is unlikely to have been reconciled with Octavian after Philippi, though Keppie does note that Longinus was pardoned by Antony.[17]

In rebuttal of Keppie, let us first note that he has not fully appreciated how Degrassi uses the Arch of the Sergii as chronological evidence.[18] Degrassi does not state that Pola was a military colony.[19] Establishing the family relationships of L. Sergius and C. Sergius (brothers) and of L. Sergius L. f. (son of L. Sergius), Degrassi uses the disbandment of Legio XXIX after Actium as a *terminus post quem* for the aedileship of L. Sergius L. f., which he dated to *c.* 25. Postulating a gap of at least ten years between the aedileships of father and son, Degrassi puts the founding of the colony in the year 35, at the latest. Degrassi then speculates that the gap between the aedileships was a few years greater, considering it unlikely that L. and Cn. Sergius would have colonized Pola when Lucius already had a grown-up child of military age. Degrassi's use of the inscriptions on the Arch of the Sergii can be criticized, but the point is not that Degrassi is wrong to use the arch's inscriptions for chronology, but that he has perhaps tried too hard to push the date back as far as he can toward 42/41. In fact, we can just as easily push the date forward a couple of years, e.g., by imagining that L. and Cn. Sergius did not arrive with the founders of the colony, but a few years later, or by not balking at the idea that L. Sergius L. f. was a teenager when his father settled in Pola.

The arguments about Piso and Longinus are also not compelling. Following Münzer's theory about Piso's demise just after Mutina is fallacious: Münzer wrote before Sticotti identified the Polan Piso as the consul of 58, so he could not take the material from Pola into account in his *RE* article; thus, following Münzer is a *petitio principii*. As for Longinus, it is likely that he was much more in Antony's debt than in Octavian's after his return from exile in Asia in 41 B.C., for it was Antony who permitted his return.[20] This can be taken as evidence supporting a triumviral date, for, invoking the model of the colonization of Capua (to be discussed in a moment in our critique of Fras-

---

[17]L. Keppie, op. cit. (*supra* n. 3) 204.

[18]Degrassi, op. cit. (supra n. 3) 66-68; cf. "Le iscrizioni dell'arco dei Sergii in Pola," in *Scritti vari*, vol. 4 (Trieste 1971) 179-185.

[19]All the evidence is against a military colony at Pola; cf. E. Polaschek, op. cit. (*supra* n. 3) col. 1246; in Degrassi's rather critical review of Polaschek (op. cit. [*supra* n. 8], he does not object to Polaschek's observation "daß Pola eine Militärcolonie gewesen wäre erfährt von keiner Seite eine Bestätigung."

[20]Appian *Bell. Civ.* 5.7.28.

chetti), we might have expected Pola to be organized precisely by a stand-in for each of the two principal triumvirs, if not by the principals themselves.[21]

Fraschetti's case is similar but more complex. Taking aim at Degrassi's date of 42/41, which is based on the theory that the colony's epithet *Pietas* makes most sense just after Octavian's vengeance against his father's murderers at the battle of Philippi,[22] Fraschetti tries to show that a date in Caesar's lifetime is also consistent with the slogan *Pietas*.[23] Of course, such a demonstration cannot be decisive, since it does not, per se, rule out a date after Philippi, nor does Fraschetti deny the possibility that Degrassi is correct. Moreover, Fraschetti's case for 46-44—which is dependent on Caesarian coins issued in 48/47 with *Pietas* themes[24]—is not very cogent. Had it been possible to argue that Pola was founded in 49/48, this evidence might have been useful: however, as Fraschetti is well aware, "Caesar's work in founding colonies did not begin before 46."[25] A date of 46/45 is, however, quite damaging to Fraschetti's thesis, since precisely in that period the slogan of *Pietas* was appropriated by the Pompeian side in the civil war. At Munda in 46, *Pietas* was the battle cry of the Pompeians, *Venus* of the Caesarians.[26] Starting the year after Munda, Sex. Pompeius made *pietas* toward his father a hallmark of his propaganda, especially through his coinage.[27] Moreover, as used by Caesar in 48/47, *pietas* was by no means a novel concept and hence one that the Romans of the period might primarily associate with him. It had been used in several political contexts during the previous fifty years and even during the early triumviral period could be exploited by Antony just as easily as Octavian, judging from the numismatic evidence.[28] The epithet, *Pietas*, then, cannot be a decisive factor in determining

---

[21]Cf. A. Fraschetti, op. cit. (*supra* n. 3) 93, who astutely recognizes the political balancing act involved in the colonization of Capua whereby a Caesarian law favored settlement of Pompeian veterans and was implemented, first in 58 by Piso—i.e., Caesar's father-in-law—and then, then next year, by Pompey himself.

[22]A. Degrassi, op. cit. (*supra* n. 3) 62.

[23]A. Fraschetti, op. cit. (*supra* n. 3) 80-90.

[24]Fraschetti refers (p. 86) to denarii minted by the Caesarian D. Iunius Brutus Albinus and by Caesar himself; for the coins, see, respectively, nrr. 450, 2 and 452, 3 in M. H. Crawford, *Roman Republican Coinage* (Cambridge 1974).

[25]P. A. Brunt, op. cit. (*supra* n. 7) 101; Z. Yavetz, *Julius Caesar and his Public Image* (London 1983) 144; L. Keppie, op. cit. (*supra* n. 3) 50. Note that Fraschetti himself writes, "nell'ambito delle due datazioni proposte (47 e primi mesi del 46 o ultimi mesi del 46 e 45 a.C.) la più probabile appare forse la seconda" (p. 102).

[26]Appian *Bell. Civ.* 2.104.

[27]Cf. nrr. 477, 3a-3b; 478, 1a; 479, 1 in M. H. Crawford, op. cit. (*supra* n. 24).

[28]Cf. M. H. Crawford, op. cit. (supra n. 24) nrr. 308 (108/107 B.C.); 374 (81 B.C.); 477, 3a-3b; 494, 19 (42 B.C.—triumviral); 516, 4 (41 B.C.—M. Anto-

the circumstances of Pola's foundation. If anything, it tends to rule out Caesar and the period 46/45.

Fraschetti next turns his attention to Piso and Longinus, whom he cogently identifies as the *primi duoviri* of the new colony, invoking the parallel case of [L.] Marcus Phi[lippus], the consul of 56 or suffect consul of 38 B.C., who served as *primus duovir* of Herculaneum.[29] Recalling the "compromise" of Capua in 59-57, whereby a notable Caesarian (Caesar's father-in-law, Piso) alternated with Pompey himself as *duovir* of the new colony (see above, n. 21), Fraschetti is perplexed to find such marginal and politically ambivalent men as Piso and Longinus serving as *duoviri* in Pola in the early triumviral period. For Fraschettti, their collaboration in Pola makes much more sense in the mids-40s, when both were ardent Caesarians.

Now, first of all, it should be noted that Fraschetti assumes that the "Capuan compromise" represented a norm in colony foundation, whereas it may only reflect the exceptional and very delicate political situation of the early years of the first triumvirate. In the 40s and 30s, so many colonies were founded that we cannot assume that the same standards obtained in the section of *primi duoviri* (always assuming that Piso and Longinus were such). Secondly, Fraschetti misrepresents Syme on Piso and the historical record when he says that Syme characterized Piso as "as ex-Caesarian turned independent."[30] When he made that statement, Syme was referring to Piso in the fall of 44 B.C.; later, he saw Piso acting as a wise statesman trying to mediate between Antony and the Senate on the eve of the battle of Mutina (April, 43): "Piso stood for concord and good sense when others...were for extreme measures against Marcus Antonius in 44 and 43."[31] Such a stance must have endeared him to Antony as much as it renewed Cicero's old feud with his erstwhile nemesis.[32] It certainly would have positioned him well to serve the interests of Antony and Octavian in the early years of the second triumvirate. As for Longinus, a strong supporter of Caesar in the civil war, his flaw was the guilt-by-association that came from being the brother of the tyrannicide, C. Cassius. Syme called him "a brother of

---

ny). For *pietas* in the Julio-Claudian period, see S. Weinstock, *Divus Julius* (Oxford 1971) 258-259.

[29] A. Fraschetti, op. cit. (*supra* n. 3) 91. As Fraschetti notes, the proposal that Piso and Longinus were *primi duoviri* of the colony was first advanced by B. Forlati Tamaro (*AMSI* 48), op. cit. (*supra* n. 3) 245.

[30] A. Fraschetti, op. cit. (*supra* n. 3) 96, incorrectly citing R. Syme, *The Roman Revolution* (Oxford 1939) 136 (not 36, as is reported at 96n78).

[31] R. Syme, "Piso and Veranius in Catullus," *C&M* 17 (1956) 129-134, at p. 130 (= *Roman Papers,* vol.1, ed. E. Badian [Oxford 1979] 300); cf. *The Augustan Aristocracy* (Oxford 1986) 330.

[32] Cf. *Ad Fam.* 12.4.1 (on Piso's embassy to Antony in January, 43): "nihil autem foedius Philippo et Pisone legatis, nihil flagitiosius."

the assassin but a Caesarian in sympathy."[33] When circumstances after Caesar's murder made it dangerous for Longinus to tarry in Rome, he fled to Asia, where, as noted above (cf. n. 20) Antony met and pardoned him in 41. Finally, Piso and Longinus are thus by no means an odd couple to be serving as *duoviri* (whether *primi duoviri* or not) in *Iulia Pietas* in the triumviral period. It was undoubtedly possession of large family estates in the neighborhood of Pola that made their choice seem not only appropriate but logical.[34]

That neither Keppie nor Fraschetti has succeeded in finding a good reason to date the colony to the Caesarian period does not, of course, mean that no good argument or decisive piece of evidence may someday be found, nor does their failure to move the date back necessarily justify our leaving it where it was before 1983. To make further progress, we need to put Pola into a larger geopolitical and archaeological context, which will present us with some evidence less ambiguous than colonial nomenclature and late-republican prosopography.

Doubtless influenced by Pola's later incorporation in regio X Italia, scholars from Mommsen onwards have viewed the problem of Pola in the context of colonial policy in Italy.[35] Yet, as noted above (see n. 8), Pola belonged to Illyria, not to Italia, when it was colonized. Seen as a key base on the eastern Adriatic coast,[36] Pola naturally takes its place among Octavian's colonial foundations or augmentations after his successful Illyrian campaign of 35-33.[37] In fact, all up and down the coast from Epidaurum to Tergeste we find evidence of Roman colonization in the period 47-33. The result was a well-spaced series of colonial ports, each one about sixteen to twenty-four hours sailing time from the next.[38] Here are the approximate sailing distances in Roman miles:

---

[33]R. Syme, op. cit. (*supra* n. 30) 132n3. On Longinus in the civil war, see Caesar *Bell. Civ.* 3.34-35.

[34]Evidence for these properties is discussed by J. Sasel, "Probleme und Möglichkeiten onomastischer Forschung," *Acta CIEGR* 4 (1964) 352-368, at pp. 363-367; cf. also M. Pavan, "Ricerche sulla provincia romana di Dalmazia," *Mem. Ist. Ven.* 32 (1958) 21, 231-233; J. J. Wilkes, *Dalmatia* (London 1969) 331.

[35]Cf. T. Mommsen, op. cit. (*supra* n. 3) 182, 192, 212; L. Keppie, op. cit. (*supra* n. 3) 203-204.

[36]As suggested, in passing, by M. P. Charlesworth, op. cit. (*supra* n. 3) 88 and J. J. Wilkes, op. cit. (*supra* n. 34) 57: "in Illyricum, the achievement of Octavian was modest and solid rather than spectacular....On the coast colonies were established at Pola in Istria and Iader in Liburnia, and the older Caesarian colonies, Salona, Narona, and Epidaurum, were strengthened by new settlements."

[37] On the campaign, see Wilkes, op. cit., (*supra* n. 34) 46-56.

[38]Roman ships averaged from 2.5 knots (unfavorable winds) to 5.0 knots (favorable); see L. Casson, *Ships and Seamanship in the Ancient World* (Princeton 1971) 281-296. It is possible that Senia should also be included here, but whether the

Appendix III: Piso in Pola

Tergeste—Pola: 70 miles
Pola—Iader: 95 miles
Iader—Salona: 100 miles
Salona—Narona: 70 miles
Narona—Epidaurum: 115 miles

This looks very much like a planned occupation of a strategically vital and agriculturally rich coast,[39] reminiscent of the early Roman maritime colonies on the Tyrhennian coast and—more pertinently—of Caesar's coastal colonies in Spain and Africa. About the date of most of these colonies, the same debate rages that we have seen in the case of Pola,[40] and so trying to settle the date of Pola by recourse to such slippery data might seem to exemplify explaining *obscurum per obscurius*. This is not, I think, the case, because once these towns are considered together—as, to my knowledge, they never have been—common features emerge that can be decisive for breaking up chronological and other logjams.

One feature common to all the eastern Adriatic colonies is a peculiar form of centuriation in which we find the usual 200-iugera unit with a rather unusual orientation on a NW-SE axis and with a rare system of *limites* demarcated by means of stones.[41] We might explain this distinctive form in one of two ways: either it results from a long-standing regional tradition, or it is the signature of a team of *agrimensores* active at all the sites. In the second case,

---

colony there (known from Tac. *Hist.* 4.45) dates from our period (46-27 B.C.) or later is not known; see the discussion in G. Alföldy, op. cit. (*supra* n. 15) 362-363.

[39] Strabo 7.5.10 attests the area's economic advantages and implies that Roman appreciation of the Illyrian coast was a relatively recent development: τοιαύτη δ'οὖσα ὠλιγωρεῖτο πρότερον ἡ Ἰλλυρικὴ παραλία, τάχα μὲν καὶ κατ' ἄγνοιαν τῆς ἀρετῆς, τὸ μέντοι πλέον διὰ τὴν ἀγριότητα τῶν ἀνθρώπων καὶ τὸ λῃστρικὸν ἔθος.

[40] On Tergeste, see L. Keppie, op. cit. (*supra* n. 3) 201-202; on the Dalmatian towns, see J. J. Wilkes, op. cit. (*supra* n. 34) 207 (Iader), 220-238 (Salona), 245-252 (Narona), 252 (Epidaurum).

[41] Cf. J. Bradford, *Ancient Landscapes* (London 1957) 175-193; M. C. Panerai, "Territori centuriati nelle provincie: il caso di Zara," in: *Misurare la terra: Centuriazione e coloni nel mondo romano*, vol. 1 (Modena 1984) 235-240, at p. 238: "elemento caratterizzante della *pertica* è l'aspetto singolare dei *limites*: questi sono costituiti da muretti di pietra, conservatisi nel corso dei secoli come confini dei campi coltivati. Questa configurazione particolare dei limiti è una peculiarità di tutta la *Provincia Dalmatiarum*: 'ubi saxa collecta ab utrisque partibus limites dederunt' (Grom. Vet., *Liber coloniarum* 2, p. 241)." For parallel cases at Cosa and in Africa vetus see F. Castagnoli, "La centuriazione di Cosa," *MAAR* 24 (1956) 149-165, at p. 161n14.

centuriation can be a factor for chronology, since the *agrimensores* will have worked along the Illyrian coast for a relatively short period of time, and if we can date one colony's centuriation, we have an approximate date for them all.[42] The second explanation seems more likely because such regional traditions are hard to find elsewhere. Of the Illyrian centuriations in question, we do have one firmly datable case—Iader, where the colony was planted in the late thirties or early twenties.[43] Such a period—after Octavian's triumph in the Illyrian campaign of 35-33—is more probable in any case on geopolitical grounds than the period 46-41, since centuriation presumes good enough regional security for exploitation of the territory and hinterlands of a colony. On the other hand, the successful conclusion of the Illyrian war provides more than a mere *post quem*: centuriation generally coincides with the founding of a colony.[44] These considerations make it likely that the colony at Pola was founded by Octavian in the period 33-27 B.C.

A second common element in these colonies is a town wall in stone. As with centuriation, we can use any firmly datable examples to give us a probable time frame for all the sites. Two walls are securely datable by inscriptions giving credit to Octavian/Augustus for their construction: Tergeste (33/32 B.C.) and Iader (27 B.C.).[45] It is sometimes assumed that, like centuriation, the construction of permanent city walls was immediately undertaken when a new colony was started; but this was not always the case. Fanum Fortunae, a triumviral colony, received its first walls decades later in 9/10 A.D.[46] Closer to home, we know that the first colony at Salona had no wall in the 40s B.C. To resist a seige by the Pompeian commander, M. Octavius, the pro-Caesarian

---

[42] On the use of centuriation for chronology, see, in general, G. Chouquer, M. Clavel-Lévêque, and F. Favory, "Catasti romani e sistemazione dei paesaggi rurali antichi," in *Misurare la terra: Centuriazione e coloni nel mondo romano* (Modena 1984), vol. 1, 39-49, at pp. 41, 42, 45.

[43] The date of the colony is approximately given by *CIL* 3.2907, where Octavian is called Imp(erator) Caesar Divi F(ilius) Aug(ustus).

[44] This is a scholarly commonplace: cf., e.g., F. Vittinghoff, op. cit. (*supra* n. 13) 24, "Landvermesserung durch Agrimensoren und Landzuweisung durch kaiserliche Beauftragte waren die selbstverständliche Begleitakte jeder Kolonisation." See also E. T. Salmon, op. cit. (*supra* n. 13) 20. Here I should note that Salona—already a colony in the Caesarian period—is not necessarily counter-evidence of a single centuriation project because it was a double foundation. For the evidence, see J. W. Kubitschek, *Imperium Romanum Tributim Discriptum* (Prague, Vienna, Leipzig 1889) 236; cf. G. Alföldy, op. cit. (*supra* n. 15) 358; J. J. Wilkes, op. cit. (*supra* n. 34) 223-224. The centuriation at Salona may thus be associated with the second colony of the late 30s.

[45] Tergeste: *Inscr. Ital.* X.iii.20-21; Iader: *CIL* III.2907.

[46] Cf. *CIL* XI.6219; A. Degrassi, op. cit. (*supra* n. 3) 52.

Appendix III: Piso in Pola

Salonians quickly erected a wooden wall that successfully served its purpose.[47] Beseiged on all sides by five *castra*, and protected only by their wooden towers, the Salonians thwarted Octavius' seige, forcing him to withdraw. This episode gives us concrete information showing why stone walls were not a high priority for new colonies, at least on the Illyrian coast. They could be built later, in times of greater peace and security, as happened at Tergeste and Iader. The parallels of these two cities—and the perpendicular of the absence of a stone wall at Salona in the 40s—make a date of *c.* 33 B.C. the likeliest for the walls of Pola, too.

In conclusion, we may say that the rare form of centuriation found at Pola and other Roman colonies on the Illyrian coast suggests that the territory of Pola and of the other cities was first exploitable after Octavian's Dalmatian campaign of the 30s firmed up Roman control of the hinterland; the date of the founding of Iader supports such a chronology of the centuriation project. At the same time the fields were centuriated, the town centers were protected by a permanent wall, as is securely known from the datable examples at Tergeste and Iader. Since their names appear on the oldest gate of the wall at Pola, the *duoviri* Piso and Longinus must have held office in the colony in the late 30s when the wall was built, and Münzer's theory of Piso's demise soon after Mutina — proposed, as we have seen, before Sticotti identified Piso in Pola—can be considered highly unlikely.

---

[47]Caesar *Bell. Civ.* 3.9: "Sed celeriter cives Romani ligneis effectis turribus his sese munierunt et, cum essent infirmi ad resistendum propter paucitatem hominum crebris confecti vulneribus, ad extremum auxilium descenderunt servosque omnes puberes liberaverunt et praesectis omnium mulierum crinibus tormenta effecerunt."

ABBREVIATIONS AND BIBLIOGRAPHY

The select bibliography that follows lists most of the books and articles mentioned in the footnotes as well as some other works I found useful but never had occasion to cite. Editions of ancient authors other than Horace, modern guidebooks, articles in standard reference works, and the like have not been included. Works quoted in *Appendix I* are also not listed here. Abbreviations are generally those used in *L'Année Philologique*. Unless otherwise noted, the text of Horace used throughout this study is the Teubner of D. R. Shackleton Bailey (Stuttgart 1985). The reader desiring a fuller list of publications on the *Ars Poetica* may consult the bibliographies found in Brink, I-III and Rudd, 234-239.

The following special abbreviations used in the notes are listed here; these works are not listed separately in the bibliography that follows:

Brink, I	= Brink, C. O. *Prolegomena to the Literary Epistles, Horace on Poetry*, vol. 1 (Cambridge 1963).
Brink, II	= Brink, C. O. *The 'Ars Poetica', Horace on Poetry*, vol. 2 (Cambridge 1971).
Brink, III	= Brink, C. O. *Epistles Book II: The Letters to Augustus and Florus, Horace on Poetry*, vol. 3 (Cambridge 1982).
Carettoni, I	= Carettoni, G. "La decorazione pittorica della Casa di Augusto sul Palatino," *MDAI(R)* 90 (1983) 373-419.
Carettoni, II	= Carettoni, G. *Das Haus des Augustus auf dem Palatin* (Mainz 1983).
Mills	= *Quintus Horatius Flaccus Editions in the United States and Canada as They Appear in the Union Catalog of the Library of Congress* (Mills College, California 1938).
Rudd	= Rudd, N. *Horace. Epistles Book II and Epistle to the Pisones ('Ars Poetica')* (Cambridge 1989).

~~~

Abrams, M. H. *The Mirror and the Lamp: Romantic Theory and the Critical Tradition* (New York 1953).
Adams, H. "Titles, Titling, and Entitlement To," *JAAC* 46 (1987) 7-21.
Agresti, A., and Finlay, B. *Statistical Methods for the Social Sciences* (San Francisco and London 1986^2).

Alföldy, G. "Caesarische und augusteische Kolonien in der Provinz Dalmatien," *Acta Antiqua* 10 (1962) 357-365.
Allen, W., Jr. "O fortunatam natam...," *TAPA* 87 (1956) 130-146.
Anderson, W. S. *Essays on Roman Satire* (Princeton 1982).
Archer, W. C. "The Paintings in the Alae of the Casa dei Vettii and a Definition of the Fourth Pompeian Style," *AJA* 94 (1990) 95-123.
Armstrong, D. *Horace* (New Haven 1989).
Asmis, E. "Philodemus' Epicureanism," *ANRW* II.36.4 (Berlin 1990) 2369-2406.
Atkins, J. W. H. *Literary Criticism in Antiquity*, 2 vols. (Cambridge 1934).
Baldwin, B. "The Date, Identity, and Career of Vitruvius," *Latomus* 49 (1990) 425-434.
Barbet, A. *La peinture murale romaine. Les styles décoratifs pompéiens* (Paris 1985).
Bardon, H. *La littérature latine inconnue*, 2 vols. (Paris 1952, 1956).
Barnes, B. *T. S. Kuhn and Social Science* (London 1982).
Barwick, K. "Zur Geschichte und Rekonstruction des Charisius-Texts," *Hermes* 59 (1924) 322-355.
Bastet, F. L. *Proposta per una classificazione del terzo stile pompeiano*, prima parte, *Archeologische Studiën van het Nederlands Instituut te Rome* 4 (1979).
Batteux, l'Abbé. *Les quartre poetiques d'Aristote, d'Horace, de Vida, de Despréaux*, vol. 1 (Paris 1771).
Becker, C. *Das Spätwerk des Horaz* (Göttingen 1963).
Bentler, P. M. *Theory and Implementation of EQS: A Structural Equations Program* (Los Angeles 1985).
Berger, K. "Hellenistische Gattungen in Neuen Testament," *ANRW* II.25.2 (Berlin 1984) 1031-1432.
Beyen, H. *Die pompejanische Wanddekoration vom zweiten bis zum vierten Stil*, 2 vols. (Den Haag 1938, 1960).
———. "Les domini de la villa de la Farnésine," in *Studia C. Vollgraff* (Amsterdam 1948) 3-21.
Blake, M. E. *The Pavements of Roman Buildings of the Republic and Early Empire*, *MAAR* 8 (1930).
———. *Ancient Roman Construction in Italy from the Prehistoric Period to Augustus* (Washington 1947).
Borda, M. *La pittura romana* (Milan 1958).
Borzsák, S. *Q. Horati Flacci Opera* (Leipzig 1984).
Bowersock, G. W. "A Date in the *Eighth Eclogue*," *HSCP* 75 (1971) 73-80.
———. "The Addressee of the *Eighth Eclogue*: A Response," *HSCP* 82 (1978) 201-202.
Bradbury, M. "An Age of Parody," *Encounter* 55 (1980) 36-53.
Bradford, J. *Ancient Landscapes* (London 1957).
Bradshaw, A. "Horace *in Sabinis*," *Collection Latomus* 206 (1986) 160-186.
Bragantini, I., and De Vos, M. *Le decorazioni della villa romana della Farnesina, Museo Nazionale Romano: Le Pitture*, II.1 (Rome 1982).
Brink, C. O. "Horatian Poetry. Thoughts on the Development of Textual Criticism and Interpretation," *Wolfenbütteler Forschungen* 12 (1981) 7-17.
Brunt, P. A. *Italian Manpower 225 B.C.—A.D. 14* (Oxford 1971).
Budd, F. E. "A Minor Italian Critic of the Sixteenth Century: Jason Denores," *Modern Language Review* 22 (1927) 421-434.
Campbell, A. Y. *Horace. A New Interpretation* (London 1924).
Casson, L. *Ships and Seamanship in the Ancient World* (Princeton 1971).

Castagnoli, F. "La centuriazione di Cosa," *MAAR* 24 (1956) 149-165.
Champlin, E. "The Life and Times of Calpurnius Piso," *MH* 46 (1989) 101-124.
Chouquer, G.; Clavel-Lévêque, M. and Favory, F. "Catasti romani e sistemazione dei paesaggi rurali antichi," in *Misurare la terra: Centuriazione e coloni nel mondo romano*, vol. 1 (Modena 1984) 39-49.
Christes, J. *Der frühe Lucilius. Rekonstruktion und Interpretation des XXVI. Buches sowie von Teilen des XXX. Buches* (Heidelberg 1971).
Cichorius, C. *Römische Studien* (Leipzig 1922).
Clark, M. E. "Horace, *Ars Poetica* 75-78. The Origin and Worth of Elegy," *CW* 77 (1983) 1-5.
Clay, E. (ed.). *Sir William Gell in Italy. Letters to the Society of Dilettanti* (London 1976).
Colie, R. L. *The Resources of Kind. Genre-Theory in the Renaissance*, ed. by B. K. Lewalski (Berkeley and Los Angeles 1973).
Crawford, J. M. *Tullius Cicero: The Lost and Unpublished Orations*, Hypomnemata 80 (1984).
Crawford, M. H. *Roman Republican Coinage*, vol. 1 (Cambridge 1974).
Crowther, N. B. "The Collegium Poetarum," *Latomus* 32 (1973) 575-580.
Cruquius, J. *Q. Horati Flacci Opera Omnia* (Antwerp 1578).
Cugusi, P. *Evoluzione e forme dell'epistolografia latina nella tarda repubblica e nei primi due secoli dell'impero con cenni sull'epistolografia preciceroniana* (Rome 1983).
Culler, J. *Structuralist Poetics* (Ithaca, New York 1975).
Cupaiuolo, F. *Tra poesia e poetica* (Naples 1966).
Damerau, F. J. "The Use of Function Word Frequencies as Indicators of Style," *Computers and the Humanities* 9 (1975) 271-280.
Dane, J. A. *Parody. Critical Concepts versus Literary Practices, Aristophanes to Sterne* (Norman and London 1988).
D'Anna, G. "La cronologia dell'epistola di Orazio ad Augusto," *Vichiana* 12 (1983) 121-135.
Degrassi, A. "La data della fondazione della colonia romana di Pola," *AIV* 102 (19-42-1943) 667-678 (= *Il confine nord-orientale dell'Italia Romana, Diss. Bernenses*, ser. I, fasc. 6 [1954] 60-68; *Scritti vari di antichità*, vol. 2 [Rome 1962] 913-924).
———. "Pietro Sticotti," *AMSI* 55 (1954) 35-41 (= *Scritti vari di antichità*, vol. 4 [Trieste 1971] 187-192).
———. "Le iscrizioni dell'arco dei Sergii in Pola," *Scritti vari di antichità*, vol. 4 (Trieste 1971) 179-185.
Dejob, C. *Marc-Antoine Muret, un professeur français en Italie dans la seconde moitié du XVIe siècle* (Paris 1881).
———. *De l'influence du Concile de Trente sur la littérature et les beaux-arts chez les peuples catholiques* (Paris 1884).
Delarue, F. "Le *Thyeste* de Varius," *Collection Latomus* 187 (1985) 100-123.
Delplace, C. *Le griffon de l'archaïsme à l'époque impériale*, Études de philologie, d'archéologie et d'histoire anciennes, l'Institut Historique Belge de Rome 20 (1980).
D'Episcopo, F. *Aulo Giano Parrasio, fondatore dell'Accademia Cosentina* (Cosenza 1982).
Dilke, O. A. W. "When Was the *Ars Poetica* Written?" *BICS* 5 (1958) 49-57.

———. "The Interpretation of Horace's 'Epistles,'" *ANRW* II.31.3 (Berlin 1981) 1837-1865.
Dillenburger, G. *Q. Horatii Flacci Opera Omnia* (Bonn 1848²).
Dionisiotti, A. C. Review of M. De Nonno, *La grammatica dell'Anonymus Bobiensis (GL* I 533-565 Keil) in *JRS* 74 (1984) 202-205.
Dorighello, F. *Q. Horatius Flaccus Illustratus* (Padua 1774).
Dubrow, H. *Genre* (London and New York 1982).
Duckworth, G. E. "Horace's Hexameters and the Date of the *Ars Poetica,*" *TAPA* 66 (1965) 73-95.
Duret, L. "Dans l'ombre des plus grands: I. Poètes et prosateurs mal connus de l'époque augustéenne," *ANRW* II.30.3 (Berlin 1983) 1447-1560.
Ehrhardt, W. *Stilgeschichtliche Untersuchungen an römischen Wandmalereien von der späten bis zur Zeit Neros* (Mainz 1987).
Elmore, J. "A New Dating of Horace's *De Arte Poetica,*" *CP* 30 (1935) 1-9.
Fantazzi, C. (ed.). *Juan Luis Vives, De conscribendis epistolis. Critical Edition with Introduction, Translation and Annotation, Selected Works of J. L. Vives,* vol. 3 (Leiden 1989).
Fantham, E. *Seneca's Troades* (Princeton 1982).
Ferrero, L. *La 'Poetica' e le poetiche di Orazio, Università di Torino Pubblicazioni della Facoltà di Lettere e Filosofia* vol. 5, fasc. 1 (1953).
Fisher, J. "Entitling," *Critical Inquiry* 11 (1984) 286-298.
Fiske, G. C. *Lucilius and Horace. A Study in the Classical Theory of Imitation* (Madison 1920).
Floriani Squarciapino, M. "Il fregio del tempio del divo Giulio," *RAL* 12 (1957) 270-284.
Forlati Tamaro, B. "Cenni preliminari sulle recenti scoperte archeologiche a Pola e Trieste," *AMSI* 44 (1932) 323-338.
———. "La fondazione della colonia romana di Pola," *AMSI* 48 (1936) 243-246.
———. *Pola* (Padua 1971).
Forni, G. "La tribù Velina degli Aquileiesi," *Antichità Alto-adriatiche* 35 (1989) 51-81.
Fowler, A. *Kinds of Literature. An Introduction to the Theory of Genres and Modes* (Oxford 1982).
Fraenkel, E. *Horace* (Oxford 1957).
Frank, T. *Catullus and Horace* (New York 1928).
Franke, C. *Fasti Horatiani* (Berlin 1839).
Fraschetti, A. "La 'Pietas' di Cesare e la colonia di Pola," *AION* 5 (1983) 77-102.
Frischer, B. *At Tu Aureus Esto. Eine Interpretation von Vergils 7. Ekloge* (Bonn 1975).
Fumaroli, M. "Genèse de l'épistolographie classique: rhétorique humaniste de la lettre, de Pétrarque a Luste Lipse," *Revue d'histoire littéraire de la France* 78 (1978) 886-905.
Gabba, E. "Sulle colonie triumvirali di Antonio in Italia," *PP* 8 (1953) 101-110.
———. "Political and Cultural Aspects of the Classicistic Revival in the Augustan Age," *CA* 1 (1982) 43-65.
Galsterer-Kröll, B. "Untersuchungen zu den Beinamen der Städte des Imperium Romanum," *Epigraphische Studien* 9 (1972) 37-145.
Gantar, K. "Die Anfangsverse und die Komposition der horazischen Epistel über die Dichtkunst," *SO* 39 (1964) 89-98.
Gargiulo, T. "Epicureismo romano," in ΣΥΖΗΤΗΣΙΣ, vol. 2 (Naples 1983) 635-648.

Gell, Sir W. *The Topography of Rome and Its Vicinity* (London 1834[1], 1846[2]) 2 vols.
Gigante, M. *Scetticismo e epicureismo* (Naples 1981).
———. "La chiusa del quarto libro 'Della morte' di Filodemo," in *Ricerche filodemee* (Naples 1983[2]) 163-234.
———. "Atakta V," *CronErc* 14 (1984) 125-134.
———. *La bibliothèque de Philodème et l'épicurisme romain, Coll. d'Etudes Anciennes* 56 (Paris 1987).
———. "Filodemo tra poesia e prosa," *SIFC* 82 (1989) 129-151.
Gigante, M. and Capasso, M. "Il ritorno di Virgilio a Ercolano," *SIFC* 7 (1989) 3-6.
Gilbert, N. W. *Renaissance Concepts of Method* (New York 1960).
Gold, B. *Literary Patronage in Greece and Rome* (Chapel Hill and London 1987).
Gori, F. *Viaggio pittorico-antiquario da Roma a Tivoli e Subiaco* (Rome 1855).
Grafton, A. *Joseph Scaliger. A Study in the History of Classical Scholarship*, vol. 1 (Oxford 1983).
Grayston, K., and Herdan, G. "The Authorship of the Pastorals in Light of Statistical Linguistics," *New Testament Studies* 6 (1959-60) 1-15.
Griffin, D. "Satiric Closure," *Genre* 18 (1985) 173-189.
Grimal, P. *Essai sur l'Art poétique d'Horace* (Paris 1968).
Gruen, E. *Studies in Greek Culture and Roman Policy, Cincinnati Classical Studies* 7 (Leiden 1990).
Guattani, G. A. *Monumenti Sabini*, tom. 3 (Rome 1830).
Habinek, T. *The Colometry of Latin Prose* (Berkeley 1985).
Hack, R. K. "The Doctrine of Literary Forms," *HSCP* 27 (1916) 1-65.
Heath, M. *Unity in Greek Poetics* (Oxford 1989).
Hendrickson, G. L. "Are the Letters of Horace Satire?" *AJP* 18 (1897) 313-324.
Hering, W. *Die Dialektik von Form und Inhalt bei Horaz* (Berlin 1979).
Holloway, J. "Two Projects to Illustrate Allan Ramsay's Treatise on Horace's Sabine Villa," *Master Drawings* 14 (1976) 280-286.
Horsfall, N. M. "The Collegium Poetarum," *BICS* 23 (1976) 79-95.
———. "Horace, *Sermones* 3?" *LCM* 4.6 (1979) 117-119.
———. "Horace, *Sermones* 3: Epilegomena," *LCM* 4.8 (1979) 169-171.
———. "Some Problems of Titulature in Roman Literary History," *BICS* 28 (1981) 103-114.
———. "Poets and Patron Reconsidered," *Ancient Society* (Macquarie) 13 (1983) 161-166.
Hurde, R. *Q. Horatii Flacci Epistolae ad Pisones et Augustum*, 2 vols. (Cambridge 17-57).
Hutcheon, L. *A Theory of Parody. The Teachings of Twentieth-Century Art Forms* (New York and London 1985).
Immisch, O. *Horazens Epistel über die Dichtkunst, Philologus* Suppl. 24.3 (1932).
Jehasse, J. *La renaissance de la critique* (Saint-Etienne 1976).
Jocelyn, H. D. "Horace, *Epistles* I," *LCM* 4.7 (1979) 145-146.
———. "Studies in the Indirect Tradition of Plautus' *Pseudolus*," *Vir Bonus Discendi Peritus. Studies in Celebration of Otto Skutsch's Eigthieth Birthday, BICS* Suppl. 51 (1988) 57-72.
Keller, O., and Holder, A. *Q. Horati Flacci Opera* (Jena 1925).
Kenny, A. J. *The Computation of Style* (Oxford 1982).
Kent, T. *Interpretation and Genre. The Role of Generic Perception in the Study of Narrative Texts* (London and Toronto 1986).
Keppie, L. *Colonisation and Veteran Settlement in Italy, 47-14 B.C.* (London 1983).

Kiessling, A., and Heinze, R. *Q. Horatius Flaccus. Briefe* (Berlin 1957[5]).
Kilpatrick, R. S. *The Poetry of Friendship. Horace, Epistles I* (Edmonton, Alberta 1986).
―――. *The Poetry of Criticism. Horace Epistles II and Ars Poetica* (Edmonton, Alberta 1990).
Kirkland, J. H. *Horace. Satires and Epistles* (Chicago 1893).
Koerte, A. "Augusteer bei Philodem,"*RhM* 45 (1890) 172-177.
Kubiak, D. P. "Piso's Madness (Cic. *In Pis.* 21 and 47)," *AJP* 110 (1989) 237-245.
Kubitschek, J. W. *Imperium Romanum Tributim Discriptum* (Prague, Vienna, Leipzig 1889).
Kuhn, T. *The Structure of Scientific Revolutions* (Chicago 1962[1], 1970[2]).
Küng, H. "Paradigm Change in Theology: A Proposal for Discussion," in *Paradigm Change in Theology*, ed. H. Küng and D. Tracy (Edinburgh 1989) 3-31.
Lakoff, G., and Turner, M. *More than Cool Reason. A Field Guide to Poetic Metaphor* (Chicago and London 1989).
Landolfi, L. "Tracce filodemee di estetica e di epigrammatica simpotica in Catullo," *CronErc* 12 (1982) 137-143
La Penna, A. *Orazio e l'ideologia del principato* (Turin 1963).
Leach, E. "Patrons, Painters, and Patterns," in *Literary and Artistic Patronage in Ancient Rome*, ed. B. Gold (Austin 1982) 135-173.
―――. *The Rhetoric of Space. Literary and Artistic Representations of Landscape in Republican and Augustan Rome* (Princeton 1988).
Lebek, W. *Verba Prisca, Hypomnemata* 25 (1970).
Lefèvre, E. "Horaz und Maecenas," *ANRW* II.31.3 (Berlin 1981) 1987-2029.
Levy, S. G. *Inferential Statistics in the Behavioral Sciences* (New York 1968).
Lindsay, K. L., and Mackay, T. W. "An Authorship Study of the Pauline Epistles," an unpublished paper given at the *International Conference on Computers in the Humanities* (Brigham Young University, June 26, 1985) 1-33.
Ling, R. E. "Studius and the Beginnings of Roman Landscape Painting," *JRS* 67 (1977) 1-16.
Lugli, G. "La villa sabina di Orazio," *Monumenti Antichi* 31 (1926) cols. 456-598.
McCuaig, W. *Carlo Sigonio. The Changing World of the Late Renaissance* (Princeton 1989).
McGann, M. J. *Studies in Horace's First Book of Epistles*, Collection Latomus 100 (1969).
Magnien, M. "Le statut d'Horace dans les Poetices Libri VII," in *La statue et l'empreinte. La poétique de Scaliger*, ed. by C. Balavoine and P. Laurens (Paris 1986) 19-33.
Manazzale, A. *Viaggio da Roma a Tivoli, Palestrina, Frascati, ed altri contorni di Roma* (Roma 1817).
Marriott, I. "The Authorship of the *Historia Augusta*," *JRS* 69 (1979) 65-77.
Mayor, J. E. B. "On Licentia Poetica," *Journal of Philology* 8 (1879) 260-262.
Meerwaldt, J. D. "Adnotationes in Epistulam ad Pisones ad picturam praesertim collatam pertinentes," *Mnemosyne* 4 (1936-37) 151-163.
Michaelis, A. "Die Horazischen Pisonen," *Commentationes Philologae in honorem Theodori Mommseni* (Berlin 1877) 420-432.
Mielsch, H. *Die römische Villa* (Munich 1987).
Moles, J. "Cynicism in Horace *Epistles* I," *PLLS* 5 (1985) 33-60.
Mommsen, T. "Die italischen Bürgercolonien von Sulla bis Vespasian," *Hermes* 18 (1883) 161-213.

Montagna Pasquinucci, M. "La decorazione architettonica del tempio del Divo Giulio nel Foro Romano," *Monumenti Antichi* 48 (1973).
Morgan, A. Q. *Literary Detection* (New York 1978).
Morricone Matini, M. L. *Roma: Reg. X Palatium, Mosaici Antichi in Italia* (Rome 1967).
Morris, E. P. *Horace. The Epistles* (New York 1911).
Mosteller, F., and Wallace, D. L. *Inference and Disputed Authorship: 'The Federalist'* (Reading, Mass. 1964).
Mueller, L. *Quintus Horatius Flaccus* (Leipzig 1880).
Nettleship, H. "The de Arte Poetica of Horace," *JP* 12 (1883) 43-61.
Neudling, C. L. *A Prosopography to Catullus, Iowa Studies in Classical Philology* 12 (1955).
Nibby, A. "Viaggio antiquario alla Villa di Orazio, a Subiaco, a Trevi, presso le sorgenti dell'Aniene," *Memorie Romane di Antichità e di Belle Arti* (Pesaro 1827) 3-81 (= *Analisi storico-topografico-antiquaria della carta de' dintorni di Roma*, tomo 3 [Rome 1849²]).
Nisbet, R. G. M., and Hubbard, M. *A Commentary on Horace: Odes Book I* (Oxford 1970).
———. *A Commentary on Horace: Odes Book II* (Oxford 1978).
Oakman, R. L. *Computer Methods for Literary Research* (Athens, Ga. 1980, 1984).
Ong, W. *Ramus, Method and the Decay of Dialogue* (Cambridge, Mass. 1958).
Opelt, I. *Die lateinischen Schimpfwörter und verwandte sprachliche Erscheinungen* (Heidelberg 1965).
Orelli, I. G.; Baiter, J. G; and Mewes, W. *Q. Horatius Flaccus*, vol. 2 (Berlin 1892).
Panerai, M. C. "Territori centuriati nelle provincie: il caso di Zara," *Misurare la terra: Centuriazione e coloni nel mondo romano*, vol. 1 (Modena 1984) 235-240.
Pasoli, E. *Le epistole letterarie di Orazio* (Rome, n. d.).
Perret, J. *Horace* (Paris 1959²).
Petrini, P.-A. *La poetica di Orazio restituita all'ordine suo* (Rome 1777).
Pigeaud, J. "La greffe du monstre," *REL* 66 (1988) 197-218.
Pöhlmann, E. "Charakteristika des römischen Lehrgedichts," *ANRW* I.3 (Berlin 1973) 813-901.
Pontani, F. M. *Orazio. Arte poetica* (Rome 1953).
Potez, H., and Préchac, F. (eds.). *Lettres galantes de Denys Lambin, 1552-1554, Publications de la Faculté de l'Université de Lille* 6 (1941).
Rawson, E. *Intellectual Life in the Late Roman Republic* (Baltimore 1985).
Reams, L. E. "The Strange Case of Sulla's Brother," *CJ* 82 (1987) 301-305.
Reckford, K. J. *Horace* (New York 1969).
Reichert, J. "More Than Kin and Less Than Kind: The Limits of Genre Theory," in *Yearbook of Comparative Criticism* 8 (1978) 57-79.
Renouard, A. A. *Annales de l'imprimerie des Estienne* (Paris 1837).
Riccoboni, A. *De Gymnasio Patavino Commentariorum Libri Sex* (Padua 1598).
Rizzo, G. E. *Pitture dell'Aula Isiaca di Caligola, Monumenti della pittura antica* III.2.2 (Rome 1936).
———. *Le pitture della 'Casa di Livia,' Monumenti della pittura antica*, III.3 (Rome 1937).
Robortello, F. *Paraphrasis in Libellum Horatii, Qui Vulgo De Arte Poetica Inscribitur* (Florence 1548).
———. *De Arte Sive Ratione Corrigendi Antiquorum Libros Disputatio*, ed. G. Pompella (Naples 1975).

Roddaz, J.-M. *Marcus Agrippa, BEFAR* 253 (1984).
Roessel, D. "The Significance of the Name *Cerinthus* in the Poems of Sulpicia," *TAPA* 120 (1990) 243-250.
Rolfe, J. C. *Horace. Satires and Epistles* (Boston 1935).
Rose, M. *Parody/Meta-Fiction. An Analysis of Parody as a Critical Mirror to the Writing and Reception of Fiction* (London 1979).
Ross, D. O. *Backgrounds to Augustan Poetry: Gallus, Elegy and Rome* (Cambridge 1975).
Rostagni, A. *Arte poetica di Orazio* (Turin 1930).
Rudd, N. "The Names in Horace's Satires," *CQ* 10 (1960) 161-178.
Rumpf, A. "Der Idolino," *La Critica D'Arte* 19-20 (1939) 17-27.
Salmon, E. T. *Roman Colonization Under the Republic* (London 1969).
Sanadon, R. P. *Les poesies d'Horace, traduites en françois*, vol. 7 (Amsterdam and Leipzig 1756[2]).
Santirocco, M. S. *Unity and Design in Horace's Odes* (Chapel Hill and London 1986).
Sasel, J. "Calpurnia L. Pisonis Auguris Filia," *ZAnt* 12 (1962-1963) 387-390.
———. "Probleme und Möglichkeiten onomastischer Forschung," *Acta CIEGR* 4 (1964) 352-368.
Scherer, W. *Poetik*, ed. G. Reiss (Tübingen 1977; first edition, 1888).
Schmidt, E. A. "The Date of Horace, Odes 2.13," *BICS* Suppl. 51 (1988) 118-125.
Schütz, H. *Q. Horatius Flaccus, Episteln* (Berlin 1883).
Scuotto, E. "Realtà umana e atteggiamenti politici e culturali di Lucio Calpurnio Pisone Cesonino," *RAAN* 47 (1972) 149-166.
Sebastiani, F. A. *Viaggio a Tivoli* (Fuligno 1828).
Segre, C. *Introduction to the Analysis of the Literary Text*, with the collaboration of T. Kemeny, trans. J. Meddemmen (Bloomington and Indianapolis 1988).
Shackleton Bailey, D. R. *Profile of Horace* (London 1982).
Sider, D. "Looking for Philodemus in P. Oxy. 54.3724," *ZPE* 76 (1989) 229-236.
Silberberg, S. R. *A Corpus of the Sacral-Idyllic Landscape Paintings in Roman Art* (Diss. UCLA 1980).
Simon, E. *Augustus. Kunst und Leben in Rom um die Zeitenwende* (Munich 1986).
Sisson, C. H. *The Poetic Art. A Translation of Horace's Ars Poetica* (Cheadle Hulme, Cheadle 1975).
Smith, C. L. *The Odes and Epodes of Horace* (Boston 1894).
Smith, W. S., Jr. "Horace Directs a Carouse: *Epistle* I.19," *TAPA* 114 (1984) 255-271.
Snyder, J. M. *The Woman and the Lyre* (Badminster, Bristol 1989).
Stephanus, H. *Q. Horatii Flacci, Opera Omnia* (Paris 1544).
Sticotti, P. "Nuova rassegna di epigrafi romani," *AMSI* 30 (1914) 113-114.
Strelka, J. P. *Theories of Literary Genre, Yearbook of Comparative Criticism* 8 (1978).
Syme, Sir R. *The Roman Revolution* (Oxford 1939).
———. "Piso and Veranius in Catullus," *Classica et Mediaevalia* 17 (1956) 129-134 (= *Roman Papers*, vol. 1, ed. E. Badian [Oxford 1979] 300-304).
———. *History in Ovid* (Oxford 1978).
———. "The Sons of Piso the Pontifex," *AJP* 101 (1980) 333-341 (= *Roman Papers*, vol. 3, ed. A. R. Birley [Oxford 1984] 1226-1232).
———. *The Augustan Aristocracy* (Oxford 1986).
Tate, J. *Horatius Restitutus, Or the Books of Horace Arranged in Chronological Order according to the Scheme of Dr. Bentley* (London 1832[1], 1837[2]).

Taylor, L. R. *The Voting Districts of the Roman Republic* (Rome 1960).
Toffanin, G. *La fine dell'umanesimo* (Milan, Turin, Rome 1920).
Toynbee, J. M. C., and Ward Perkins, J. B.. "Peopled Scrolls: A Hellenistic Motif in Imperial Art," *PBSR* 18 (1950) 1-43.
Turney, P. "The Curve Fitting Problem: A Solution," *The British Journal for the Philosophy of Science* 41 (1990) 509-530.
Ulmer, G. L. "The Parodic Tone Recently Adopted in Criticism," *New Literary History* 13 (1982) 543-560.
Vahlen, J. "Über Zeit und Abfolge der Literaturbriefe des Horaz," *Monatsberichten der Berliner Akademie* 1878, 688-704 (= *Gesammelte philologische Schriften* II [Leipzig and Berlin 1923] 46-61).
Van Reenen, J. H. *Disputatio philologico-critica de Horatii Epistola ad Pisones* (Amsterdam 1806).
Van Rooy, C. A. *Studies in Classical Satire and Related Literary Theory* (London 1965).
Van Sickle, J. "The Book Roll and Some Conventions of the Poetic Book," *Arethusa* 13 (1980) 5-42.
Villa, C. "'Ut Poesis Pictura': Appunti iconografici sui codici dell'*Ars Poetica*," *Aevum* 62 (1988) 186-197.
Villeneuve, F. *Horace, Epîtres* (Paris 1934).
Vittinghoff, F. *Römische Kolonisation und Bürgerrechtspolitik, Akad. Wiss. Mainz, Abh. Geistes- und Sozialwiss. Kl.* 14 (1951).
Vollmer, F. "Die Überlieferungsgeschichte des Horaz," *Philologus Suppl.* 10 (1907).
von Blanckenhagen, P. H., and Alexander, C. *The Paintings from Boscotrecase, MDAI(R) Ergänzungsheft* 6 (1962).
von Rohden, H., and Winnefeld, H. *Architektonische römische Tonreliefs der Kaiserzeit* (Stuttgart 1911).
Waltz, A. *Des variations de la langue et de la métrique d'Horace dans ses différents ouvrages* (Paris 1881).
Watson, P. "Axelson Revisited: The Selection of Vocabulary in Latin Poetry," *CQ* 35 (1985) 430-448.
Weichert, A. "Commentatio de Q. Horatii Flacci Obtrectatoribus," in *Memoriam Anniversariam Dedicatae ante hos CCLXXI Annos Regiae Scholae Grimensis* (Grimae 1821).
Weinberg, B. *A History of Literary Criticism in the Italian Renaissance*, 2 vols. (Chicago 1961).
Weinstock, S. *Divus Julius* (Oxford 1971).
Westphal, J. H. *Die römische Kampagne* (Berlin und Stettin 1829).
White, J. L. "New Testament Epistolary Literature in the Framework of Ancient Epistolography," *ANRW* II.25.2 (Berlin 1984) 1730-1756.
White, P. "*Amicitia* and the Profession of Poetry in Early Imperial Rome," *JRS* 68 (1978) 74-92.
———. "Positions for Poets in Early Imperial Rome," in *Literary and Artistic Patronage in Ancient Rome*, ed. B. Gold (Austin, Texas 1982) 50-66.
Wickham, E. C. *Quinti Horatii Flacci, Opera Omnia*, vol. 2 (Oxford 1891).
Wieland, C. M. *Horaz, Über die Dichtkunst*, in *Christoph Martin Wieland Werke*, 5. Band, ed. H. W. Seiffert (Munich 1968) 586-628.
Wili, W. *Horaz und die Augusteische Kultur* (Basel 1948).
Wilkes, J. J. *Dalmatia* (London 1969).
Wilkins, A. S. *The Epistles of Horace* (London 1902).

Wilsmore, S. J. "The Role of Titles in Identifying Literary Works," *JAAC* 45 (1987) 403-408.
Wimsatt, W. K., Jr., and Brooks, C. *Literary Criticism. A Short History* (New York 1957).
Wiseman, T. P. *Catullan Questions* (Leicester 1969).
———. "Legendary Genealogies in Late-Republican Rome," *Greece & Rome* 21 (1974) 153-164.
———. "Catullus, His Life and Times," Review of F. Stoessl, *C. Valerius Catullus. Mensch, Leben, Dichtung* (Meisenheim am Glan 1977) in *JRS* 69 (1979) 161-168.
———. *Catullus and His World. A Reappraisal* (Cambridge 1985).
———. "Satyrs in Rome? The Background to Horace's *Ars Poetica*," *JRS* 78 (1988) 1-13.
Witting, G. "Über einige Schwierigkeiten beim Isolieren einer Schreibweise," in *Zur Terminologie der Literaturwissenschaft. Akten des IX. Germanistischen Symposions der Deutschen Forschungsgemeinschaft Würzburg 1986*, ed. C. Wagenknecht (Stuttgart 1986) 274-288.
Wood, A. G. *Literary Satire and Theory. A Study of Horace, Boileau, and Pope* (New York and London 1985).
Yavetz, Z. *Julius Caesar and his Public Image* (London 1983).
Zangemeister, C. "Über die älteste Horaz-Ausgabe des Cruquius," *RhM* 23 (1864) 321-339.
Zanker, P. *Augustus und die Macht der Bilder* (Munich 1987).
Zetzel, J. E. G. *Latin Textual Criticism in Antiquity* (New York, 1981; reprinted Salem, N.H. 1984).
———. "Re-creating the Canon: Augustan Poetry and the Alexandrian Past," *Critical Inquiry* 10 (1983) 83-105.

GENERAL INDEX

Accius, L.: 63n
Actium: 119
ad: 32, 36, 47-48
addressee: changeable in didactic poem, 95-96; characteristics in *Ars Poetica*, 96
adynaton: 69
Anonymous Bobiensis: 14n
Antonius, M. (Antony): 119-121
archaism: Varronian, 63; Sallustian, 63n
Aristarchus: 64
Aristotle: 69, 71
Asinius: C. Asinius Pollio: 63n, 90n
association tests: 32; controlling for "rest": 33-34, 37; defined: 23n
Augustus: colonies of: 117-118
Becichemo, Marino: 9, 101
binomial test: 109
book-length: 11-12
Borussus, Joannes Lobartus: 11
Boscotrecase: 80-81
Bradbury, Malcolm: 61, 100
Caecilius: Q. Caecilius Epirota: 60n
Caesar: (see under Julius)
Calpurnia: 54
Calpurnius: identification of family in *Ars Poetica*: 52-59; and Horace's contemporary reader: 56-58; Cn. Calpurnius Piso (cos. 23): 3, 51, 52, 56; L. Calpurnius Piso Caesoninus (cos. 58): 3; and Cicero, 54, 57; dedicatee of *Ars Poetica*, 66; in Pola, 115-125; is Piso père of *Ars Poetica*, 54, 59; property in Illyria, 122; year of his death, 55-56; L. Calpurnius Piso Pontifex (cos. 15): 51-53, is *maior iuvenum* of *Ars Poetica*, 54, 59
Calpus: 53; and legendary genealogies: 53n
Campania: late Second Pompeian Style in, 80
Capua: 116, 119, 121
Cascellius, A.: 20
Cassius: L. Cassius Longinus: 55, 116, 119, 121
Catius: in Sat. II.4: 97
Catullus: 1, 4, 65, 66; and Piso: 57
centuriation: and regional security, 124; on Illyrian coast: 123
Chabotius, Petrus Gualterius: 11
Charisius: 12-16; erroneous titles in: 13; two classes of citations: 14; erroneous names of authors in: 15
Charisius-group: 14n

chi-square test: 23-25; and nominal variables, 28; defined: 23n
Cicero: 3; and L. Calpurnius Piso Caesoninus: 54, 64; attacks on Piso known to Horace: 58-59; opinion of Maecius: 62;
colonies: and centuriation: 123-124; nomenclature: 116-117; on Illyrian coast: 122-123
Colonius, Nicolaus: 88n
Concordia Iulia Felix Augusta: 116n
Contingency test: 32
Cosentia: 65
Cramer V test: 32
Crispinus: in *Sat.* II.7: 97
Cruquius, Iacobus: 11
cum: no trend in Horace's use: 31
Damasippus: in *Sat.* II.3: 97
De Nores, Jason: 8-9, 88n, 91n, 102
descriptio: 73
didactic letters: 89
didactic poem: addressee of: 90; relevance of addressee in: 96
Digentia: 80 (see also under Licenza)
Domitii Pisones: 53n
drama: in decline in Horace's lifetime: 63
Du Verdier, Claude: 10
Duckworth, G.: critique of dating of *Ars Poetica*: 20-25
duoviri: 121
Epicureanism: 59; and poetry: 67
Epidaurum: 123
epistle-theory: and De Nores: 9
Erasmus: 9
Fabricius, Georgius: 8
fantasy-style: 76-77
Fanum Fortunae: 124
Federalist Papers: authorship of: 27
function words: 113; and connotation: 27, 29-30; and genre: 30; and random fluctuation in use of: 27, 30; and trends in use of: 27, 29; defined: 26; and Horace: 31

Gabriele, Trifone: 9
Gell, Sir William: 80n
genre: and interpretation: 87; Horatian mixed: 99; of *Ars Poetica*: 87-99
grammatici: unreceptive to new poetry: 60
griffins: 80, 83, 84
Heinsius, Daniel: 88n
Hesiod: 90
Horace: and critics, 59-61; drama: 63; and mixture of genres: 99; and Philodemus: 64n; characteristics of his verse epistles: 92-96; chronology of his poetry: 27; hexameter poems and five-point lines: 111; knew Cicero's attacks on Piso: 58-59; lyric poems and three-point lines: 110; opinion of Maecius: 62; Sabine villa of: 82;
——*Ars Poetica*: = *Epistula ad Pisones*? 3, 5; = *Epist.* II.3? 6, 11; echoes of Horatian poems in: 19; and *Epist.* I.19: 59-61; and *Epist.* II: 3; and persona-theory: 2-3; and Roman painting: 52, 74-85; and *sermo*: 4, 98; *ante quem* date: 20, 48-49; classified as didactic: 90n; confessional? 2; date: 3, 17-49; date and strings: 42-47; dated with *Epist.* I: 22, 29, 39, 43, 59; didactic features of: 89-92, 96; ending of: 93; epistolary features of: 92-95; genre: 4, 52, 87-100; history-of-ideas and dating: 19; independent work in corpus: 3; meter and date: 21-25; methods for dating: 18-19; not dated with *Epist.* II.1: 36; not technical hand-book: 88; position in

General Index

mss.: 2-3, 6-7; *post quem* date: 20, 49; problem of its structure: 74, 88n; reception of: 2; senior addressee of: 3; speaker's abuse of license: 73; speaker's authority in: 4, 61-85; speaker's conservatism: 63; speaker's ignorance: 85; speaker's inconsistency: 63-64; speaker's misuse of metaphor: 73-74; speaker's pedantry: 4, 61; title: 5-16; titles in Charisius: 12-16

Iader: 123; date of founding: 124; date of city wall: 124

interval variables: 29; and absolute chronology: 43-44; defined: 23n

iste: 96

Iunius: M. Iunius Congus: 65

iuvenis: defined: 54n, 56n

Julius: C. Julius Caesar: 115, 116, 117, 118

Laelius, D.: 65

Laelius, Q.: 72n

Laelius Archelaus: 72n

Lambda test: 32

Lambinus, Dionysius (= Denis Lambin): 8, 10, 103-104, 107

legio XXIX: 119

letter: informality of: 91

license: poetic: 69, 71-74

Licenza: Horace's (?) villa at: 80, 82-83

lines: conversion of three-point to five-point: 111-112; definition of "similarity": 112; three- and five-point types: 32; typology of: 110-111

Livy: 89n

Lodge, David: 61

Lucilius, C.: 65

Lucretius: 89, 90

macrochronometers: and length of words, words per sentence, unique vs. non-unique strings: 41; defined: 41

Maecenas, C.: 63, 66, 93; gave Horace his Sabine villa? 82n

Maecius: Sp. Maecius Tarpa: 4, 20, 52, 61-63

Manutius, Aldus (II): 13, 105

Melissus, C.: 63

metaphor: mixed: 73; sign of genius: 74

meter: controlling for: 30; Horace's lyric and hexameter poems: 30; misuse of: 72

method: Morellian: 27

methodology: and persona-theory: 2-3; art-historical: 2; statistical: 2, 26-30

model-building: principle of parsimony: 36, 37n, 40

modelling: exploratory: 47; of data: 29, 36, 39, 43

monsters: in late Second Pompeian Style: 75-85; interpretation of in *Ars Poetica*: 70-73

Muret, Marc-Antoine: 10, 103-104

Mutina: Battle of: 115; and death of Piso: 55

Nabokov, Vladimir: 61

Narona: 123

nec: 37, 47-48; and *ne*: 40

Neoptolemus of Parium: 65

nominal variables: 28; defined: 23n

Numa Pompilius, king: 53

obtrectatores: of Virgil and Horace: 60

Octavian: 118, 119, 120, 122, 124, 125; Illyrian campaign: 122 (see also under Augustus)

Octavius, M.: beseiges Salona: 124-125

Ofellus: in *Sat.* II.2: 97

ordinal variables: defined: 23n

paradigm: 99-100

parody: xi, 4, 19, 51, 52, 61, 77, 97, 100; at beginning of *Ars Poetica*: 68-85

Parrasio, Aulo Giano: 7
Peacham, Henry: 10
per: 37, 47-48
Persius, C.: 65
Phalaris: 3, 57, 64
Philodemus: 65, 67; and Horace: 64n; and Piso: 57, 64; poems about Piso: 66
pietas: 120
Pietas Iulia: (see under Pola.)
pinacotheca: 84n
Pisones: (see under Calpurnius.)
Plautus: 64
Pliny: colony names in: 116-117
Pola: 3; Arch of the Sergii: 118-119; centuriation of: 123-124; city wall of: 56, 125; founded by Caesar or Octavian? 115-117; incorporated into regio X Italia: 122; inscriptions mentioning L. Calpurnius Piso Caesoninus in: 55-56, 115-125; part of Illyria: 122; Pietas Iulia: 116, 120
Pompeian Styles: first and second: 75
Pompeii: Casa del Cinghiale: 82n; Caserma of the Gladiators: 80; House of the Labyrinth: 84; House of Obellius Firmus: 80;
Pompey: Cn. Pompeius Magnus: 64
Porphyrio: 53, 56, 70, 82n, 89; and mistaken identifications in: 54
Priapus: in *Sat*. I.8: 98
prosopography: 3
Ps.-Acro: 16, 70, 82n, 89
Pupii Pisones: 53n
Quintilian: 9, 16, 70, 72
Quintilius: Quintilius Varus Cremonensis: 20, 28, 36, 66-68
Ramus, Petrus: 11
regression analysis: 44-48
rhetoric: misuse of: 4, 72
Riccoboni, Antonio: 9n, 88n

Robortello, Francesco: 9, 88n, 102
Rome: Aula Isiaca: 79; House of Augustus: 78; House of Livia: 79, 82; Temple of Julius Caesar: 78; Villa of the Farnesina: 79, 81, 83
Sallust: 63n
Salona: 123; city wall of: 124-125
Sanchez, Francisco: 89n
Σαρδισμός: 70, 74n
Scaliger, Julius Caesar: 10, 104
Scaliger, Joseph: 88n
Scylla: 84-85
Sebastiani, Filippo Alessandro: 80n
sed: 32, 37, 47-48
sermo: 4; and Horatian persona: 98; and monologues: 97; Horace's definition: 96-97; open-ended: 93; mock-didactic features of: 97; parody in: 97
Sicily: 65
Sinnius Capito: 90n
Sosii: 20
sphinx: 80
Stephanus, Henricus (= Henri Estienne): 7, 10, 12, 105, 106-107
Stertinius: in *Sat*. II.5: 97
stops: and sentence length, 41-42
Strabo: on advantages of Illyrian coast: 123n
strings: defined: 42; unique vs. non-unique: 41, 42-43, 44-47; and date of *Ars Poetica*: 47
Sturm, Johann: 11, 105-106
stylistics: statistical: 2, 26-30
Suetonius: 60
Tarentum: 65
Tergeste: 123, 124
time-order: 28
Timon of Phlius: 100
Tiresias: in *Sat*. II.5: 98
titles: and interpretation: 5
Tuscanus, Joannes Aloisius: 7n
Ulysses: in *Sat*. II.5: 98

Uncertainty test: 32
unity: in Aristotle's *Poetics*: 69n
Valerius: M. Valerius Messalla Corvinus: 20, 90n; C. Valerius Catullus: (see under Catullus)
Valgius: C. Valgius Rufus: 90n
variables: three kinds defined: 23n
Varus: (see under Quintilius)
Venus: 120
verisimilitude: 73, 76
Verrius: M. Verrius Flaccus: 16, 90n
Virgil: 20, 67, 89, 90
Vitruvius: a "pedantic conservative": 76; condemnation of late Second Pompeian Style: 74-76
vocabulary: misuse of: 72; and stylometrics: 26
walls: of Illyrian colonies: 124-125; wood vs. stone: 125
wisdom literature: 90n
word-length: 41
Zeuxis: 77n

WORD	EPD	S1	S2	C1	C2	C3	EP1	AP	EP2.2	EP2.1	C4	TOT	NOTE
A	3	10	7	2	1	0	1	0	2	0	1	27	L.F.
AB	3	9	8	5	3	14	4	4	1	3	6	60	L.F.
AC	2	29	13	7	1	1	15	6	2	2	0	78	L.F.
AD	12	21	28	6	1	5	21	13	7	9	8	131	√
AN	8	9	22	3	2	4	22	12	3	3	1	89	L.F.
AT	4	34	9	2	2	1	3	1	2	1	0	59	L.F.
ATQUE	12	65	36	11	4	2	12	6	6	5	2	161	N.P.
AUT	32	36	35	21	9	16	23	28	13	11	6	230	N.P.
AU	0	0	0	0	0	0	0	1	0	2	0	3	L.F.
CUM	7	65	61	20	8	16	34	9	7	16	9	262	N.P.
CUR	3	8	8	7	2	4	7	6	1	0	5	51	L.F.
DE	2	8	10	4	4	2	12	4	3	1	1	51	L.F.
DONEC	1	2	3	1	0	3	5	1	0	1	0	17	L.F.
DUM	2	14	8	9	3	9	16	3	2	3	2	71	L.F.
ENIM	0	3	10	1	2	1	7	5	1	4	4	38	L.F.
ET	78	134	142	121	86	179	268	147	134	76	85	1450	N.P.
ETIAM	0	5	4	0	0	1	6	6	4	4	1	31	L.F.
IAM	6	8	15	7	10	8	9	5	1	5	14	88	N.P.
IN	36	65	69	36	27	35	58	35	12	17	27	417	N.P.
INTER	7	14	7	5	0	9	14	2	4	6	3	71	L.F.
MOX	0	0	2	2	1	3	3	3	2	2	3	21	L.F.
NAM	5	17	18	2	1	1	2	1	0	3	1	51	L.F.
NE	2	25	23	9	2	8	29	10	2	2	2	114	L.F.
NEC	26	23	23	47	32	39	35	22	1	5	16	269	√
NEQUE	14	26	22	16	13	18	5	2	2	3	5	126	L.F.
NEU	1	3	3	9	0	0	3	3	0	0	0	22	L.F.
NISI	1	9	10	2	3	2	8	2	1	4	0	42	L.F.
NON	30	74	73	38	29	46	94	39	17	13	41	494	N.P.
NUNC	8	13	16	16	4	13	12	6	10	6	6	110	N.P.
PER	11	5	13	10	9	13	16	5	1	10	22	115	√
POST	1	10	6	4	0	5	7	5	2	4	3	47	L.F.
QUIA	0	5	7	0	0	0	8	0	0	1	0	21	L.F.
QUIDEM	0	1	0	0	1	0	2	0	0	2	0	6	L.F.
QUODSI	4	0	1	1	0	1	8	0	0	1	0	16	L.F.
QUOQUE	0	5	8	4	3	3	4	0	1	5	1	34	L.F.
SAEPE	1	17	1	5	3	3	10	1	0	2	0	43	L.F.
SED	7	12	21	4	6	6	15	6	5	11	10	103	√
SEU	2	2	19	12	5	12	7	3	0	1	2	65	L.F.
SI	7	56	61	7	9	29	80	34	13	18	9	323	N.P.
SIC	4	21	15	7	6	2	13	11	3	5	3	90	N.P.
SINE	0	7	10	5	1	10	7	5	1	0	3	49	L.F.
SIVE	1	2	12	13	2	2	0	1	0	1	1	35	L.F.
SUB	4	4	9	13	5	8	7	4	2	1	4	61	L.F.
TAM	0	4	5	3	0	0	0	0	0	3	0	15	L.F.
TAMEN	0	7	12	6	1	5	12	5	5	3	3	59	L.F.
TANDEM	1	1	3	2	1	1	2	1	0	3	1	16	L.F.
UBI	5	8	5	1	5	2	12	1	2	1	2	44	L.F.
UNDE	3	8	13	4	2	4	1	3	1	1	1	41	L.F.
UT	34	92	75	13	1	8	60	23	11	12	8	337	N.P.
VEL	7	5	8	6	3	5	15	5	4	8	3	69	N.P.

L.F.=low frequency (25% of cells [i.e., 2.25, rounded up to 3] have fewer than 5 cases; C.I-III count as one cell)   **N.P.**=no pattern   √=meets conditions for consideration as chronometer.

TABLE A: FREQUENCY OF CERTAIN FUNCTION WORDS IN HORACE

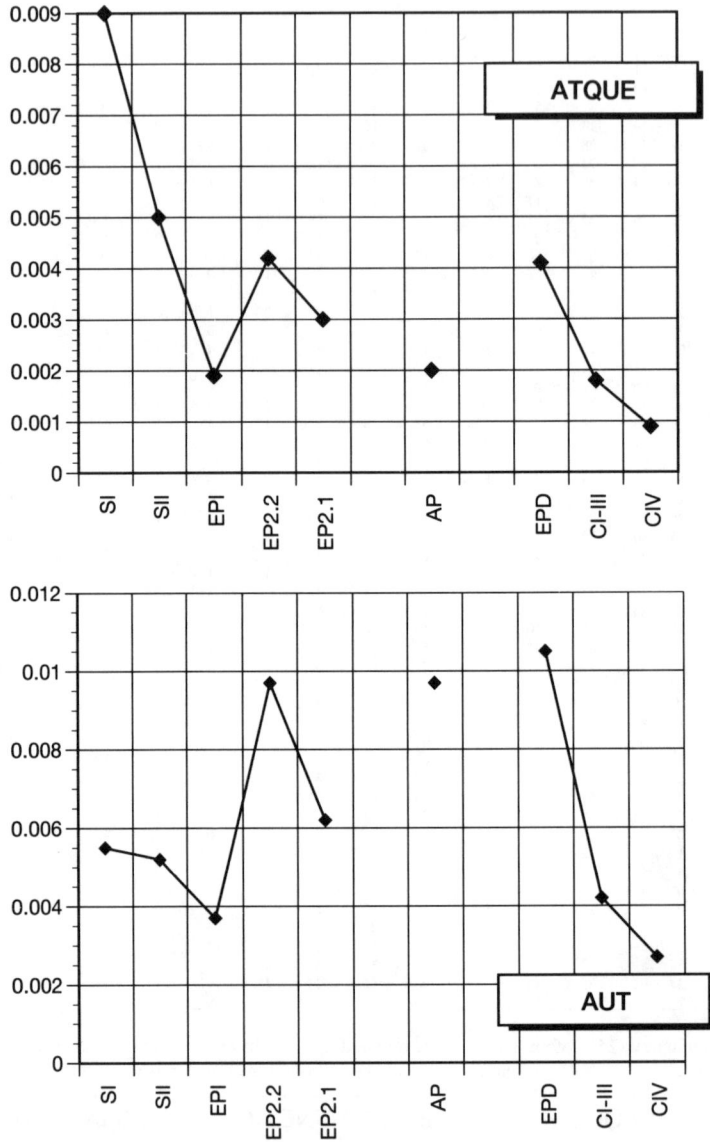

TABLE B: GRAPHS OF RANDOMLY OCCURRING
FUNCTION WORDS (1)

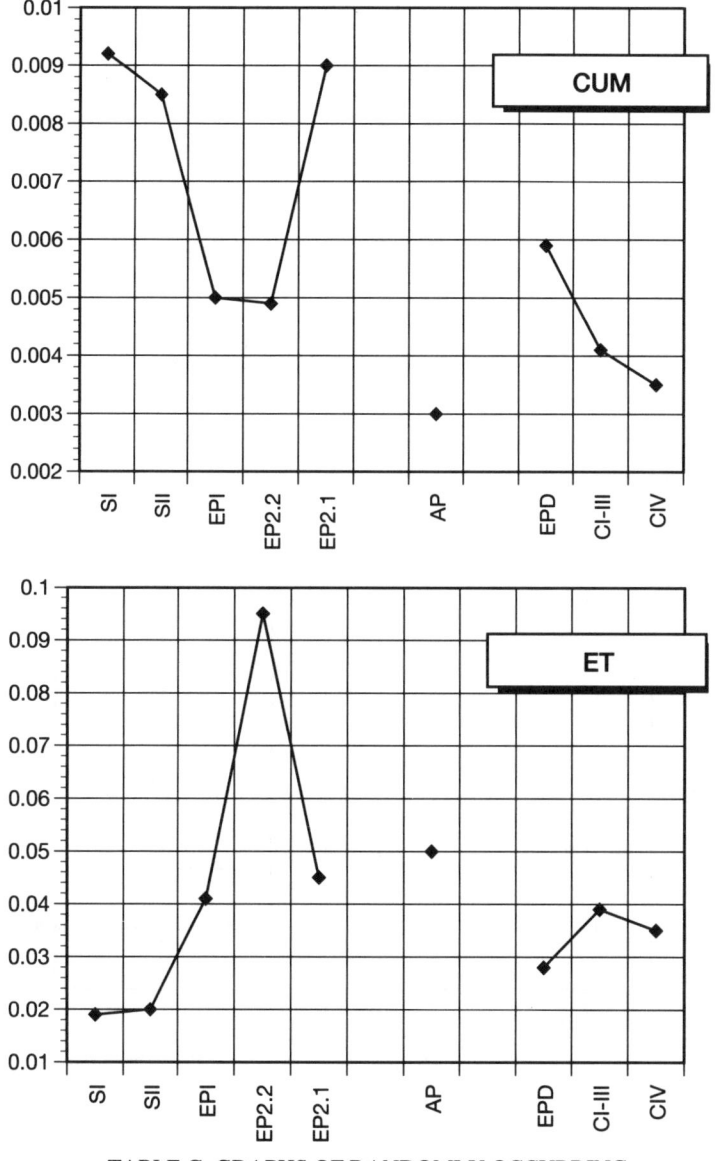

TABLE C: GRAPHS OF RANDOMLY OCCURRING
FUNCTION WORDS (2)

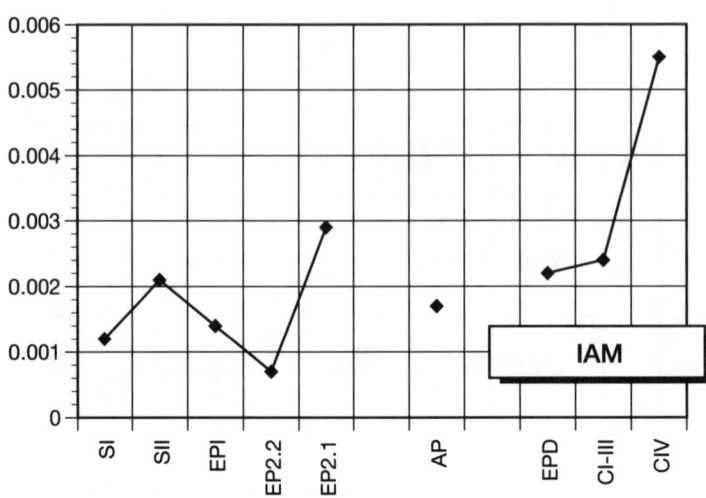

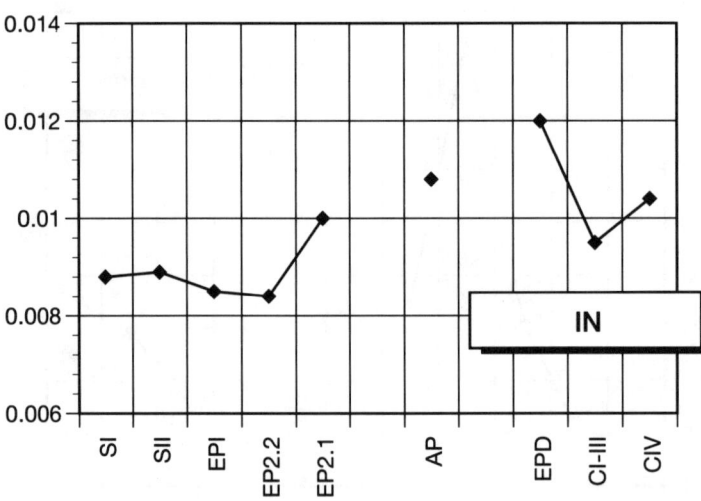

TABLE D: GRAPHS OF RANDOMLY OCCURRING
FUNCTION WORDS (3)

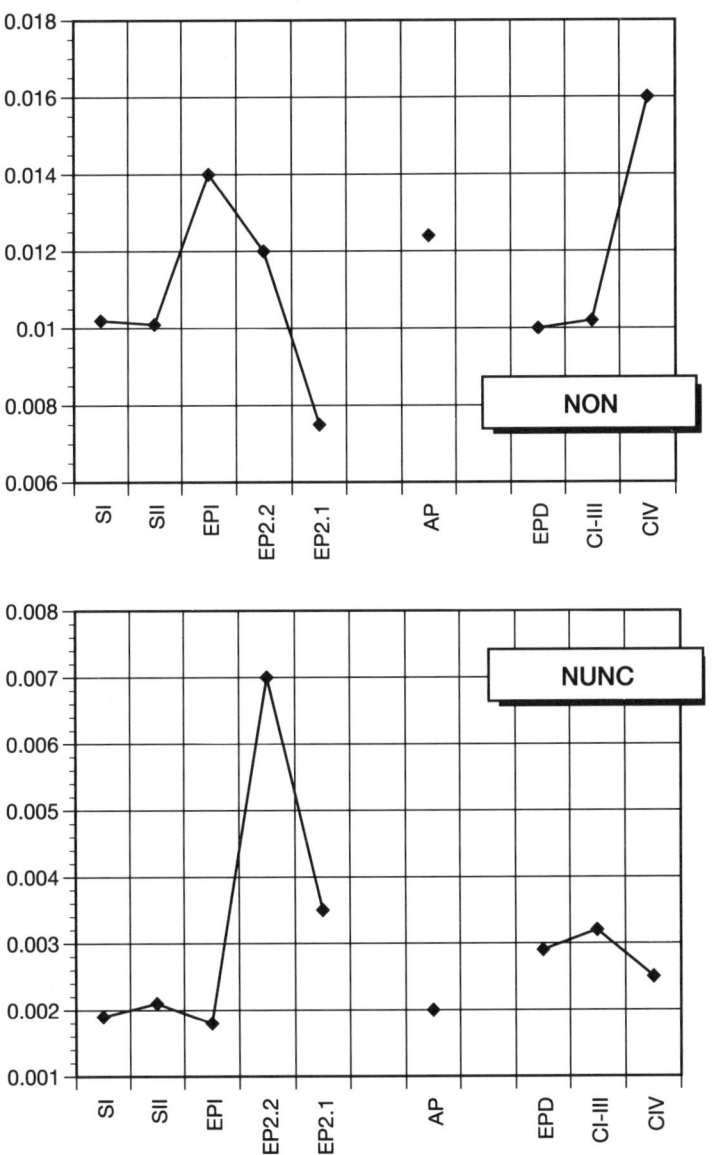

TABLE E: GRAPHS OF RANDOMLY OCCURRING
FUNCTION WORDS (4)

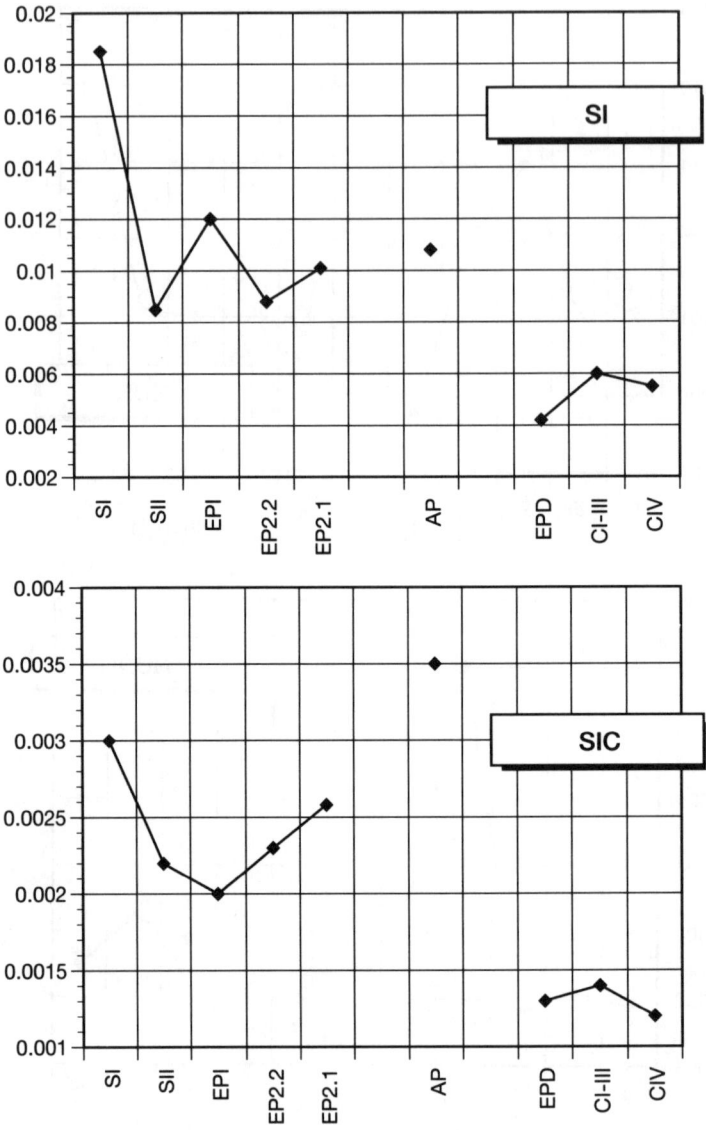

TABLE F: GRAPHS OF RANDOMLY OCCURRING
FUNCTION WORDS (5)

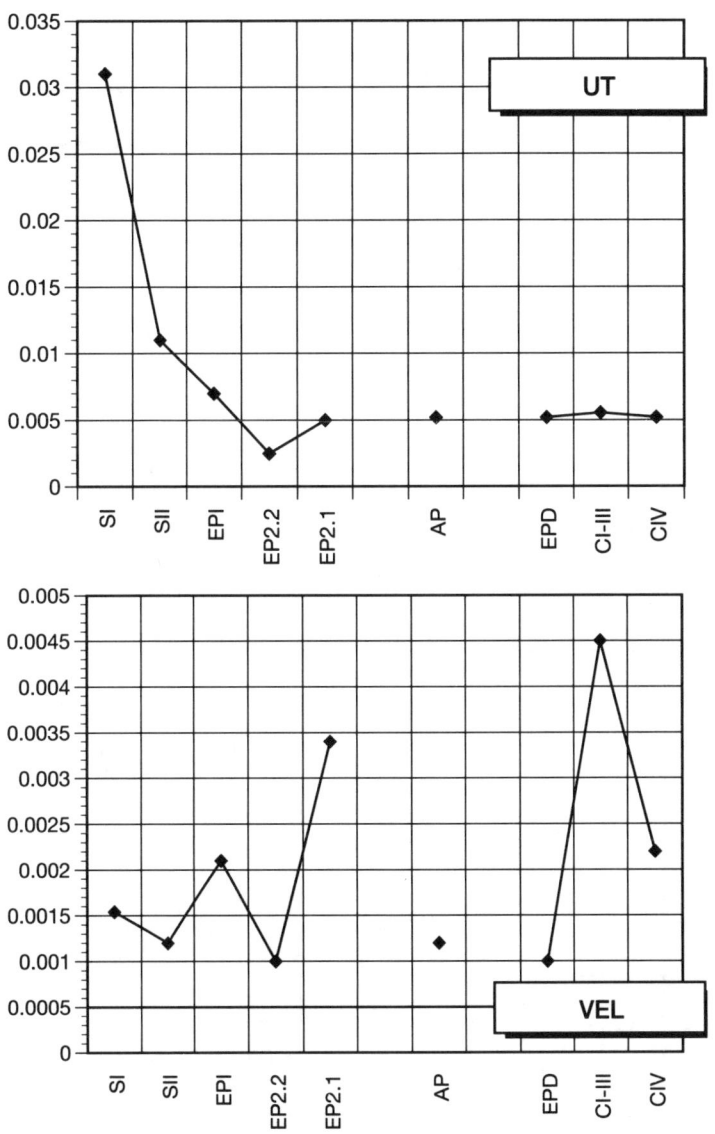

TABLE G: GRAPHS OF RANDOMLY OCCURRING
FUNCTION WORDS (6)

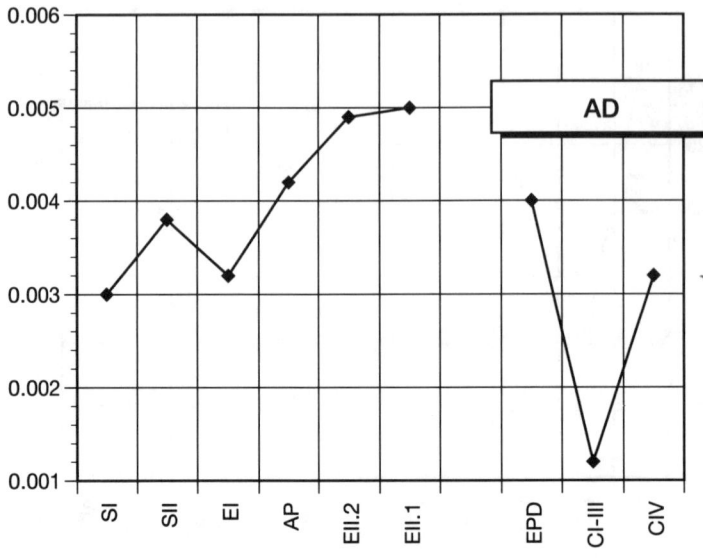

TABLE H: FREQUENCY OF "AD" IN HORACE

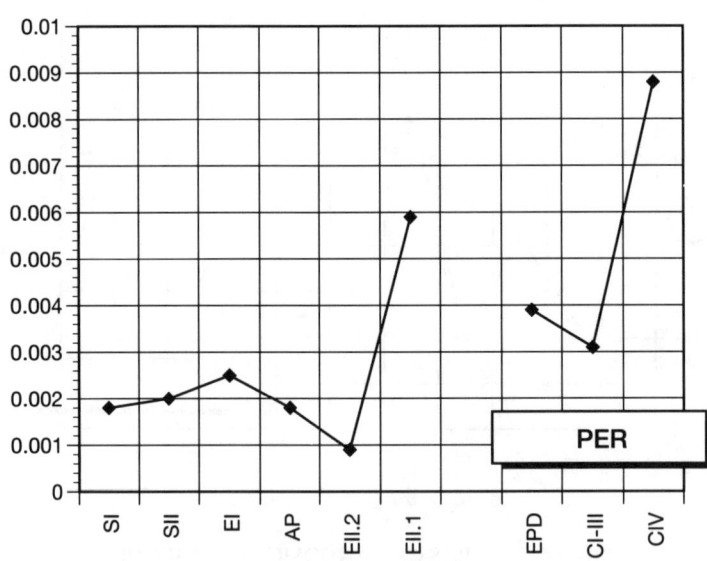

TABLE I: FREQUENCY OF "PER" IN HORACE

Tables 151

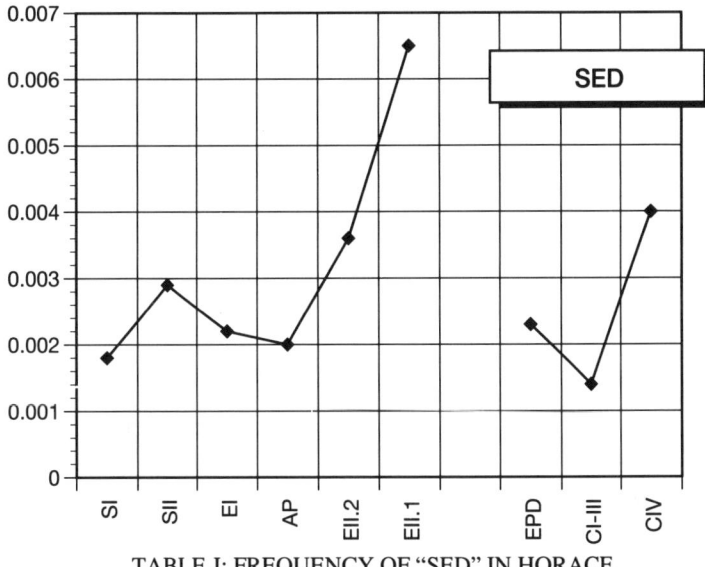

TABLE J: FREQUENCY OF "SED" IN HORACE

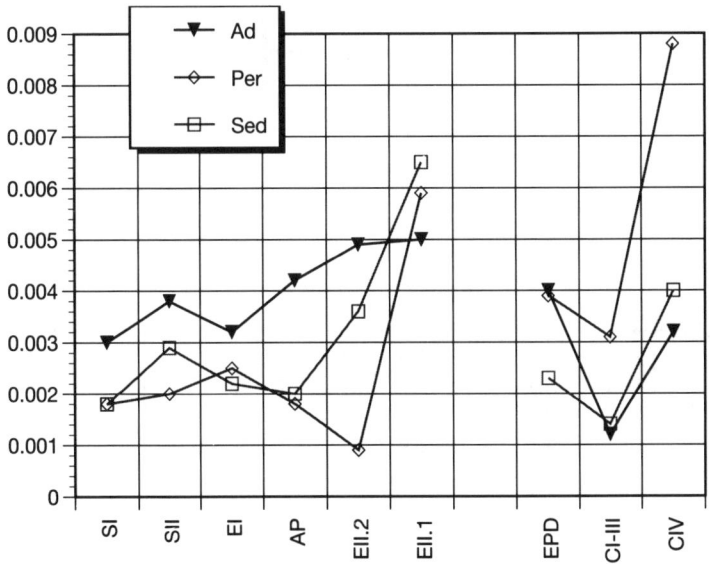

TABLE K: FREQUENCY OF "AD," "PER," AND "SED" IN HORACE

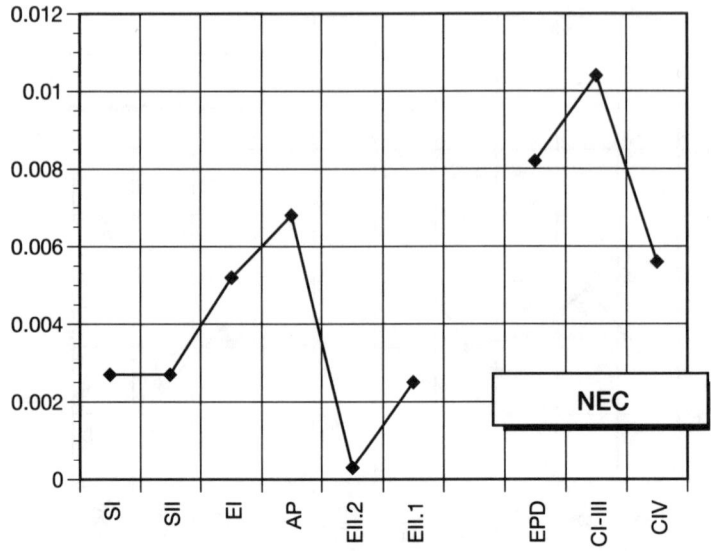

TABLE L: FREQUENCY OF "NEC" IN HORACE

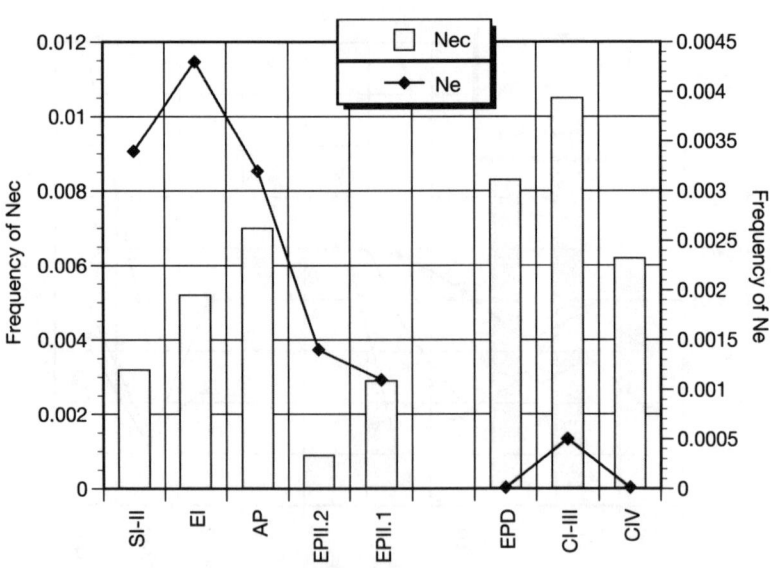

TABLE M: FREQUENCY OF "NEC" AND "NE" IN HORACE

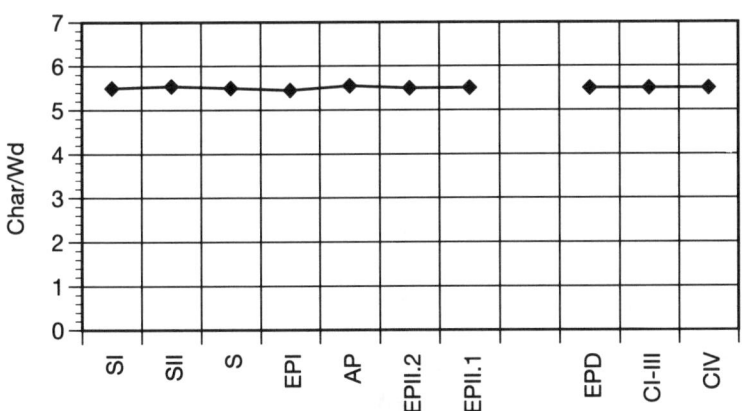

TABLE N: AVERAGE NUMBER OF CHARACTERS
PER WORD IN HORACE

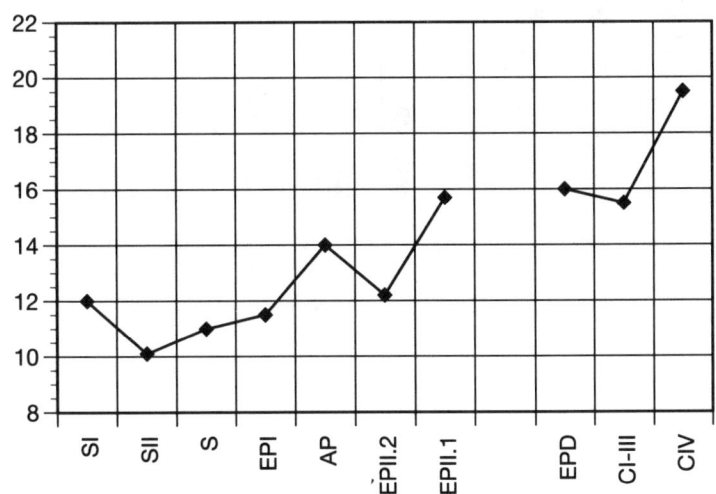

TABLE O: RATIO OF WORDS TO STOPS IN HORACE

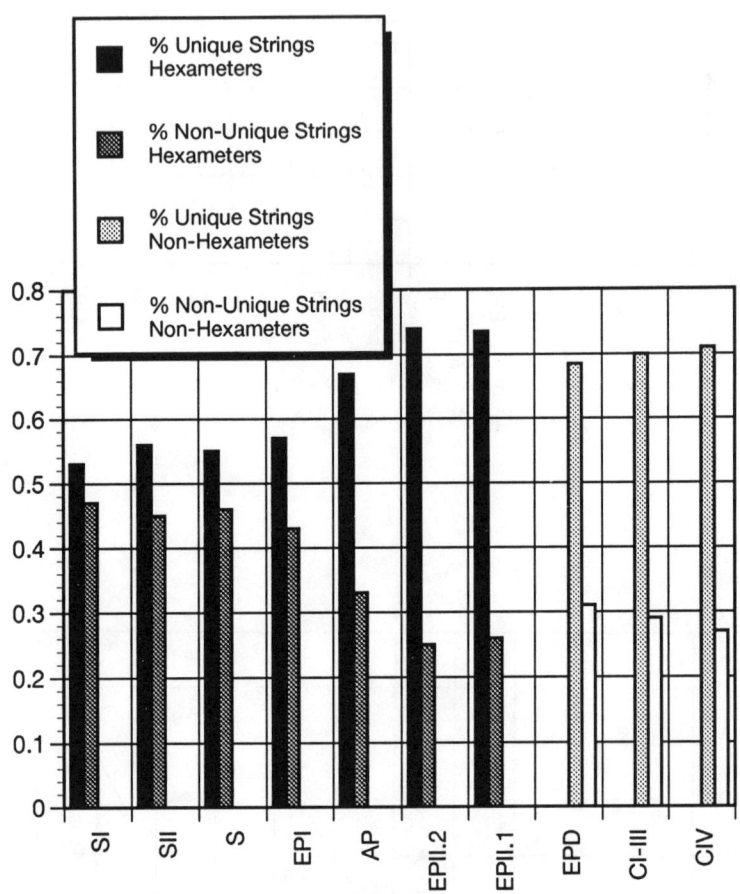

TABLE P: UNIQUE AND NON-UNIQUE STRINGS
IN HORACE'S POETRY

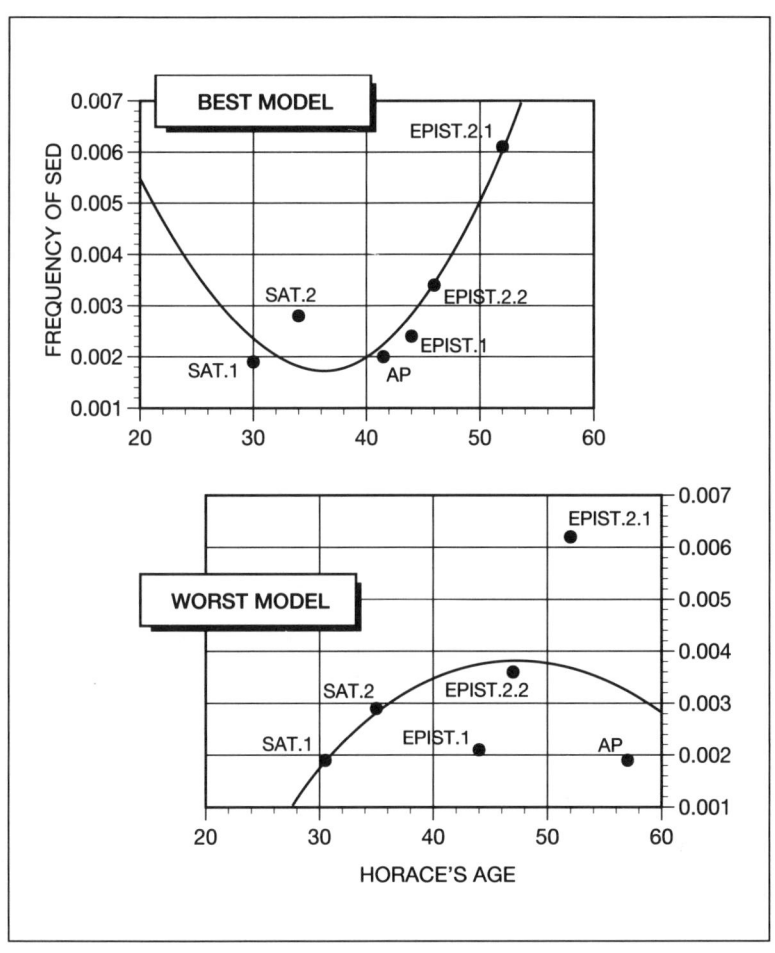

TABLE Q: BEST AND WORST REGRESSION
MODELS FOR "SED"

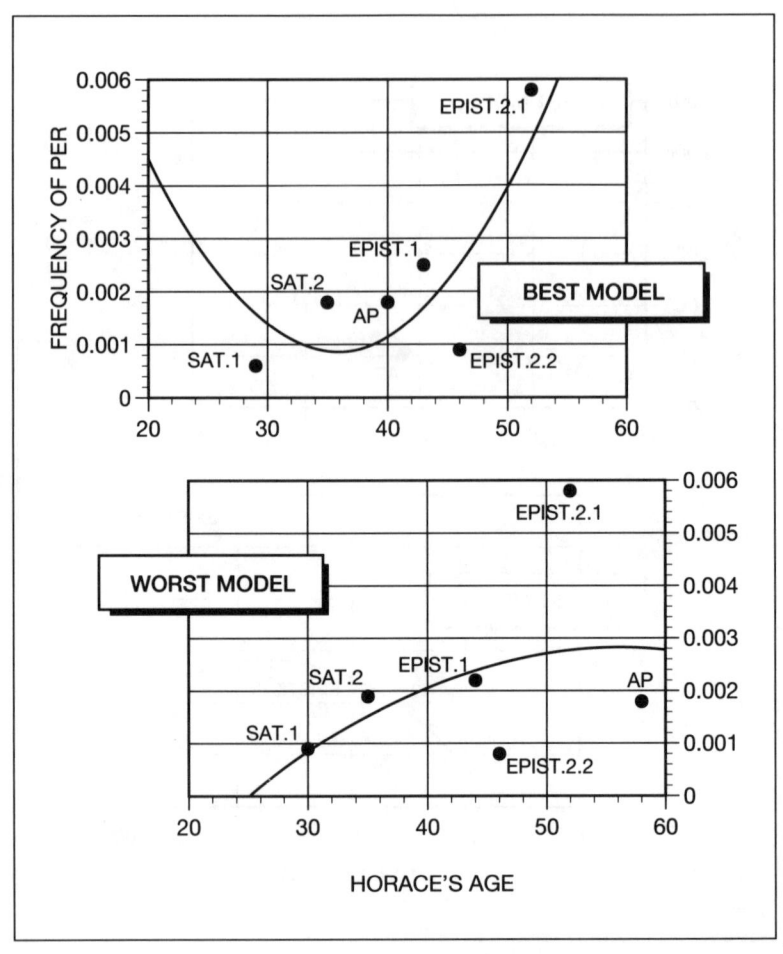

TABLE R: BEST AND WORST REGRESSION
MODELS FOR "PER"

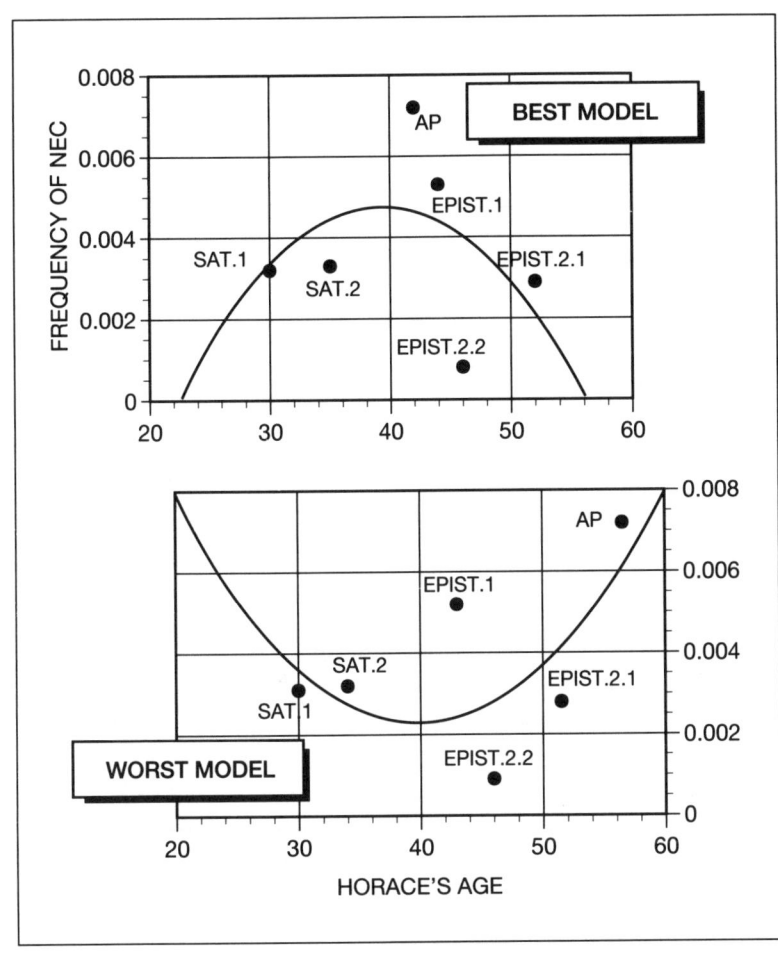

TABLE S: BEST AND WORST REGRESSION
MODELS FOR "NEC"

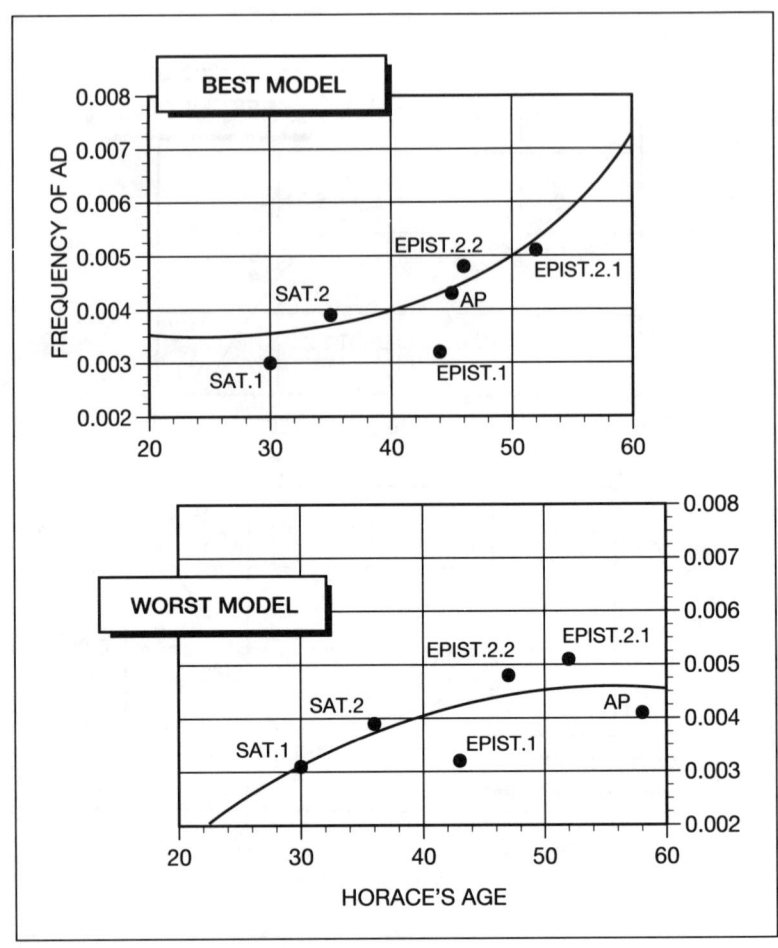

TABLE T: BEST AND WORST REGRESSION
MODELS FOR "AD"

Fig. 1—*Inscr. Ital.* X.i.65 (Pola, Lapidarium of Arheoloski muzej Istre 214)

Fig. 2—Detail from Frieze of the Temple of the Divine Julius Caesar, Rome (DAI Rome 63.1233)

Fig. 3—Detail of Wall Painting from Left Ala, House of Livia, Rome (DAI Rome 56.435)